Scots in the
Mid-Atlantic States
1783–1883

Scots

in the

Mid-Atlantic States

1783–1883

David Dobson

Introduction

Scottish emigration to the British colonies in America, which had been suspended during the American Revolution, recommenced soon after 1783. The British government did attempt to direct emigrants to Canada through incentives such as land grants, while the cost of passage across the Atlantic being cheaper to Canada than to the United States did result in an emphasis of emigration to the Canadian colonies. At the same time the growing industrial economy of Scotland did offer economic opportunities at home while the Napoleonic Wars provided employment as soldiers or sailors for thousands of Scots who otherwise would have emigrated.

Traditionally many of the Scottish emigrants had been farmers, merchants or professional workers, and while such people still crossed the Atlantic to settle in America opportunities there increasingly attracted skilled industrial workers from Scotland initially to the Atlantic States but later to the Mid-West. New York and Philadelphia as two of America's leading ports were the major gateways to Scots entering America and consequently many of them settled there or in their hinterlands.

Who were these Scottish immigrants to the Mid-Atlantic States? Little exists to record their departure from Scotland but from around 1820 there are passenger arrival records in USA which briefly identify immigrants. Also the US Census Records provide vital information on them. In Scotland probably the most informative source of vital data on Scots who settled abroad are the births, marriages and deaths columns of local newspapers, sources not usually available to researchers in America. This compilation depends heavily on such sources, together with certain documentary sources located in the National Archives of Scotland as well as a few other sources both printed and manuscript. In America, the published records of the St Andrew's Societies of both New York and of Philadelphia, both dating from the mid-eighteenth century, which contain much biographical material on their members who were Scots or of Scottish origin, were particularly useful.

David Dobson
St Andrews, Scotland, 2002

References

ARCHIVES

BM = British Museum, London
DGA = Dumfries & Galloway Archives, Dumfries
DU.lib = Dundee University Library
EUL = Edinburgh University Library
GA = Glasgow Archives
GRH = General Register House, Edinburgh
NAS = National Archives of Scotland, Edinburgh
NJSA = New Jersey State Archives, Trenton
NLS = National Library of Scotland, Edinburgh
NRH = New Register House, Edinburgh
NYPL = New York Public Library
PCC = Prerogative Court of Canterbury
PRO = Public Record Office, London
USNA = United States National Archives

PUBLICATIONS

ACK = Alexander Cowan—His Kinsfolk and Connections
    [Perth, 1915]
AJ = Aberdeen Journal, series
ANY = Biographical Register of the St Andrew's Society of New
    York, A. McBean [New York, 1911]
AO = Annandale Observer, series
AP = An Historical Account of the St Andrew's Society of
    Philadelphia,1749–1907 [Philadelphia, 1907]
CEG = Compendium of Edinburgh Graduates [Edinburgh]
CM = Caledonian Mercury, series
DA = Dundee Advertiser, series
DC = Dundee Courier, series
DGC = Dumfries & Galloway Courier, series
DGH = Dumfries & Galloway Herald, series
DP = Dunfermline Post, series
DPCA = Dundee, Perth and Cupar Advertiser, series
DRC = Dutch Reformed Church, New York, registers
EC = Edinburgh Courant, series
EEC = Edinburgh Evening Courant, series
EFR = East Fife Record, series
F = Fasti Ecclesiae Scoticanae, J. Scott [Edinburgh]
FFP = Fife Free Press, series
FJ = Fife Journal, series

FPA = Fulham Papers in the Lambeth Palace Library,
    W. Manross [Oxford, 1965]
GCr = Glasgow Courier, series
GkAd = Greenock Advertiser, series
GM = Glasgow Mercury, series
GM = Gentleman's Magazine, London, series
HA = House of Alexander [Edinburgh, 1877]
BFH = History of the Bethune Family
KCA = Officers and Graduates of King's College, P.J. Anderson
    [Aberdeen, 1893]
MAGU = Matriculation Albums of Glasgow University
    1727–1858, W.I. Addison [Glasgow, 1913]
MB = The Macleans of Boreray, H.H. Mackenzie [Inverness]
MCA = Records of Marischal College, P.J. Anderson [Aberdeen,
    1898]
MG = McClellans in Galloway, D.R. Torrance [Edinburgh, 1996]
NWI = New World Immigrants, M. Tepper [Baltimore, 1980]
Pa.Chron = Pennsylvania Chronicle, series
PaGaz = Philadelphia Gazette, series
PC = Perth Courier, series
PCR = Records of the 1st and 2nd Presbyterian Churches of the
    City of New York
PI = Passengers from Ireland, D. Schlegel [Baltimore, 1980]
PJ = People's Journal, series
PMHB = Pennsylvania Magazine of History & Biography, series
S = Scotsman, series
SG = Scottish Guardian, series
Sgen = Scottish Genealogist, series
SM = Scots Magazine, series
SSA = Scots and Scots Descendants in America [NY, 1917]
UPC = Annals of the United Presbyterian Church, W. McKelvie
    [Edinburgh, 1873]
W = Witness, series
WMQ = William and Mary Quarterly, series

ABBREVIATIONS

Cnf = confirmation of testament
G/s = gravestone inscription
OPR = Old Parish Register
Pro. = probate

SCOTS IN THE MID-ATLANTIC STATES
1783-1883

ABEL, ARCHIBALD, naturalised, Supreme Court of
Pennsylvania, 24 March 1813, Quarter Session Court of
Philadelphia 20 September 1813.

ABEL, WILLIAM, naturalised, Quarter Session Court of
Philadelphia, 29 September 1813.

ABERCROMBY, ANDREW, born in 1843, late of the Northern
Insurance Co in Aberdeen, died NY, 3 July 1872.
[AJ:31.7.1872]

ADAIR, JOHN, born in Portpatrick, Wigtownshire, on 3 July 1824,
in 1848 to Quebec on the Collingwood, settled in NY during
1850, died in Newark, NJ, on 10 Nov. 1912. [ANY#2.287]

ADAM, JAMES, naturalised, Quarter Session Court of
Philadelphia, 7 June 1819.

ADAM, ROBERT, naturalised, Supreme Court of Pennsylvania,
17 February 1798.

ADAMS, WILLIAM, a cooper late in NY, settled in Halifax, Nova
Scotia, by 1786. [NAS.CS17.1.5/303]

ADAMSON, ALEXANDER, late a merchant in NY, by 1801 in
Glasgow.[NAS.CS17.1.9/330]; in 1808.
[NAS.CS17.1.28/139]

ADAMSON, THOMAS, from Halbeath, Fife, died in St Mary's, Elk
County, PA, on 30 June 1883. [DJ]

ADDISON, ALEXANDER, born 1759, educated at Aberdeen
University, a minister, settled in western PA by 1785, a
lawyer in Washington County, PA, from 1787, a Judge from
1790 to 1803, died in Pittsburgh, PA, on 27 Nov. 1807.
[AP#99]

AIKEN, JAMES, a merchant in NY in 1789. [NAS.CS17.1.8/346]

AIKEN, ROBERT, born in Dalkeith, Midlothian, during 1734, a
publisher in PA, died in 1802. [SSA#86]

AIKENHEAD, JESSIE, born 1825, daughter of Rev. Robert
Aitkenhead in Kirkcaldy, Fife, and wife of Robert Wood, died
in Newark, NJ, 22 September 1871. [S#8879]

AIKMAN, JOHN, in NY 1831. [NAS.RD5.435.207]

AIKMAN, MARY BROWN, daughter of George Aikman an
engraver in Edinburgh, married J. Gray from Canada West,
in NY on 21 Mar. 1853. [EEC#22416]

AIKMAN, PETER, born in 1819, second son of George Aikman an engraver, and Alison Mackay, died in NY on 15 Sep. 1883. [Edinburgh, St Cuthbert's g/s]

AIMER, JAMES, a joiner from Westhaven, Angus, with 4 or 5 children, from Dundee on the Providence of Perth, master Robert Nicoll, to New York in May 1819. [NAS.CE70.1.15]

AINSLIE, ROBERT, a merchant from PA, married Elizabeth Ann Telfar, daughter of the late John Telfar a farmer in Edinburgh, at the Kirk of the Canongate, Edinburgh, on 28 Feb. 1800. [Canongate Marriage Register]

AITCHISON, REBECCA, born in the 1780s, daughter of Thomas Aitchison in Kellwood, Caerlaverock, Dumfries-shire, marrie d .... Dobie, a farmer, settled in Binghamton, Broome County, NY, died there in Dec. 1857. [DGH:5.2.1858]

AITKEN, JOHN, born in Cumbernauld, Dunbarton, 1806, merchant in NY, died 31 West 52nd Street on 6 Jan.1879. [ANY.2.272]

AITKEN, R. EASTON, from Glasgow, married Olivia Augusta Jones, daughter of Jesse Jones, from Glasgow but in NY, in London 7 March 1872. [S#8928]

AITKEN, WILLIAM, naturalised, Supreme Court of Pennsylvania, 20 February 1798.

ALEXANDER, F., from Kirkcudbrightshire, to NY during June 1850, died in Alabama on 20 Sep. 1850. [DGH:3.10.1850]

ALEXANDER, MARGARET, born in 1791, daughter of John Shaw Alexander of Mackilston, married John Johnston, died in Geneva, Ontario County, NY, on 30 Aug. 1854. [Dalry g/s, Ayrshire]

ALEXANDER, ROBERT, in Jackson, NY, cnf 1866 Edinburgh. [NAS.SC70.1.128/921]

ALEXANDER, WILLIAM, naturalised, Supreme Court of Pennsylvania, 13 February 1798.

ALLEN, ALEXANDER, naturalised, Supreme Court of Pennsylvania, 13 February 1798.

ALLISON, AGNES, in Mifflintown, PA, died on 19 Feb. 1863, cnf 1865. [NAS.SC70.1.123]

ALLAN, CHRISTIAN, born in 1824, wife of William Martin late of Craigrothie, Fife, died in Buffalo, NY, on 5 Jan. 1872. [PJ]

ALLAN, GEORGE, a currier from Anstruther, Fife, son of George Allan a currier there, married [1] Janet Hollingworth,daughter of Charles Hollingworth in Haddington, East Lothian, in Newark, NJ, on 2 Nov. 1858, she died on 6 Oct. 1867, [2] Emma C. Price in Harlem, NY, on 5 May 1873. [EFR]

ALLAN, JOHN, son of George Allan from Townhill, Dunfermline, Fife, died at Beechtree, Jefferson County, PA, in 1886. [DJ, 3.7.1886]

ALLAN, ROBERT, born in 1774, married Mary Bailey in 1801, a shipmaster in Philadelphia later a grocer/cartman in NY, died on 14 Sep1832. [ANY.2.13]

ALLAN, ROBERT, born 1786 in Kilbarchan, a poet who to America Apr. 1841, died in NY 1842. [GM.NS18.331]

ALLAN, Mrs THOMAS, from Tweedale, Peebles-shire, died in Hoboken, NY, in Sep. 1822. [EEC#17482]

ALLAN, WILLIAM, born in Kilconquhar, Fife, during 1842 son of George Allan a currier, a printer-compositor who emigrated to NY in 1862, married Lizzie McCaig in Bloomfield, NJ, on 18 Feb. 1869, died in Brooklyn on 28 July 1910. [EFR]

ALLAN, W. CLEVELAND, son of Lewis F. Allan, married May M. Barclay, daughter of William Barclay from Banff, in Buffalo, NY, 3 March 1874. [S#9563]

ALLAN, ..., daughter of George Allan, from Townhill, Dunfermline, Fife, born in Reynoldsville, Jefferson, PA, on 10 Sep. 1883. [DJ]

ALSTON, WILLIAM, son of James Alston of Muirburn, died in NY on 24 Nov. 1820. [S#4/203]

AMOS, SUSAN, eldest daughter of John Amos a letterpress printer in Edinburgh, relict of Walter Buchanan Thomson, died in NY on 17 November 1875. [S#10114]

ANDERSON, ALEXANDER, born in 1810 son of John Anderson [1780-1851] and Ann White [1780-1876], died in NY on 18 Dec. 1845. [Montrose g/s]

ANDERSON, ALEXANDER, naturalised, Quarter Session Court of Philadelphia, 17 October 1805.

ANDERSON, ALEXANDER G., merchant in NY 1827-1835. [ANY.2.149]

ANDERSON, ANDREW, naturalised US District Court, Philadelphia, 1 November 1805.

ANDERSON, ANN, born in 1792, daughter of Laurence Anderson and Jane Watson, died in NY on 24 Nov. 1825. [St Andrews, Fife, g/s]

ANDERSON, ANN WHITE, or BROWN, in Morristown, NY, daughter of David Anderson in Arbroath who died 8 Oct.1886. [NAS.SH.5.6.1889]

ANDERSON, CATHERINE, daughter of Robert Anderson,
Woodbine, Corstorphine, Midlothian, wife of T. Mitchell in
Philadelphia, died there 28 Dec.1861. [S#2042]

ANDERSON, CHARLES, born 1849, from Nenthorn, died in NY
on 11 February 1875. [S#9871]

ANDERSON, CLEMENT, born in North Queensferry, Fife, 1850,
died in NY 30 June 1871. [S#8729]

ANDERSON, DAVID, born in 1775, a stonecutter who settled in
America around 1800, married Jean Pitcaithly in 1806, died
in Brooklyn on 28 May 1839. [ANY.2.96]

ANDERSON, Reverend DAVID, born during 1785, late of
Boghole, Scotland, died in Philadelphia on 8 Nov. 1841.
[AJ#4902]

ANDERSON, DAVID, born on 1 July 1801 in Kilmarnock,
Ayrshire, via Liverpool to America, arrived in NY City on 12
Sep. 1821 aiming to settle in Philadelphia, nat. in NY on 15
Dec. 1830.[Court of Common Pleas Records]

ANDERSON, DAVID, an engineer from Angus, married Miss
Phillis Irving from Annan, Dumfries-shire, in NY during 1857.
[AO]

ANDERSON, HENRY R., married Elizabeth G. S. Diaper,
daughter of Henry Diaper, in NY on 20 Oct. 1859.
[EEC#23452]

ANDERSON, HUGH, born in Edinburgh, secretary of the NY
Insurance Co from 1804 to 1810, died in NY on 24 Dec.
1812. [ANY#1.374]

ANDERSON, JAMES, born in 1797, son of Laurence Anderson
and Jane Watson, died in Newark on 12 Apr. 1830. [St
Andrews g/s]; a merchant in NY, brother of Laurence
Anderson, deacon of the shoemakers of St Andrews, 1805.
[NAS.B65.5.8.238; B65.5.8.240]

ANDERSON, JAMES, naturalised, Philadelphia Court of
Common Pleas, 26 September 1820.

ANDERSON, JAMES, late in Dundee, third son of James
Anderson a wine merchant in Arbroath, Angus, died in NY 1
November 1868. [S#7897]

ANDERSON, JAMES, from Edinburgh, married Balmain,
youngest daughter of Walter Black from Hamilton, in the
house of her uncle William Semple, Alleghany County, Pa.,
1 January 1867. [S#7326]

ANDERSON, JAMES KEITH, from Leith, married Maggie Bruce
Baxter, youngest daughter of Laurence Baxter a sculptor in

Edinburgh, at 370 State Street, Brooklyn, NY, on 19 October 1878. [S#11,014]

ANDERSON, JOHN, eldest son of James Anderson a clothier in Edinburgh, married Annie E. Bavington, third daughter of Thomas Bavington of Bavington County, PA., in Alleghany City, PA., 17 June 1868. [S#7781]

ANDERSON, JOHN LETHAM, from Amoy, China, married Ella, eldest daughter of John S. Harberger, of the Manhattan Bank in NY, at 145 Lexington Avenue, NY, on 25 Mar. 1879. [EC#29498]

ANDERSON, MARGARET, born in 1790, daughter of Alexander Anderson of Udall, Cromarty, died in Canandaigua, NY state, on 30 Aug.1855. [EEC#788792]

ANDERSON, MARGARET, in Brooklyn, 1882. [NAS.SC70.1.125]

ANDERSON, MARY, daughter of George Anderson in Aberchirder, Banffshire, married Francis L. Farquharson from Baltimore, in NY on 10 June 1867.[AJ#6233]

ANDERSON, ROBERT MUNRO, son of John Anderson (1789-1840) and Mary Ross (1806-1871), died in NY. [Kincardine Ardgay g/s]

ANDERSON, WILLIAM, in Philadelphia, 1882. [NAS.PS3.17.70]

ANDERSON, ... , daughter of John Anderson from Edinburgh, was born in NY on 13 Jan. 1839. [SG#742]

ANDERSON, ..., daughter of Walter Anderson from Dunkeld, Perthshire, was born in Pittsburg, PA., 16 september 1868. [S#7860]

ANDREW, ELIZABETH, born in New Galloway, Kirkcudbrightshire, during 1818, married Thomas Harper, died in NY on 15 Dec. 1855. [DGC:15.1.1856]

ANDREW, JOHN MCADAM, born on 16 Sep. 1807, son of John Andrew in Gillsburn [1771-1856] and Jean McAdam [1780-1807], died in NY on 24 May 1835. [Kilmarnock g/s, Ayrshire]

ANGUS, WILLIAM, born in Stirling during 1780, a carpenter who settled in NY City then in Brooklyn, nat. in NY on 7 Nov.1826. [Marine Court Records]

ANNAN, ROBERT, a Presbyterian minister in Baltimore then at Mount Pleasant, Lancaster Co., PA, 1817. [NAS.CS17.1.37/80]

ANNAN, ROBERT, minister in York Co., PA, 1891.[NAS.SC70.1.292]

ANTON, ..., son of John Gray Anton formerly a public-house keeper in Hillside, Montrose, was born in Elizabeth, NJ, on 24 Jan. 1876. [DA#4635]

ARCHIBALD, ANNIE, born in 1844, wife of Frank Davis, from Dunfermline, Fife, died in Portage, PA, on 4 Jan. 1907. [DJ]

ARCHIBALD, CHARLES, son of Thomas Dickson Archibald Senator of the Dominion of Canada, married Edith Jessie Archibald, daughter of E. M. Archibald, HM Consul General in NY, in NY on 2 June 1874. [EC#27689]

ARCHIBALD, ..., son of William Archibald a jeweller, was born at 128 Elem Street, Newark, NJ, 23 May 1872. [S#9006]

ARCHIBALD,......, son of William Archibald a bookbinder from Edinburgh, was born at 204 East 36th Street, NY, on 24 Jan.1878. [S#10,788]

ARMET, ..., son of William Armet a bookbinder, was born in NY 22 August 1868. [S#7733]

ARMET, ..., son of William Armet, a book-keeper from Edinburgh, and his wife Maria Dodds, was born at 31 Lewis Street, N.Y. on 19 January 1870. [S#8278]

ARMSTRONG, GEORGE, born in Roxburghshire, to America in 1818, settled in Ovid, NY, [Sgen#32.3]

ARMSTRONG, JANE, born in 1817, from Garlieston, Sorbie, Wigtownshire, settled at Mount Pleasant, Saratoga County, NY, died there on 27 Jan. 1859. [DGH:18.3.1859]

ARMSTRONG, THOMAS, from Roxburghshire, to America in 1819, settled in Ovid, NY. [Sgen#32.3]

ARMSTRONG, WILLIAM, from Roxburghshire, to NY in 1819, settled in Ovid, NY. [Sgen#32.3]

ARMSTRONG, WILLIAM, born in Kirleton, Gilnockie, Dumfriesshire, son of David Armstrong the Sheriff of Dumfries, a British Army officer from 1775 to 1783, settled in NY during 1790, married (1) Margaret Marshal in 1793, (2) Elizabeth Roberts in 1810, died in Elisabethtown, NJ, on 27 Jan. 1830.[ANY.1.284]

ARNOLD, ..., son of Dr Edmund Arnold, was born in Yonkers, NY, in 1856.[EEC#21067]

ARNOT, ANDREW, a stonecutter from Crossgates, Fife, married Annie Cowan, fourth daughter of John Cowan in Forfar, Angus, in Newark, NJ, on 11 Sep. 1872. [FFP]

ARNOT, JAMES, born in 1767, a merchant, to NY on the <u>George of NY</u>, on 12 Aug. 1807. [PRO.PC1/3790]

ARROTT, JAMES, naturalised, US District Court, Phiadelphia, 19 June 1801.

ARTHUR, Captain JAMES, born in 1798, son of .... Arthur and Elizabeth Herald, died in NY during Apr. 1838. [Dundee g/s]

ARTHUR, JAMES, naturalised, Court of Common Pleas, Philadelphia, 4 October 1813.

ARTHUR, WILLIAM, son of Reverend Michael Arthur in Aberdeen, a minister in Edinburgh 1790, Glasgow 1793, and in Pegua, PA, to 1818, died there during 1827. [UPC#1.441]

ARTHUR, WILLIAM, in Brooklyn, NY, cnf 1876. [NAS.SC70.1.179]

ARTHUR, ... , daughter of Mr Arthur, was born in NY on 25 Dec. 1847.   [SG#17.1685]

ASKEW, Mr, sr., Sciba, Oswego, NY, died on 24 Jan. 1875. [EC#28242]

ASPINWALL, ANNA ROSS, in Pittsburgh, cnf 1895. [NAS.SC70.1.350]

AUCHINCLOSS, HUGH, a merchant in NY, 1818. [NAS.CS17.1.37/670]

AUCHINCLOSS, JAMES, born in Paisley on 19 Apr. 1794, son of James Auchincloss and Jean Lyle, to NY around 1815, a merchant there, married Anna Steuart Shaw in 1821, died on 17 Oct. 1855. [ANY.2.81]

AUCHINVOLE, DAVID, a merchant in NY, 1801. [NAS.CS17.1.9/325]

AUCHTERLONIE, JANE, youngest daughter of James Auchterlonie, St Andrews, Fife, married Joseph Robertson from Brechin, Angus, in Brooklyn on 17 June 1873. [S#9345]

AULD, JAMES WARDROP, third son of Patrick Auld, died in NY on   6 Sep. 1844. [AJ#5050]

AUSTIN, ADAM, from Milton, Moffat, Dumfries-shire, settled in Franklinville, Cattaraugus County, NY, by 1849. [DGH:2.8.1849]

AUSTIN, JOHN B., naturalised, Court of Quarter Session, Philadelphia, 12 May 1807.

AUSTIE, THOMAS, naturalised, US District Court, Philadelphia, 16 May 1797.

BABCOCK, B. F., from Glasgow, married Maria Aug.a Bicknell, daughter of W. T. Bicknell, in Patterson, NJ, on 3 Apr. 1844. [GEP#857]

BAIN, JAMES, in NY, died in July 1848, cnf 1853.
[NAS.SC70.1.79]

BAIN, JOHN, a typefounder in St Andrews, Fife, in 1742, later in Camlachie, Glasgow, settled in Philadelphia. [SA#86]

BAIN, JOHN IRELAND TUCKER, in Brooklyn, grandson of John Bain and Elizabeth McEwan who died 29 Jan.1855.
[NAS.SH.6.8.1889]

BAINE, JOHN, naturalised, Court of Common Pleas, Philadelphia, 17 June 1799.

BAIRD, ROBERT, in NY, 1809. [NAS.CS17.1.28/501]

BALD, ROBERT, naturalised, Court of Common Pleas, Philadelphia, 16 March 1813, and 20 October 1817.

BALFOUR, ..., son of Dr Lewis Balfour, was born in Eldred, McKean County, PA, on 10 June 1887. [EC#30499]

BALIEFF, JOSEPH, born in 1819, drowned near NY on 21 Nov. 1836. [St Michael's Dumfries g/s]

BALLANTINE, WILLIAM, naturalised, Court of Common Pleas, Philadelphia, 9 October 1822 and 17 April 1827.

BANKS, JOHN, born in Stirling around 1763 son of John Banks a merchant in Kilwinning, Ayrshire, educated at Glasgow University in 1787, an Associate Congregation minister from Edinburgh who to America during 1796, settled in NY 1796-1802, moved to Montgomery County, Philadelphia, in 1816 as a schoolmaster and pastor, died there on 10 Apr. 1826. [AP#106][MAGU#149][UPC#1.149]

BARBOUR, WILLIAM, born 31 March 1814 at Castle Douglas, Kirkcudbrightshire, son of Thomas Barbour and Margaret Cochran, a merchant in NY, died at 11 West 32nd St., NY, 13 November 1885. [ANY.2.221]

BARR, MATTHEW, born in Lochwinnoch, a baker who emigrated via Greenock, naturalised in NY on 29 Sep. 1818. [Court of Common Pleas Records]

BARR, ROBERT, master of the Fifeshire of Glasgow married Agnes Moxey Cattenach, youngest daughter of Archibald Cattenach in Philadelphia, in London 7 Feb.1872. [S#8904]

BARRIE, PETER, naturalised, 11 March 1799, Court of Common Pleas, Philadelphia.

BARRON, JOHN, born in 1810, a watchmaker, son of John Barron, [1765-1852] and Ann Allan, 83 Crown Street, Aberdeen, died in NY on 30 Aug. 1851.
[AJ#5408][Aberdeen, Old Machar g/s]

BARRY, CHARLES HENDERSON, in Jefferson, NY, by 1845. [NAS.Perth.SC#45/60]

BAXTER, ARCHIBALD, born Greenock 1823, to NY in 1856, merchant, died in Brooklyn 22 Oct.1884. [ANY.2.288]

BAXTER, MAGGIE BRUCE, daughter of Laurence Baxter a sculptor in Edinburgh, married James Keith Anderson from Leith, at 370 State St., Brooklyn, NY, on 19 Oct.1878. [S#11,014]

BAXTER, THOMAS, from Tranent, East Lothian, died in Philadelphia on 20 March 1870. [S#8325]

BAXTER, ..., son of Thomas W. Baxter, was born in NY on 17 July 1877.[EC#28966]

BAYLEY, THOMAS ELDER, son of Isaac Bayley of Manuel, died in Franklin, PA, 28 January 1875. [S#9849]

BAYNE, PENELOPE SOBER, 29E 29th Street, NY, cnf 1884 Edinburgh.[NAS.SC70.1.231/903]

BEATSON, GEORGE, born 1849, son of John Beatson a miller in Abernethy, Perthshire, died in Trenton, NJ, on 4 August 1873. [S#9385]

BEATTIE, JAMES C., born in 1825, from Kells, Kirkcudbrightshire, died in NY on 11 Nov. 1857. [DGH:11.12.1857]

BEATTIE, LIZZIE, youngest daughter of P.C.Beattie in Edinburgh, married M. Jenkinson, in NY 3 Sept.1870. [S#8470]

BEATTIE, NICHOLAS ARBUTHNOTT DUN, youngest daughter of William Beattie in Edinburgh, married William M. Gow, in NY 18 June 1869. [S#8088]

BEATTIE, WALTER, born in 1789, from Ruthwell, Dumfries-shire, died in Iruxton, Cortland County, NY, on 23 Feb. 1863. [AO]

BECK, JAMES, born in Dumfries 12 January 1814, eldest son of Thomas Beck of Lincluden College Mains, emigrated to NY in 1834, a merchant, quartermaster of the Caledonian Fusiliers, died in NY 24 January 1853. [ANY.2.215]

BECK, JOHN, born in Dumfries 2 September 1817, son of Thomas Beck, emigrated to NY 1842, a merchant, married Janet Johnston from Dumfries-shire in 1853, died in Scotland 13 November 1874. [ANY.2.221]

BECK, MARION, daughter of Thomas Beck in Lincluden Mains, Dumfriesshire, married Charles Bathgate of Morrissiana, West Chester County, in NY on 25 Apr. 1855. [DGC:22.5.1855]

BECK, WILLIAM JOHNSTON, born in Dumfries 14 May 1820, son of Thomas Beck of Tynron, died at West Farms, NY, in Apr. 1877. [ANY#2.242]

BEGBIE, RICHARD, son of John Begbie, painter, 62 Bristo Street, Edinburgh, died in NY on 25 December 1873. [S#9504]

BEGG, ARCHIBALD, in Damascus on the Delaware River 1815. [NAS.CS17.1.34/570]

BEGG, HUGH, a merchant from Glasgow, in NY 1809. [NAS.CS17.1.28/541]

BELL, JAMES, born in 1809, son of David Bell [1778-1859] and Elizabeth Hunter [1780-1837], died in NY on 25 Aug. 1859. [Duns g/s, Berwickshire]

BELL, JOHN,naturalised, Court of Common Pleas, Philadelphia, 11 Nov. 1812, Supreme Court of Pennsylvania, 20 February 1816.

BELL, JOHN L., born in Dumfries 1792, a merchant in NY, died 26 January 1838. [ANY.2.166]

BELL, MARY ANNE, second daughter of John Bell in Ruthwell, Dumfries-shire, and wife of Alexander Hardgrave, died in NY on 27 Oct. 1864.[AO]

BELL, RICHARD, son of Richard Bell in Tanlawhill, Dumfries-shire, settled in New York, died in June 1857, cnf 1860. [NAS.SC70.1.103]

BELL, THOMAS, born 1794, third son of William Bell, Blackadder Mains, Berwickshire, and brother of Mrs Hastie, Colville House, Ayton, died in Eatontown, NJ, on 3 June 1876. [S#10,272]

BELL, WILLIAM, naturalised Court of Common Pleas, Philadelphia, 10 October 1806.

BELL, WILLIAM, born in 1789, a laborer from Methven, Perthshire, via Greenock on 4 Sep. 1817 bound for NY on the William of New York, arrived in NY on 17 Oct. 1817. [NYMunicipal Archives][NY Comm. Advertiser,18.10.1817]

BELL, ..., infant son of William Bell, from Dumfries, and his wife Jane, died in Brooklyn Royal, NY, on 12 Dec. 1854. [DGC:2.1.1855]

BENNETT, JAMES GORDON, born 1795 in Enzie, Banffshire, son of James Bennett and Janet Reid, emigrated to Nova Scotia in 1819, moved to NY 1822, founder of the *New York Herald*, died 2 June 1872. [ANY.2.139]

BENNET, ..., daughter of William Bennet and Elizabeth Martin from Edinburgh, was born in Brooklyn, NY, on 6 July 1854. [EEC#22614]

BERTRAM, GEORGE, born in Cranshaws, Berwickshire, on 2 Dec. 1803, died in Philadelphia on 21 Apr. 1887. [AP#109]

BERTRAM, JAMES, in Salem, NJ, 1807. [NAS.CS17.1.26/257]

BETHUNE, DAVID, born in Dingwall, Ross and Cromarty, during 1771, to Tobago, settled in NY around 1792, a merchant in NY, married Joanna Graham in 1795, died on 18 Sep. 1824 in NY. [ANY.I.318][AP#110]

BETT, JOHN, born in Coupar Angus, Perthshire, during 1825, son of William Bett, settled on Staten Island, NY, by 1864, died in St Andrews, Scotland, on 14 Mar. 1910. [ANY#2.273]

BIGGAM, HAMILTON, born in Doune, Stirlingshire, in 1799, a merchant who was naturalised in NY on 10 Oct. 1826. [Marine Court Records]

BIGGAR, ELIZABETH, from Dundrennan, Kirkcudbrightshire, died in Lewiston, PA, on 14 Oct. 1849. [DGH:17.1.1850]

BIGGAR, GEORGE, in NJ, cnf 1899. [NAS.SC70.1.377]

BIGGAR, JOHN, from Dundrennan, Kirkcudbrightshire, died in Lewiston, PA, on 7 Oct. 1849. [DGH:17.1.1850]

BINNEY, ARCHIBALD, born in Portobello, Midlothian, during 1763, a typefounder in Philadelphia by 1796, died in 1838. [SSA#86]

BISHOP, AGNES, daughter of James Bishop a land-surveyor in Tipperline, married W. Bain, MD, in Torrington, NY, on 16 July 1875. [S#9992]

BISSET, JAMES, a tailor from Edinburgh, then in NY 1796. [NAS.CS17.1.15/403]

BISSETT, SAMUEL, born in Aberdeenshire during 1793, a saddler, and his wife Anne, born in Banffshire in 1793, from Aberdeen, naturalised in NY on 20 Apr.1821. [N.Y. Court of Common Pleas]

BLACK, J. FRANCIS, son of William Black in Leven, Fife, married Sadie M. Swingle, daughter of William Swingle of Forrestville, NY, in Albany, NY, on 2 Dec. 1886. [FFP]

BLACK, JAMES, son of Robert Black of Easter Portsburgh [died on 16 Mar. 1790] and Rachel Ray [died on 8 Mar. 1798], settled in Philadelphia.[St Cuthbert's g/s, Edinburgh]

BLACK, JAMES, naturalised, Court of Common Pleas, Philadelphia, 3 June 1805.

BLACK, JAMES, late of Philadelphia, died at 1 East Claremont Street, Edinburgh, on 24 Mar. 1843. [EEC#20585]

BLACK, JOHN, born in 1791, a laborer from Lundy, Angus, from Greenock on 4 Sep. 1817 bound for NY on the William of NewYork, arrived in NY on 17 Oct. 1817. [NYMunicipalArchives] [NY Commercial Advertiser, 18.10.1817]

BLACK, JOSEPH, a soldier of the Voluntary Artillery in NY, died on 21 July 1847, cnf 1857. [NAS.SC70.1.94]

BLACK, WILLIAM, from Ayrshire, died in Troy, Rensselaer County, NY, on 19 January 1823. [DGC:10.2.1836]

BLACKBURN, WILLIAM, naturalised, Supreme Court of Pennsylvania, 15 June 1799.

BLACKIE, WILLIAM, born in 1792, late a merchant in Glasgow, died in NY on 21 May 1823. [DPCA#1092][EEC#17474]

BLADWORTH, GEORGE HILL, from Edinburgh, married Jessie Bonthron, eldest daughter of James Swirles a merchant in Edinburgh, in NY 9 Sept.1870. [S#8476]

BLADWORTH, ..., daughter of George Bladworth was born in NY 3 Sept. 1871. [S#8770]

BLAIR, ANDREW, born in Stirlingshire during 1787, his wife Janet born in Glasgow during 1793, and their son Thomas R. Blair born in Glasgow during 1815, to America via Liverpool, naturalised in NY on 11 May 1821. [N.Y.Court of Common Pleas]

BLAIR, JOHN, in Philadelphia 1784. [NAS.CS17.1.2/53]

BLAIR, JOHN G., a merchant, eldest son of William Blair of Fintry, died in Sengerties, NY, on 31 Oct. 1839. [SG#8/823]

BLAKIE, JAMES, naturalised, Supreme Court of Pennsylvania, 17 June 1799.

BLANE, THOMAS, late a merchant in NY, now in London, 1787.[NAS.CS17.1.6,271]

BLOUNT, GEORGE, a cabinetmaker from Dumfries, died in NY on 26 Oct. 1840. [DGH:10.12.1840]

BLUNT, AGNES OLIVER, from Roxburghshire, married John McGeorge in Philadelphia during 1850. [DGH:19.12.1850]

BOGIE, JAMES, a florist, son of William Bogie in Kimmental Green, Annan, Dumfries-shire, died in Boulevard Grove, Brooklyn, on 4 Jan. 1870. [AO]

BOGLE, ROBERT, a merchant, late of NY, died in Wilmington, North Carolina, in Dec. 1785. [GM#IX.427.80]

BONE, ROBERT, son of Robert Bone in Edinburgh, died in Philadelphia on 27 March 1872. [S#8974]

BONNAR, Rev. JAMES, born in Edinburgh 2 September 1810, to Ohio 1835, an Episcopalian minister and schoolmaster in Pennsylvania from 1840, died 29 June 1880. [AP#123]

BONNAR, WILLIAM, naturalised, Court of Common Pleas, Philadelphia, 25 May 1797.

BONTHRON, JOHN, born in 1789, to Philadelphia in 1817, naturalised in Washington DC in 1828.

BORRIE, RALPH, naturalised, Supreme Court of Pennsylvania, 3 May 1799.

BORTHWICK, ROBERT, naturalised, Court of Common Pleas, Philadelphia, 4 October 1823, and 6 October 1827.

BOSTON, JOHN, born 1741, emigrated via Liverpool to NY on the Stephen 28 May 1804, slater, died Belleville, NJ, 10 Aug.1819. [ANY.27]

BOSTON, ROBERT, born in Kelso, Roxburghshire, during 1779, a slater in NY from 1806 to 1813, naturalised in NY on 17 Apr. 1811, died on 11 Dec. 1813. [ANY#2.7]

BOSWELL, Mrs ELIZABETH, born in 1815, relict of David Boswell MD, from Edinburgh, died in NY on 15 Apr. 1878. [EC#29201]

BOTT, JAMES, naturalised, Supreme Court of Pennsylvania, 17 January 1812

BOWES, ..., an architect from Edinburgh, then in Philadelphia 1796.   [NAS.CS17.1.15/403]

BOWIE, ELIZABETH LEIGHTON, daughter of William Bowie in NY, married William Dickson a stationer from Dundee, in Edinburgh on 20 June 1842. [SG#11.1199]

BOWIE, JOHN HENRY, born in Aberdeen during 1808, to NY 1825, a leather merchant in NY, a member of the legislature 1847-1848, died in Brooklyn 3 July 1859. [AJ: 3.8.1859][ANY.2.263]

BOWIE, RALPH, a lawyer, to America in 1783, settled in Philadelphia and York, PA, a counsellor at law in Philadelphia,married Anna Bartholemew, daughter of George Bartholemew a merchant in Linlithgow, West Lothian, in Edinburgh 15 July 1788. [Edinburgh Marriage Register], died in 1816. [AP]

BOWMAN, ARCHIBALD, a merchant in NY who died in Glasgow during May 1790, cnf 3 Nov. 1790 Commissariat of Glasgow. [NAS.CC9.7.74][NAS.CS17.1.23/84]

BOWMAN, SARAH, from Edinburgh, settled in Staten Island, NY, cnf 1889. [NAS.SC70.1.273]

BOX, THOMAS, in Buffalo, cnf 1862. [NAS.SC70.1.212]

BOYCE,....., dau. of Joseph Boyce, was born in NY on 28 August 1867. [S#7531]

BOYD, THOMAS, of 278 West 31st Street, NY, died on 27 May 1860, cnf 1865. [NAS.SC70.1.124]

BOYD, WILLIAM, born in Alloway 1799, a merchant in NY, married Mrs Agnes Crerar 14 May 1835, died NY 12 July 1864. [ANY.2.156]

BRAND, JAMES, born in Dumfries on 31 Jan. 1822, son of James Brand [1781-1840] and Jean McQueen, a merchant in Ceylon and later in New York, died in NY on 12 May 1897. [ANY#2.242][Dumfries g/s]

BRAND, WILLIAM, born in Dundee during Oct. 1813, son of James Brand and Isabella Nicoll, later a linen merchant in NY from 1841 to 1865, died near Dundee on 11 Dec. 1882. [ANY#2.205]

BRAND, GEORGE, married Annie Laing, daughter of Captain Laing, in Brooklyn   on 2 Sep. 1879. [AO]

BRANDER, JAMES S., born on 31 Dec. 1795 in Inverness, to USA around 1810, married Harriet A. McCulloch in Petersburg, Virginia, during 1820, a merchant in NY, New Orleans and Virginia, also a shipowner and marine insurance broker, died in NY on 13 Feb. 1876. [ANY.2.184]

BRANDER, JOHN, in Vernon, PA, died on 14 Oct. 1863, cnf 1865. [NAS.SC70.1.128]

BRANDS, ROBERT ABERCROMBY, a writer in Forres, Morayshire, then in Sugar Grove, Warren Co., PA.,1838. [NAS.RS.Elgin#254]

BRASH, ..., son of James Brash from Edinburgh, died at Broomfield Avenue, Newark, NJ, 25 July 1873. [S#9373]

BREEDON, BENJAMIN F., a merchant in NY, cnf 1874. [NAS.SC70.1.168]

BRIGGS, DAVID, a merchant, brother of Alexander Briggs a merchant in Dalkeith, Midlothian, died in NY on 1 July 1796. [CM#11701, 1.9.1796]

BROADFOOT, G.S., a gardener, married Agnes Drysdale, youngest daughter of John Drysdale in Rosehall, Haddington, East Lothian, at 15th Street, 7th Avenue, NY, on 28 february 1874. [S#9563]

BROCKIE, WILLIAM, born in Edinburgh on 23 Dec. 1834, shipping agent in Philadelphia from 1865, died there on 12 Sep. 1890, buried in Northwood Cemetery. [AP#125]

BROCKIE, ..., son of William Brockie, was born in Germantown, PA, 18 July 1872. [S#9058]

BROCKIE, ..., son of William Brockie, was born in Germantown, PA, 19 January 1875. [S#9841]

BRODIE, ALEXANDER OSWALD, born on 25 Sep. 1787, son of Rev. Alexander Brodie and Helen Pitcairn, a merchant in NY from 1816, died in Edinburgh 1856. [F#5.190][ANY.2.45]

BRODIE, ANDREW, naturalised, Court of Quarter Session, Philadelphia, 2 October 1811.

BRODIE, ELIZABETH, in NY, died in Edinburgh on 13 Oct. 1857, cnf 1859. [NAS.SC70.1.101]

BRODIE, GEORGE, born in Meggatdale, Selkirkshire, 1814, to US in 1846, settled in NY, died there on 2 May 1866. [ANY#2.289]

BRODIE, JAMES WEBSTER, born in Selkirkshire during 1804, a distiller, via Greenock to America, nat. in NY on 14 May 1828.[Southern District Court Records]; a merchant in NY, died 3 December 1879. [ANY.2.185]

BRODIE, JOHN, born in Perthshire during 1767, a slater, with his wife Elizabeth Archibald, daughter Lindsay born 1798, sons John born 1800 and James born 1802, via Liverpool to NY, naturalised in NY on 15 Nov. 1819.

BRODIE, JOHN, born in Dundee in 1799 son of John Brodie and Elizabeth Archibald, to USA in 1819, a slater in NY, married Helen Pirnie on 2 Jan. 1835, died in NY in 1866. [ANY.2.205]

BRODIE, WILLIAM, sr., from Edinburgh, died NY 5 May 1879. [S#11,180]

BROWN, ALEXANDER, Greenwich Street, NY, 22 Aug. 1853. [NAS.RS.Edinburgh#64/110]

BROWN, ANDREW, from Leith, died in NY on 1 Aug. 1828. [DGC:25.11.1828]

BROWN, CATHERINE, wife of James Greenfield, late of Causewayside, Edinburgh, died in NY on 28 Sept.1862. [S#2288]

BROWN, ELIZABETH, from Dumfries-shire, married Thomas Nichol a compositor from Dumfries-shire, Brooklyn 24 Feb. 1870. [AO]

BROWN, FRANCIS, born in Earlston on 4 March 1816, company director in NY, died at Tarrytown 12 April 1886. [ANY.2.166]

BROWN, Rev. GEORGE, MA, died in New Brunswick, NJ, 23 March 1860. [S#1525]

BROWN, GEORGE, in Buffalo, died on 25 Jan. 1863, cnf Edinburgh 1864.[NAS.SC70.1.123]

BROWN, JAMES, naturalised, Supreme Court of Pennsylvania, 20 Feb.1798.

BROWN, JAMES, naturalised, Court of Common Pleas, Philadelphia, 20 September 1825, and 3 March 1826.

BROWN, JAMES N., a tailor in NY, 1863. [NAS.SC58.59.26.165]

BROWN, JOHN, a stonecutter in Woodbury, Gloucester County, NJ, probate 23 Dec.1788 NJ [NJA.Liber 31/37]

BROWN, JOHN, born 1843, third son of Robert Brown, 1 Cheyne Street, Edinburgh, died in Philadelphia 1870. [S#8335]

BROWN, MARY, second daughter of William Brown a seedsman in Glasgow, wife of Reverend Archibald MacLay, died in NY on 20 Sep. 1848. [SG#1765]

BROWN, RACHEL, in Mearville, PA, cnf 1877 Edinburgh. [NAS.SC70.1.182/1018]

BROWN, ROBERT, born in 1767, formerly of Perth Nurseries, died in Philadelphia on 20 Sep. 1845. [EEC#21257][W#616][DGH:23.10.1845]

BROWN, THOMAS, born 1857, sixth son of William Brown a wright in Pittenweem, Fife, died in Philadelphia on 18 March 1874. [S#9582]

BROWN, ..., son of David Brown, died NY 9 Aug.1863. [S#2559]

BROWN, ..., daughter of William Brown from Langholm, Dumfries-shire, was born in Brooklyn on 28 Oct. 1866. [AO]

BROWN,......, daughter of David Brown, was born in Brooklyn on 25 April 1868. [S#7732]

BROWN,......, son of James C. Brown, Superintendent of Thomson Road Steamers, was born in Paterson, NJ, 5 Oct.1870.[S#8497]

BROWNLEE, WILLIAM CRAIG, born in Torfoot, Lanarkshire, during 1783, son of James Brownlee of Torfoot and Margaret Craig, graduated MA from Glasgow University 1803, to America around 1808, a minister of the Associate Presbyterian Church at Mount Pleasant, Washington County, PA, also in Philadelphia, and in Basking Ridge, NJ, professor at Rutgers College in 1825, and pastor of the

SCOTS IN THE MID-ATLANTIC STATES, 1783-1883

Reformed Dutch Church in NY, died there on 10 Feb. 1860, buried in Second Street Cemetery, NY, husband of Maria MacDougall; naturalised, Supreme Court of Pennsylvania, 20 April 1813, and Court of Common Pleas, Philadelphia, 23 May 1820. [AP#129][MAGU#189][ANY.2.149]

BRUCE, ALEXANDER, born in Aberdeen during 1789, a grocer who emigrated via Grangemouth to NY, naturalised there on 18 Apr. 1821 and on 20 Sep. 1827. [N.Y. Marine Court Records][N.Y.Court of Common Pleas Records]

BRUCE, CHARLES KEY, from Musselburgh, Midlothian, a physician in Philadelphia, died in 1826. [Inveresk g/s, Midlothian]

BRUCE, DAVID, naturalised, Court of Common Pleas, Philadelphia, 27 June 1803.

BRUCE, GEORGE, born in Edinburgh on 26 June 1781, son of John Bruce, to Philadelphia in 1795, a printer and typefounder in New York, married (1) Margaret Watson in 1803, (2) Catherine Wolfe, father of David, died in 1866. [ANY#1.383]

BRUNNER, WILLIAM, from Glasgow, settled in NY, cnf Edinburgh 1894.[NAS.SC70.1.336]

BRUNTON, ARCHIBALD, son of William Brunton {1776-1841} and Elizabeth Richardson, Tinwald, Dumfries-shire, died in Philadelphia on 26 Aug.1839. [DGH:11.10.1839]

BRYCE, JAMES, from Edinburgh, married Mary Anne Wares, second daughter of David Wares in Pultneytown, Wick, Caithness, in NY on 23 March 1872. [S#8955]

BRYCE, Mrs JAMES, second daughter of David Wares, Pulyneytown, Wick, Caithness, late of Edinburgh, died in NY on 5 July 1878. [S#10,924]

BRYCE, JOHN, a merchant from Glasgow, in NY 1805. [NAS.CS17.1.24/118]

BRYCE, WILLIAM, born in Midcalder 1782, saddler in NY by 1806, died 27 May 1830. [ANY.2.31]

BRYCE, ..., daughter of David Bryce from Glasgow, was born at 12 Sheridan Ave., Totowa, Paterson, NY, on 27 July 1874. [S#9701]

BRYDEN, JAMES, born 1751, innkeeper in Baltimore by 1796, settled in NY 1808, owner of the Tontine Coffee House, died in Baltimore 1820. [ANY.2.8]

BRYDEN, JOHN, born in Dumfries-shire during 1800, died at Clark's Hill, Oneida County, NY, on 10 Jan. 1875. [AO]

BRYSON, CHRISTIAN, born in 1793, a spinster from Chapehill, Moneddy, Perthshire, from Greenock on 4 Sep. 1817 bound for NY on the William of NewYork, arrived in NY on 17 Oct. 1817.
[NYMunicipal Archives][NY Commercial Adv., 18.10.1817]

BRYSON, JAMES, born in 1794, a laborer from House of Burn, Monivaird, Perthshire, from Greenock on 4 Sep. 1817 bound for NY on the William of New York arrived in NY on 17 Oct. 1817.
[NYMunicipal Archives][NY Commercial Adv., 18.10.1817]

BRYSON, ROBERT, born in 1787, a laborer, his wife Elizabeth born in 1795, and daughter Jean born in 1815, from the House of Burn, Monyvaird, Perthshire, from Greenock on 4 Sep. 1817 bound for NY on the William of New York, arrived in NY 17 Oct.1817. [NYMunicipal Archives#2999][NY Comml Adv.,18.10.1817]

BRYSON, ROBERT, born in 1787, a laborer from Chapelhill, Moneddy, Perthshire, from Greenock on 4 Sep. 1817 bound for NY on the William of New York, arrived in NY on 17 Oct. 1817. [NYMunicipal Archives][NY Commercial Adv., 18.10.1817]

BUCHAN, JAMES, born at Harelaw Mains in Linton, Roxburghshire, on 3 Sep. 1812, via Leith to Montreal in 1833, settled in NY during 1835, died there on 29 Apr. 1887. [ANY#2.235]

BUCHAN, JOHN GENTLES, a linen agent in NY, cnf Edinburgh 1884. [NAS.SC70.1.236]

BUCHAN, ROBERT, in NY, 1801. [NAS.CS17.1.9/242]

BUCHANAN, ALEXANDER, shipmaster in NY, executor of Alexander Buchanan, sometime of Tobago then in Campbeltown, Argyll, edict of executry, 1811.[NAS.CC2.8.115,13]

BUCHANAN, ALEXANDER, in NY, then in Campbelltown, Argyll, cnf 20 Dec. 1811 Commissariot of Argyll. [NAS.CC2/3.14, 224]

BUCHANAN, HENRY, from Edinburgh, in Toronto or NY state, 30 Jan. 1837. [NAS.RS-Edinburgh#46/125]

BUCHANAN, JAMES, baptised on 6 Nov. 1769, son of David Buchanan and Margaret Grubb in Montrose, Angus, later a merchant in NY, died there during 1786. [ANY#1.219]

BUCHANAN, JAMES, British Consul for NY and NJ, 1833. [NAS.SC58.59.13.247]

BUCHANAN, JOHN, born in Glasgow around 1786, a tallow chandler, emigrated via Greenock, naturalised in NY on 4 Mar. 1826. [N.Y.Court of Common Pleas Records]

BUCHANAN, MARY, from Glasgow, in NY 1816. [NAS.CS17.1.35/196]

BUCHANAN, THOMAS, born 24 Dec. 1744 in Glasgow son of George Buchanan, maltman in Glasgow, and Jean Lowden, educated at Glasgow University, to NY in 1763, a merchant there, died 10 Sep. 1815. [ANY][NAS.RS54.PR36/308] [NAS.CS17.1.23/124]

BUCHANAN, ..., son of Isaac Buchanan, was born in NY on 29 Feb. 1848. [SG#1702]

BUCKHAM, ANDREW, born in Edinburgh during 1780, a physician in NY from 1825 to 1844, died there on 21 Apr. 1844. [ANY#2.144]

BUCKHAM, JOHN, born in Edinburgh during 1806, son of Dr Andrew Buckham and his wife Jane, to USA in 1819, a merchant in NY, died there on 24 Sep. 1835. [ANY.2.145]

BUDGE, HELEN COPLAND SUTHERLAND, second daughter of John Budge in Skerpie, Burray, Orkney, married James, second son of John Johnstone in Burray, at 108, 10th St., Williamsburgh, NY, 23 Nov.1870. [S#8543]

BUIST, ROBERT, born Cupar, Fife 1805, horticulturalist, to Philadelphia in 1828, died there on 13 July 1880. [AP#129]

BUNZEA, WILLIAM, a weaver, portioner of Newstead, then in Lignor Valley, Westmoor County, Pennsylvania, 1797. [NAS.CS26.1906.13]

BURD, ALEXANDER, born 1825, son of Robert Burd, 2 Dunbar's Close, Edinburgh, died in PA on 7 June 1874. [S#9664]

BURDEN, HENRY, born in Dunblane, Perthshire, on 22 Apr. 1791, son of Peter Burden and Elizabeth Abercrombie, settled in Troy, NY, during 1819, died in 1871. [BLG#2591]

BURGESS, JOHN, in NJ, cnf Edinburgh 1878. [NAS.SC70.1.187]

BURGESS, WILLIAM, from Kells, Kirkcudbrightshire, died in NY on 31 May 1823. [DGH:9.7.1823]

BURGESS, WILLIAM, from NY, son of Rev. William Burgess in Glasgow, married Adelaide Richardson Goodlade, youngest daughter of D. R. Goodlade in County Armagh, there on 7 July 1869. [S#8095]

BURNETT, CATHERINE, born in 1852, wife of Duncan McPherson, died at 101 East 40th Street, NY, on 22 Jan. 1875. [AO]

BURNETT, ELIZABETH, second daughter of John Burnett in Edinburgh, married James B. Baillie a pianoforte manufacturer, in NY on 31 May 1875. [S#9975]

BURNETT, JAMES G., of Friendville, Aberdeen, married Mary Grace Tyrel, youngest daughter of Nathan Tyrel of Providence, Rhode Island, in NY during 1837. [AJ#4683]

BURNETT, JOHN, naturalised, Court of Quarter Sessions, Philadelphia, 1 June 1813.

BURNETT, JONATHAN, a grocer from Bannockburn, Stirlingshire, naturalised in NY on 18 June 1830. [Superior Court Records]

BURNETT, WILLIAM, born in 1827, from Banff, died in Greenwich, NY State, on 9 May 1854. [AJ: 12.7.1854]

BURNETT, WILLIAM, a merchant in NY, cnf Edinburgh 1857. [NAS.SC70.1.94]

BURNIE, ROBERT, from Dumfries-shire, died NY in Nov.1875. [AO]

BURNS, ANN LOCKHART, born in 1772, relict of James Darsie, died in Alleghany City on 2 Jan. 1847. [EEC#21463]

BURNS, CHARLES, born 1828, fr. Edinburgh, died 20 Mar.1861 at 1005 Broadway, 27th Street, NY. [S#1817]

BURNS, JAMES, born in Hamilton, Lanarkshire, around 1775, died in Sterling, Cayuga County, NY, on 8 Feb. 1845. [DGH:27.3.1845]

BURNS, JOHN, naturalised, Supreme Court of Pennsylvania, 20 February 1798.

BURNS, Dr ROBERT, born in Glasgow on 9 Nov. 1809, educated at Glasgow University, to Philadelphia on the 5 May 1828, a physician who graduated from the University of PA 5Apr.1839, died in Frankford, Philadelphia, on 12 Mar. 1883. [AP#134]

BURNS, ROBERT, born in Dumfries, mate in the US Navy, died in Brooklyn Naval Hospital, USA, on 28 Jan. 1865.[AO]

BURNS, WILLIAM, born around 1796, to America by 1824, a merchant in NY, died there on 30 Sep. 1845. [ANY.2.105]

BURT, ANDREW, in Baltimore 1812, eldest son of John Burt, tacksman of the Pittencrieff Coalworks. [NAS.CS17.1.31/397]

CAIRNS, JAMES MILN, born near Longforgan, Perthshire, during 1806, son of Rev. Adam Cairns and ... Miln, graduated from Glasgow University, a schoolmaster in NY, died on 24 July 1832 in Peebles, Scotland. [ANY#2.27/135]

CAIRNS, WILLIAM, of Torr, in the Stewartry of Kirkcudbright, a merchant in NY 1819. [NAS.CS17.1.39/203]

CALDERHEAD, ALEXANDER, born around 1751, from Cambuslang, Lanarkshire, a minister in Berwickshire from 1787 to 1802, settled in West Middleton, PA and later in Ohio, died 31 Jan. 1812. [UPC.I.419]

CALDWELL, JAMES, born in Kilmarnock, Ayrshire, 1822, a merchant in NY 1856, died there 16 Feb.1862.[ANY.2.264]

CALLENDAR, JAMES, born in Leith on 4 June 1829, to NY in 1850, a merchant there, died in Brooklyn on 23 Apr. 1903. [ANY#2.264]

CAMERON, ALEXANDER, born in 1796, from Perthshire, from Greenock to NY on the Recovery on 4 Aug. 1803. [NLS#MS1053]

CAMERON, ALEXANDER, son of James Cameron a merchant in Leith, married Isabella Thompson, eldest daughter of Andrew Craig Johnstone, in NY on 17 October 1867. [S#7593]

CAMERON, ALEXANDER, in Brooklyn, NY, cnf 1884 Edinburgh. [NAS.SC70.1.231/577]

CAMERON, CHARLOTTE SARAH, second daughter of D. Cameron in Inverness-shire, married Robert Dey from Dufftown, Banffshire, in NY on 3 Apr. 1873. [EC#27629]

CAMERON, DANIEL, naturalised, Court of Common Pleas, Philadelphia, 24 September 1808.

CAMERON, Dr JAMES, born in 1785 at Craigie, Kinross, son of James Cameron [1752-1832] and Magdalene Gordon [1757-1830], educated at Glasgow University, settled in NY, died 12 Dec.1851.[Milnathort g/s] [ANY.2.157]

CAMERON, JAMES, naturalised, Supreme Court of Pennsylvania, 19 February 1798.

CAMERON, JAMES, born in Perthshire during 1774, a grocer in NY, died on 22 Jan. 1851. [ANY]

CAMERON, JAMES WATSON, from Dundee, a merchant in NY during the 1840s, settled on Staten Island, possibly died in Dundee. [ANY#2.201]

CAMERON, JEAN, born in 1827, widow of James MacMillan in West Chester County, NY, died in Inverness on 14 July 1877. [Inverness, Chapel Yard g/s]

CAMERON, JEMIMA FISHER, daughter of D. A. Cameron in Glasgow, married Humphrey Ewing Buchan MD from Toronto, in NY 2 Aug.1870. [S#8441]

CAMERON, JOHN, and his wife Kitty, in Caledonia, Genessee County, NY, 1816. [NAS.CS16.1.35/268]

CAMERON, JOHN, MD, born in Kinross, died at North Moore St., NY, 1851. [S.17.1.1852]

CAMERON, JOHN, a commission agent in NY, son of .... Cameron and Margaret Webster in Dundee, 1857. [NAS.SC20.34.32.82/87]

CAMERON, KITTY, in Caledonia, Genesee County, NY, daughter of Alexander Cameron former tacksman of Auchnanellen, wife of John Cameron in Caledonia, 1813. [NAS.CS17.1.33/49]

CAMERON, ..., daughter of William Cameron from Leith, was born in Philadelphia, NY, (sic), on 23 March 1875. [S#9949]

CAMERON, ..., son of William Cameron from Leith, was born at Lime Lake, Macias, Catterangus County, NY, on 20 January 1877. [S#10,468]

CAMPBELL, ADAM, infant son of William Campbell late of the Parcels Department, North British Railway, Edinburgh, died in Tayre, PA., on 20 Oct.1876. [S#10,399]

CAMPBELL, ALEXANDER, naturalised, Supreme Court of PA, 19 February 1798.

CAMPBELL, ALEXANDER A., born in Auchterarder, Perthshire, on 16 Feb. 1823, a carpenter and builder, to Philadelphia in May 1861, died there on 26 Aug. 1903. [AP#138]

CAMPBELL, ANGUS WILLIAM, in NY, cnf Edinburgh 1893. [NAS.SC70.1.315]

CAMPBELL. ARCHIBALD, born in Glen Lyon, Perthshire, on 16 Nov. 1779, son of Donald Campbell and Mary Campbell, to Saratoga, NY, in 1798, married Mary Grant on 30 June 1806, settled in Albany, NY, died there on 14 July 1865. [CCS/USA]

CAMPBELL, ARCHIBALD, from Glasgow, married Grace Victoria Gibson, youngest daughter of John Gibson, in NY on 15 Nov. 1849. [SG#1879]

CAMPBELL, ARCHIBALD, born on 31 Dec. 1824, to Philadelphia in 1842, cotton goods manufacturer in Manayunk, Philadelphia, died in Germantown, PA, 23 Oct. 1874. [AP#139]

CAMPBELL, DANIEL, in NY, wife Susanna, father of Archibald, Jane, Mary, Margaret and Catherine, probate 20 Sep. 1779 NY.

CAMPBELL, DANIEL, naturalised, Court of Quarter Sessions, Philadelphia, 14 Feb.1821.

CAMPBELL, DAVID, son of John Campbell of Barcaldine, a prisoner in NY, 1787. [NAS.GD170.1628.40]

CAMPBELL, DAVID, naturalised, Supreme Court of Pennsylvania, 20 February 1798.

CAMPBELL, DONALD, born in 1754, a Loyalist and British Army officer from 1776 to 1783, married Margaret Campbell in NY on 2 Aug. 1815, died 18 Aug.1825, probate 31 Aug.1825 NY. [Loyalists of NJ in the Revolution, p.39]

CAMPBELL, GEORGE, a farmer in Chautague County, NY, 1843. [NAS.RS.Wigtown.4.16]

CAMPBELL, HUGH, naturalised, Court of Quarter Session, Philadelphia, 28 September 1808.

CAMPBELL, JAMES, settled in Elizabethtown, NY, by 1791. [NAS.NRAS#0934/98]

CAMPBELL, JAMES, naturalised, Supreme Court of Pennsylvania, 28 December 1798.

CAMPBELL, JAMES KIRKLAND, born Aug.1802 near Edinburgh, educated at Edinburgh University, a minister in NJ 1838-1855, and in NY, died 29 Sept.1873. [ANY.2.290]

CAMPBELL, JANE, eldest daughter of Samuel Campbell in NY, died 19 May 1806. [EEC]

CAMPBELL, JEAN, born in 1788, daughter of David Campbell [1756-1821] and Janet McNish [1756-1834], died in Delaware City, USA, on 13 Nov.1853. [Balmaghie g/s, Kirkcudbrightshire]

CAMPBELL, JOHN, naturalised, Supreme Court of Pennsylvania, 3 July 1802.

CAMPBELL, JOHN, born in 1792, a cooper from Aberdeen, arrived in NY on the brig Gowan in Sep. 1822. [USNA/par]

CAMPBELL, JOHN, born in Kincardine-on-Forth 1815, died in Jersey City on 28 April 1871. [S#8674]

CAMPBELL, JOSEPH, jr., from Glasgow, married Mary Abby Hague, only daughter of Reverend William Hague DD, in Orange, NJ, on 2 July 1873.   [EC#27695]

CAMPBELL, MALCOLM, born 1781, a farmer from Argyll, with his wife and five children, arrived in America during Sep. 1807, settled in Russia, Herkimer County, NY. [1812]

CAMPBELL, MARY, born in Glen Lyon, Perthshire, in 1753, daughter of Peter Campbell and Margaret Stewart, married

Donald Campbell (1750-1782), to NY in 1798, died in York, Genesee County, NY, during 1823. [CCS/USA]

CAMPBELL, MARY A., or WHYTE, 194 Brooklyn Street, NY, 3 Jan. 1884. [NAS.RS.Edinburgh#149/230]

CAMPBELL, MARY ANN, in Fonda, Montgomery County, NY, cnf Edinburgh 1885. [NAS.SC70.1.247/620]

CAMPBELL, PETER, from Killin, Perthshire, to Canada on the Harmony in 1817, later settled in Glovesville, NY. [CGS#274]

CAMPBELL, QUINTIN, born in Nov. 1774 in Glenfairn, Galloway, son of Reverend Campbell, arrived in Philadelphia in Sep. 1790, a banker in Philadelphia, died there on 6 Apr. 1863. [AP#141]

CAMPBELL, RACHEL, alias McMunn, in NJ, 1801. [NAS.CS17.1.20/401]

CAMPBELL, ROBERT, born in Edinburgh on 28 Apr. 1767, son of Samuel Campbell, a bookseller, stationer and publisher in Philadelphia, died in Frankford, Philadelphia, on 14 Aug. 1800. [ANY#1.254][EEC]

CAMPBELL, ROBERT, naturalised, Court of common Pleas, Philadelphia, 17 Feb.1795, and US District Court, Philadelphia, 1 May 1798.

CAMPBELL, ROSE, naturalised US District Court, Philadelphia, 1 May 1798.

CAMPBELL, ROSS, of Ross Campbell and Company of NY and Baltimore,died on 3 Mar. 1876. [EC#28532][DA#4652]

CAMPBELL, SAMUEL, born in Edinburgh or St Andrews during 1738, died in NY on 17 April 1813. [SM#75.639][EEC#1813] [NAS.CS17.1.26/10, 58] [NAS.B65.7.1.122]

CAMPBELL, WILLIAM, a merchant in NY, 1787. [NAS.CS17.1.6, 382]

CAMPBELL, WILLIAM, naturalised, Court of Common Pleas, Philadelphia, 7 Sept. 1819, and 27 Sept. 1822.

CAMPBELL, WILLIAM, youngest son of William Campbell of Queenshill, died in Philadelphia on 22 June 1842. [EEC#20393][DGH:28.7.1842]

CAMPBELL, WILLIAM, born in 1796, son of William Campbell [1763-1816] and Jane Herron [1752-1835], died in NY in June 1850. [Crossmichael g/s, Kirkcudbrightshire]

CAMPBELL, WILLIAM HENRY, in Brooklyn, grand-nephew of Margaret Waldie who died 1 Feb.1868, wife of Henry Linn in Edinburgh. [NAS.SH.6.9.1886]

CANDLISH, THOMAS CHARLES, in NY, brother of William Candlish, a draper in Kirkcudbright, who died on 7 January 1887. [NAS.SH.4.8.1896]

CANNON, ELIZA M., in NY, cnf Edinburgh 1881. [NAS.SC70.1.204/899]

CARLOW, ALEXANDER, born around 1785, a truckman, via Liverpool, naturalised in NY on 10 Apr. 1821. [N.Y. Court of Common Pleas Records]

CARMICHAEL, JAMES, and his wife Jean Miller, at Albany Mills 1812.[NAS.CS17.1.32/432]

CARMICHAEL, JOHN, late of Albany, and his son Douglas, 1809. [NAS.CS17.1.29/30]

CARR, ANDREW, born in Auchencairn, Kirkcudbrightshire, during 1745, via London to NY in 1784, a shipbuilder who died in NY on 12 Apr. 1812. [ANY#2.304]

CARR, CATHERINE P., born in Scotland during 1791, arrived in NY on the Camillus in 1821. [USNA.par]

CARRICK, ALEXANDER, born in Paisley 1789,to USA in 1807, a merchant and manufacturer in NY and NJ, died Paterson, NJ, 1 Jan. 1834. [ANY.2.75]

CARRICK, ROBERT, born in Paisley 1789, to USA in 1807, a merchant and manufacturer in NY and NJ died in Paterson, NJ, in 1867. [ANY.2.71]

CARRICK, ROBERT, born in Glasgow in 1802, to America via Liverpool, a merchant, naturalised in NY on 9 May 1827.[Marine Court Records]

CARRINGTON, ISURA, born in 1810, daughter of E. Carrington, Oswego, NY, and wife of James MacFarlane, died in Kingston, Upper Canada, on 10 Nov. 1838. [SG#7/723]

CARRUTH, ..., son of Robert Carruth from Paisley, was born in NY at 631 3rd Avenue, on 29 June 1874. [EC#28022]

CARRUTHERS, JANE, eldest daughter of Captain James Carruthers, Port Street, Annan, Dumfries-shire, married Joseph K. Smith, in Jersey City on 27 Oct. 1865. [AO]

CARRUTHERS, WILLIAM, born in Annan, Dumfries-shire, a millwright who died in Newcastle, Lawrence County, PA, on 8 Dec. 1862.[AO]

CARSON, ANDREW, from Castle Douglas, Kirkcudbrightshire, a merchant, died in NY in May 1849. [DGH:26.7.1849]

CARSTAIRS, THOMAS, a farmer and fruiterer from Edinburgh, died in NY 25 Aug. 1871. [S#8774]

CARSWELL, ALLAN, born 1794, from Colvend, Kirkcudbrightshire, died in East Worcester, Otsego County, NY, on 29 June 1833. [DGC:31.7.1833]

CARTER, PETER, born in Earlston, Berwickshire, 19 July 1825, settled in Galway, Satatoga, NY, 1832, a publisher in NY, died 19 March 1900 in Bloomfield, N.J. [ANY.2.249]

CARTER, ROBERT, born in Earlston, Berwickshire, 2 November 1807, schoolmaster educated at Edinburgh University, settled in NY 1831, a publisher and bookseller in NY, died there 28 December 1889. [ANY.2.212]

CARTER, WALTER, born in Earlston, Berwickshire, on 19 May 1823, son of Thomas Carter and Agnes Ewing, to America in 1831, settled in Saratoga County, NY, died at Montclair, N.J. [ANY#2.254]

CARTLEDGE, .. a son and daughter of John Cartledge, born in Williamsburgh, NY, on 9 Aug.1862. [S#2243]

CARTLEDGE, ..., daughter of John Cartledge, was born in Williamsburgh, NY, on 7 March 1867. [S#7378]

CARY, ELIZABETH C., daughter of T. G. Cary, married Louis Agassix, a Professor at Harvard, in NY on 25 Apr.1850. [W#1109]

CASSIDY, NINA, wife of John Lindsay a type setter from Seton Place, Grange, died in NY on 26 March 1875. [S#9897]

CATTENACH, ARCHIBALD, from Edinburgh, died at 1345 Lombard St., Philadelphia, on 3 December 1872. [S#9181]

CATTENACH, DONALD, naturalised, Supreme Court of Pennsylvania, 16 February 1798.

CAULDCLEUGH, ANDREW, in PA, 1789. [NAS.CS17.1.8,182]

CAULDCLEUGH, ROBERT, in PA, 1789. [NAS.CS17.1.8,182]

CHALMERS, HUGH, a merchant in NY, husband of Charlotte the daughter of William Gordon, 1798. [NAS.CS17.1.17/49]

CHALMERS, JAMES, a carpenter at 1014, 10th Avenue, NY, cnf 1887. [NAS.SC70.1.259]

CHALMERS, PETER, a mechanic at Great Bend Village, PA, late of Gorgie Mills, Edinburgh, married Agnes Donaldson, daughter of Daniel Donaldson, Blair Drummond, Perthshire, at 41 Fillay Street, Brooklyn, on 25 April 1872. [S#8990]

CHALMERS, THOMAS H., born in Fife during 1793, a grocer who was nat.in NY on 7 May 1821. [N.Y.Court of Common Pleas]

CHALMERS, ..., son of James Chalmers an engineer from Edinburgh, was born at Susquehanna Depot, PA, 26 December 1872. [S#9197]

CHALMERS, ..., daughter of Peter Chalmers from Gorgie, Edinburgh, was born at Susquehanna Depot, PA, 23 April 1873. [S#9294]

CHALMERS, ..., daughter of Peter Chalmers a gelatine manufacturer from Gorgie Mills, Edinburgh, was born in Williamsville, NY, on 2 August 1875. [S#10006]

CHILLAS, DAVID, third son of Robert Chillas in Paisley, died in NY on 21 Aug. 1843. [SG#1243]

CHISHOLM, JOHN, born 1857, grandson of Alexander Chisholm of the Edinburgh City Mission, died in Darlington, NJ, on 13 June 1879. [S#11228]

CHRISTIE, CAROLINE ANNE, youngest daughter of Thomas Christie, Springbank, Stirlingshire, Captain of the 70th Regiment, died in Philadelphia on 28 July 1871. [S#8759]

CHRISTIE, JENNIE, eldest daughter of Robert Christie, born in Auchterarder,Perthshire, married A. Gibson from Dumfries-shire, in Philadelphia on 3 July 1873. [AO]

CHRISTIE, JOHN, born in 1745, married Janet McGregor (1757-1852), from Killin, Perthshire, to America, settled at Creek Road, Mumford, New York, in 1797, died on 3 July 1843. ["Genealogy of Miller and Tillotson",Scottsville, NY, 1951]

CHRISTIE, WILLIAM, naturalised, Court of Quarter Session, Philadelphia, 24 September 1813, Court of Common Pleas, Philadelphia,22 September 1818.

CLAPPERTON, THOMAS, from Edinburgh, died in Albany, NY, on 12 September 1867. [S#7549]

CLARK, ALEXANDER, in NJ, cnf 1877 Edinburgh. [NAS.SC70.1.184/147]

CLARK, DANIEL, naturalised, Supreme Court of Pennsylvania, 24 September 1799.

CLARK, DANIEL, naturalised, Supreme Court of Pennsylvania, 4 May 1799.

CLARK, DAVID, naturalised, Court of Quarter Session, Philadelphia, 17 June 1829.

CLARK, DAVID, born in Auchencairn, Kirkcudbright, a lumber merchant in NY from 1799 to 1833, married Mary Buchan in Feb. 1803, died in NY on 30 Dec. 1835. [ANY#2.358]

CLERK, FRANCIS, naturalised, Court of Quarter Session, Philadelphia, 9 October 1802.

CLARK, GEORGE B., from Hamilton, Ontario, married Virginia S. Carr, daughter of John Carr, at Clark's Mills, Oneida County, NY, on 22 Sep.1869. [AO]

CLARK, JAMES, in NY, cnf 1877 Edinburgh. [NAS.SC70.1.181/974]

CLARK, JOHN, naturalised, Court of Common Pleas, Philadelphia, 19 November 1817.

CLARK, JOHN, eldest son of Robert Clark, Clark's Mill, Oneida County, NY, late of Windmill, Annan, Dumfries-shire, died in Hartford, Connecticut, on 2 Mar. 1864. [AO]

CLARK, MARY, from Brechin, Angus, married Donald Fraser from Middlesex County, Ontario, in NY on 30 Apr. 1877. [EC#28899]

CLARK, THOMAS, born in 1772, a farmer from Lochwinnoch, from Greenock on 4 Sep. 1817 bound for NY on the William of New York arrived in NY on 17 Oct. 1817.[NYMunicipal Archives] [NY Commercial Advertiser, 18.10.1817]

CLARK, THOMAS MCLEOD, a merchant in NY, late of Tain, Ross-shire, married Jessie McKay, youngest daughter of Thomas McKay, in Rideau Hall, Bytown, Canada West, on 6 June 1854. [EEC#22604]

CLARK, WILLIAM, born in 1768, from Ballater, Aberdeenshire, died in Jersey City, NY, on 10 Feb. 1851. [AJ:19.3.1851]

CLARKSON, JAMES, son of James and Helen Clarkson, died in NY on 29 September 1867. [S#7553]

CLEGHORN, WILLIAM, a druggist in NY, who died 12 Aug.1853. [NAS.SH.6.11.1897]

CLELAND, ALEXANDER BROWN, MD, of the Royal Canadian Rifle Regiment, married Fanny K. Roberts, youngest daughter of John Roberts of Bristol, in NY on 3 June 1845. [SG#14/1416]

CLELAND, GEORGE, an ironmonger in NY 1812, husband of Ann Smith. [NAS.CS17.1.31/352]

CLEVELAND, CHAS. D., died Philadelphia 18 Aug. 1869. [S#8148]

CLUNIE, MICHAEL, naturalised, Supreme Court of Pennsylvania, 1 March 1810.

COATS, ANDREW, born in Paisley 22 June 1814, son of James Coats a thread manufacturer and Catherine Mitchell, educated at Edinburgh University, a merchant in NY and in Philadelphia 1839-1860, died in Perth 10 Feb. 1900. [ANY.2.214][AP#150]

COATS, Dr DAVID, born in Paisley 1817 son of James Coats and Catherine Mitchell, emigrated to USA in 1839, settled in NY and Philadelphia, died 20 Bleecker St., NY, 18 May1856.[ANY.2.214]

COBURN, ROBERT, naturalised, Court of Quarter Session, Philadelphia, 14 August 1813, and Court of Common Pleas, Philadelphia, 20 September 1813.

COCHRAN, ALEXANDER, naturalised, Supreme Court of Pennsylvania, 2 April 1794.

COCHRAN, ALEXANDER, naturalised, Court of Common Pleas, Philadelphia, 9 October 1813.

COCHRAN, CHARLES PATTERSON, born on 6 Jan. 1804 in Kirkcudbright son of Robert Cochran and Elizabeth Guthrie, educated at Edinburgh University, a physician in Jamaica from 1825 to 1834, then a merchant in NY, died there on 28 Dec. 1869. [ANY#2.250]

COCHRAN, DUNCAN, born in 1797, son of Alexander Cochran, [1763-1820], and Christine MacFarlane, [1769-1841], died in NY 3 June 1827.[Dunbarton g/s]

COCHRAN, FERGUS, born during Dec. 1804 in Kirkcudbright, son of Robert Cochran and Elizabeth Guthrie, a merchant in NY about1830, died in St Croix on 8 Dec. 1831. [ANY#2.135]

COCHRAN, ISABELLA, from Kirkcudbrightshire, died in Dunedin on the Hudson River, NY, on 6 June 1864. [DGH:8.7.1864]

COCHRANE, ISABELLA RAMSAY, daughter of Rupert Cochrane, wife of Edward King in NY, died in Highwood during 1873. [EC#27598]

COCHRAN, JAMES BLAIR, born in Kirkcudbright on 25 Nov. 1799, son of Robert Cochran and Elizabeth Guthrie, an importer in NY from 1831, died in Sing Sing, NY, on 25 Apr. 1859. [ANY#2.266][DGH:13.5.1859]

COCHRAN, JOHN, naturalised, Supreme Court of Pennsylvania, 17 February 1798.

COCHRANE, RICHARD, from Edinburgh, died in Brooklyn on 3 July 1868. [S#7796]

COCHRANE, ROBERT, born Kirkcudbright 9 May 1788, son of Robert Cochrane and Elizabeth Guthrie, married Helen ....., merchant in NY, in Natchez, Mississippi, ca.1845, 'many years resident in NY', died in Albany, NY, on 30 July 1849. [ANY.2.172][SG#1847][DGH:23.8.1849]

COCHRAN, SAMUEL, born in Kirkcudbright 23 February 1806, son of Robert Cochrane and Margaret Guthrie, a merchant in NY, died at Dobbs Ferry, NY, 31 August 1859. [ANY.2.206]

COCHRAN, SAMUEL, a merchant from Kirkcudbrightshire, died in NY on 31 Aug. 1859. [DGH:23.9.1859]

COCHRANE, THOMAS, a watchmaker in Glasgow, married Agnes .... from Vermont, father of Charles, Anna, Archibald and James born 1810, to USA in 1812, settled in NY, died in 1840. [WMQ]

COCHRANE, THOMAS, born in Kirkcudbright 2 June 1807, son of Robert Cochrane and Margaret Guthrie, settled in NY 1831, a lace merchant, died in NY 28 November 1889. [ANY.2.215]

COCHRANE, WILLIAM, partner in Cochrane and Meekier, merchants in Baltimore, 1796. [NAS.CS18.712.24]

COCHRAN, WILLIAM JOHNSON, born in Dundee on 1 May 1797, son of John Cochran and Helen Thornton, a tailor who from Dundee to America on 1 May 1820, naturalised in NY on 27 Mar. 1834.[Superior Court Records]

COCKBURN, JAMES, naturalised, Court of Common Pleas, Philadelphia, 8 December 1813.

COLQUHOUN, ADAM, a weaver in Govan, later in NY 1794. [NAS.CS17.1.13,400]

COLQUHOUN, MARY, daughter of Dugald Colquhoun in Sheein, Argyll, wife of William Fergusson, died in Philadelphia on 18 Aug. 1879. [EC#29621]

COLVILL, MAGGIE VIVERS, born in 1858, daughter of James and Margaret Colvill, died in Trenton, NJ, on 3 Feb. 1874. [AO]

COMBS, MATTHEW, naturalised, Court of Quarter Session, Philadelphia, 29 Sept. 1808.

CONDELL, Mrs THOMAS H., from Aberdeen, died in Brooklyn during 1860.   [AJ:31.10.1860]

CONNELL, JANET GALLETLY, in NY, cnf 1883. [NAS.SC70.1.225/510]

CONNELL, ROBERT, naturalised, US District court, Philadelphia, 19 Sept. 1806.

CONNELL, THOMAS, naturalised, Supreme Court of Pennsylvania, 19 February 1798

CONNELL, THOMAS, born 1858, second son of Captain James Connell of <u>SS Paris</u>, Leith, drowned in the <u>Swiftsure</u> bound from Leith to NY 1 Sept. 1870. [S#8607]

CONNELL, WILLIAM M., son in law of Andrew Turnbull a painter and stationer in Edinburgh, died in NY 27 Aug.1871. [S#8777]

CONNELLY, PATRICK J., from 50 Buccleuch Street, Edinburgh, married Mary Jane Cox of Union Port Hotel, West Chester, NY, in West Chester on 4 Jan. 1873; late of Buccleuch Street, Edinburgh, died Union Port Hotel, Westchester, NY, 1875. [EC#27550][S#9202/10,109]

COOK, DUNCAN, naturalised, US District Court, Philadelphia, 15 August 1817.

COOK, GEORGE FREDERICK, born during 1755 in Berwick-on-Tweed, a tragedian who died in NY on 26 Sep. 1812. [GM#82.494]

COOK, WILLIAM, born in 1825, from New Pitsligo, Aberdeenshire, died in Albany on 27 Aug. 1861. [AJ:18.9.1861]

COOPER, ALEXANDER, second son of James Cooper an upholsterer in Edinburgh, died in NY during Aug. 1832. [EEC#18868]

COOPER, BELFORD, naturalised, Court of Common Pleas, Philadelphia, 3 January 1809.

COOPER, JAMES, naturalised, Court of Quarter Sessions, Philadelphia, 28 September 1808.

COOPER, JOHN, born 1838, a compositor, eldest son of John Cooper in Edinburgh, died in Brooklyn, NY, in Aug. 1878.[S#11,043]

COPELAND, GEORGE, born in Shetland, a grocer who settled in NY before 1785, died there on 25 Dec. 1820. [ANY#1.377]

COPLEY, JANET, in NY, died on 27 Nov. 1850, cnf 1854. [NAS.SC70.1.83]

CORMACK, DANIEL, '50 years a mason in Edinburgh', died in NY 7 Oct.1860. [S#1684]

COSKRY, NATHANIEL, born in Kelton Hill, Kirkcudbright, a hosier and haberdasher in NY from 1807, died at sea in Aug.1811.[ANY#2.6]

COSKRY, SAMUEL, born in Keltonhill, Kirkcudbright, during 1797, to USA by 1830, a merchant in NY who died 17 Oct. 1835. [ANY.2.135]

COVENTRY, ALEXANDER, in Hudson, Columbia County, NY, 1794. [NAS.CS17.1.13,325]

COWAN, S. HUNTER, Captain of the Bengal Staff Corps, married Frances Brown, daughter of D. Brown a merchant in Siam and widow of Henry S. Dean, Rochester, NY, in NY on 27 July 1876. [S#10,321]

CRAIG, ARCHIBALD CUMMING, son of George Craig, in PA before 1820. [NAS.GD1.495/35]

CRAIG, BELLA, elder daughter of Andrew Caraig from Johnstone, Renfrewshire, then NY, wife of Alexander Cameron, died at 533 Pavonia Ave., Hudson City, NJ, on 8 Oct.1877.[S#10,691]

CRAIG, DAVID, at West 31 Street, NY, 1854. [NAS.RS.Auchtermuchty,5,8]

CRAIG, JOHN, born in 1788, son of Thomas Craig and Helen Young, died in Albany, NY, on 11 Jan. 1832. [Llanbryde g/s, Morayshire]

CRAIG, WILLIAM, born in 1822, from Kinnoull, Perthshire, died in NY on 15 Jan. 1873. [EC#27558]

CRAMOND, JAMES, son of Jane Cramond in Tain, Ross and Cromarty, later a merchant in Philadelphia and NY, died in NY on 29 Sep. 1799. [ANY#1.200]; naturalised, Supreme Court of Pennsylvania, 5 Jan.1795.

CRAWFORD, DAVID ROSE, born in 1829, a solicitor from Greenock, died in NY on 6 Oct. 1877. [EC#29035][S#10,687]

CRAWFORD, JAMES, born in 1815, son of Hugh Crawford [1782-1866], a farmer in Galston, and Euphemia White [1788-1878], died in Del. on 29 Aug. 1848.[Loudoun g/s, Ayrshire]

CRAWFORD, JOHN, son of James Crawford [1810-1863] and Margaret Mitchell[1811-1856], settled in Patterson, NJ. [Old Cumnock g/s, Ayrshire]

CRAWFORD, JOHN, son of John Crawford a surgeon in Glasgow, in Newark near NY, 1821. [NAS.CS17.1.40/564]

CRAWFORD, PETER, son of Peter Crawford in Barbieston, Ayrshire, died in NY on 5 Sep. 1843. [SG#xi.1239]

CRAWFORD, ROBERT, son of James Crawford [1810-1863] and Margaret Mitchell[1811-1856], settled in Patterson, NJ. [Old Cumnock g/s, Ayrshire]

CRAWFORD, STEPHEN R., born in Port Glasgow on 22 Jan. 1798, a merchant in Calcutta, India, married Jane Wilson in

Scotland during 1838, to Philadelphia in 1840, died in Fox Chase, Philadelphia, on 28 Apr. 1864. [AP#155]

CROLL, NELLIE TURNBULL, only daughter of David Croll in Edinburgh, married Francis William Lewis of NJ, in Glasgow on 12 April 1878. [S#10,839]

CROMBIE, HUGH, of Humphrey Crombie and Company merchants in Glasgow, a merchant and clerk in NY in 1807. [NAS.CS235.seqn.C2/2]

CROOKS, RAMSAY, born in Greenock on 28 Jan. 1786, a fur trader and explorer in Oregon and Washington, then a merchant and insurance company director in NY, married Emilie Maison in St Louis during 1825, died in NY on 8 Jan. 1859. [ANY.2.150]

CROSBIE, JAMES, born during 1794 in Sanquhar, Dumfriesshire, died in NY on 18 June 1858. [DGH:9.7.1858]

CROSBIE, MARGARET, born in 1824, daughter of William Crosbie a gardener in Dalskairth, Troqueer parish, Kirkcudbrightshire, died in NY on 20 Nov. 1843. [DGH:21.12.1843]

CROSS, ..., son of Reverend James Cross, was born on 20 May 1845 in Blairsville, PA. [AJ#5088]

CROSS, ROBERT, clerk, a Presbyterian in NY 1724. [NAS.CH1.2.49.55]

CROSSLY, THOMAS BALDWIN, in East Orange, NJ, cnf 1897. [NAS.SC70.1.355]

CROW, ALEXANDER, born in Campbelltown, Argyll, on 8 Apr. 1812, to America in 1840, textile manufacturer in Fairmount, Philadelphia, died there on 1 Oct. 1889. [AP#156]

CRUICKSHANK, JAMES, from Glasgow, married Martha Dyer, in Loda, NJ, on 27 May 1860. [S#1557]

CUDDIE, JEAN, wife of John Keir, in Philadelphia, cnf 1831. [NAS.SC70.1.44]

CUMMINGS, WILLIAM, naturalised, Court of Common Pleas, Philadelphia, 30 Nov.1802.

CUNNINGHAM, JAMES, born in Govan during 1801, to USA in 1823, settled in NY, Boston and San Francisco, a mechanical engineer and shipowner, died in Irvington-on-Hudson on 28 Apr. 1870. [ANY.2.292]

CUNNINGHAM, JOHN, born in Scotland during 1781, a laborer, arrived in NY on the Camillus during 1821. [USNA.par]

CUNNINGHAM, WILLIAM, a merchant in NY, 1787. [NAS.CS17.1.6]

CURRIE, ARCHIBALD, from Argyll, a merchant in NY, died in Martinique during 1802. [EA#4048]

CURRIE, GEORGE, born in Scotland during 1799, a laborer, arrived in NY on the Camillus during 1821. [USNA.par]

CURRIE, GILBERT E., born Glasgow 31 Dec.1818, to US 1853, published in NY 1854-1859. [ANY.2.295]

CURRIE, WILLIAM, born 1808, from Crocketfield, Kirkcudbright, died Lynden, Cattaraugus Co, NY, 10 Oct. 1858. [DGH:9.11.1858]

CURRIE, ..., daughter of David C. Currie, was born in Morrissiana, Westchester County, NY, on 20 Dec. 1870. [AO]

CUTHBERT, ARTHUR ANDREW, from Ayr, married Emily Selina Fawcett, daughter of Colonel William Fawcett of London, at Schroon Lake, Warren County, NY, 17 Aug.1861. [S#1947]

CUTHBERTSON, JAMES, naturalised, Supreme Court of Pennsylvania, 13 July 1813.

DALGLEISH, SIMON, born 1790 probably in Glasgow, to USA 1817, a commission agent in NY, died on 21 Jan. 1819. [ANY.2.51]

DALLAS, ALEXANDER, MD, NY, married Gilberta A. Fraser, daughter of Rev. Daniel Fraser in Helmsdale, in Westfield, NJ, on 23 Jan.1878. [s#10,782]

DALYELL, JOHN, from Glenroan, Crossmichael, Dumfries-shire, died in Del. on 18 Oct. 1838. [DGC:26.8.1838]

DALZIEL, JOHN, an overseer on Sir William Pulteney's estate in NY, 1798. [NAS.CS17.1.1.7/95]

DARSIE, GEORGE, to America as a boy, trained as a cabinetmaker in Pittsburgh, PA, a politician from 1842 to 1854, died in Pittsburgh on 3 Mar. 1865. [EFR, 5.5.1865]

DARSIE, JANE, born in Edinburgh on 19 Aug. 1802, with her family to NY in 1812, settled in Pittsburgh during 1817, married .... McGrew, died on Observatory Hill, Alleghany, on 13 Jan. 1888. [Pittsburgh Commercial Gazette]

DARSIE, THOMAS CHALMERS, from Anstruther, Fife, married Edith, dau. of Jas. Benny, in Alleghany City 14 Jan. 1886. [EFR]

DAVIDSON, DAVID S. GOODBURN, born in 1852, eldest son of Andrew Davidson, Burnhead Cottage, Lockerbie, Dumfries-shire, died in Brewster, Putnam, NY, on 20 Mar. 1878. [AO]

DAVIDSON, ELSPETH, born during Dec. 1781, daughter of William Davidson and Anne McLean in Croy, Dalcross

parish, a spinster in Lanniwelg, Almy, Inverness-shire, to
NY on the George of New York on 12 Aug.
1807.[PRO.PC1.3790]

DAVIDSON, EUPHEMIA, in Albany City, cnf 1874.
[NAS.SC70.1.169]

DAVIDSON, JAMES, youngest son of Alexander Davidson,
Clune, Nairnshire, married Elizabeth Brander, youngest
daughter of Alexander Brander of Ormiston, East Lothian, in
NY 23 June 1871. [S#8727]

DAVIDSON, JOHN, naturalised, Court of Common Pleas,
Philadelphia, 28 October 1828

DAVIDSON, WALTER, engineer, son of John Davidson in
Sibbaldbie Mill, Lockerbie, died Bordentown, NJ, 17 Nov.
1868. [AO]

DAVIE, ARCHIBALD, married Margaret Smith in NY 19 May
1798, both from Dalziel, Lanarkshire, [ANY.2.190]; a
merchant in NY, 1803. [NAS.CS17.1.22/488]

DAVIE, JOHN, from Kirkcaldy died Livingston, NJ, 21 April 1870.
[S#8368]

DAVNIE, ELIZABETH JANET, from Aberdeen, married James
Law, a merchant in Auburn, in NY on 24 July 1838.
[AJ#4730]

DAWSON, MARGARET, 2nd dau. Robert Dawson in Alloa,
Clackmannan, married Henry A. Oakman of Troy, NY, in
South Brooklyn, Long Island, 20 Mar.1861. [S#1817]

DEAN, ..., son of Robert Dean, late of 40 Reid Terrace,
Edinburgh, was born in Buffalo on 14 November 1866.
[S#7308]

DEANE, MARIA, eldest daughter of Robert Deane a wine
merchant in Glasgow, married Henry Heaton Bury from NY,
in Glasgow during 1856. [CM#20734]

DEANS, JOHN, a shoemaker in Orange, NJ, 1820.
[NAS.CS17.1.39/382]

DEANS, JOHN, born in 1823, formerly a gardener in Kinmount,
died in Astoria, Long Island, in 1869. [AO]

DEMPSTER, Mrs BEATRIX, wife of John Gardiner late tenant in
Pitkeathly Wells, Perthshire, died in Charleton, NY, in 1807.
[DPCA#262]

DEMPSTER, DAVID, late of Gettysburg, York County, America,
then of Wester Talliochie, Kinross, 1800.
[NAS.CS18.712.24]

DENHAM, PETER, naturalised, Supreme Court of Pennsylvania, 20 February 1798.

DEWAR, JOHN, late of 1 Mound Place, Edinburgh, died in Sayre, PA, on 13 March 1875. [S#9904]

DEWAR, THOMAS, born in 1748, with his wife E. O., from Perthshire, from Greenock to NY on the <u>Recovery</u> 4 Aug.1808. [NLS.MS#1053]

DEY, ROBERT, from Dufftown, Banffshire, married Charlotte Sarah Cameron,second daughter of D. Cameron from Inverness-shire, in NY on 3 Apr. 1873. [EC#27629]

DICK, JAMES, born in 1782, from Scotland to America in 1803, a tanner and currier, with his wife and four children, settled in Plattsburgh, Clinton County, NY. [1812]

DICK, JOHN B., naturalised, Court of Common Pleas, Philadelphia, 8 October 1827.

DICK, JOHN, settled in NY during 1835. [EUL:Gen#717/14]

DICK, JOHN, a horticulturalist in Philadelphia around 1850. [AP#257]

DICK, PETER, son of John Dick a farmer in Laighmoor, Kennethmont,Aberdeenshire, died in NY on 24 Apr. 1855. [AJ:5.12.1855]

DICK, ROBERT, settled in NY during 1835. [EUL:Gen#717/14]

DICK, WILLIAM, naturalised, Court of Common Pleas, Philadelphia, 7 May 1813, and 8 October 1827.

DICKIE, ALEXANDER, from Ayrshire, settled in Buffalo, Washington County, PA, cnf 1888. [NAS.SC70.1.269]

DICKIE, BETSY ANDERSON, eldest daughter of Robert Dickie in Gallowridge, Perthshire, married Robert Garrow, at 182 7th Avenue, NY, 17 September 1869. [S#8170]

DICKIE, JAMES, a manufacturer from Glasgow, in NY by 1801. [NAS.CS17.1.9/63; CS17.1.21/319; CS17.1.18/421]

DICKISON, JANET KERR, born 1854, from Glasgow, wife of William F. Bassett, died in Ogdenburgh, NY, on 21 July 1875. [S#10011]

DICKSON, EDWARD, from NY, married Isobel Gordon, second daughter of William Gordon, in Montrose, Angus, on 16 May 1843.   [AJ#4973]

DICKSON, JAMES, born 1807 in Peebles, a slater, died in Albany, NY, on 28 Feb. 1867. [S#7380]

DICKSON, JAMES, in Brooklyn, NY, cnf 1869. [NAS.SC70.1.143]

DICKSON, JOHN, naturalised, Supeme Court of Pennsylvania, 16 February 1798.

DICKSON, MARY, born in 1830, daughter of David Dickson a solicitor in Maxwelltown, Dumfries-shire, died in Jersey City, NJ, 1856. [DGC:16.9.1856]

DICKSON, PETER, naturalised, Quarter Session Court, Philadelphia, 3 October 1828.

DICKSON, ROBERT, a surgeon in PA and in South Carolina, 26 Sep. 1861. [NAS.RS.Lochmaben#5/226]

DICKSON, WILLIAM, in NY, cnf 1869 Edinburgh. [NAS.SC70.1.144/452]

DINWIDDIE, JANE ISABELLA, born in 1854, daughter of Robert Dinwiddie a merchant, died in NY on 10 Aug. 1859. [AO]

DINWIDDIE, ROBERT, born Dumfries 23 July 1811, a banker in NY from 1835, died there on 12 July 1888. [ANY#2.255]

DINWOODIE, WILLIAM, born in 1841, a joiner, son of David Dinwoodie in Annan, Dumfries-shire, died in Jefferson St., Brooklyn, 11 Jan. 1873. [AO]

DIVINS, MARGARET, daughter of Roger Divins and Margaret Blain, died in Brooklyn on 24 Jan. 1881. [Mochrum g/s, Wigtownshire]

DOBSON, ROBERT, naturalised, Court of Common Pleas, Philadelphia, 11 October 1826.

DODD, THOMAS, naturalised, Court of Quarter Sessions, Philadelphia, 5 June 1809.

DOIG, JOHN, naturalised, Court of Quarter Sessions, Philadelphia, 9 October 1802.

DOLLAR, THOMAS, naturalised, Supreme Court of Pennsylvania, 20 February 1798.

DONALD, ANDREW, naturalised, Court of Quarter Sessions, Philadelphia, 5 October 1824.

DONALD, PETER, born in Dunfermline, Fife, on 10 Dec. 1825, son of David Donald [1796-1881] and Margaret McGregor [1792-1874], a linen merchant in NY by 1859, died there on 9 Apr. 1915, buried in Greenwood Cemetery. [DJ,17.4.1915]

DONALD, ROBERT, a merchant in NY, 21 Jan. 1875. [NAS.RS.Edinburgh#141/58]

DONALDSON, ANDREW, naturalised, Court of Quarter Sessions, Philadelphia, 24 September 1806.

DONALDSON, ROBERT, born in Barnkiss, Dumfries, on 4 Mar. 1764, son of John Donaldson and Margaret Tait, a merchant in NY, died in Brunswick County, NC, on 8 July 1808. [ANY#2.391]

DONALDSON, THOMAS, from Cupar, Fife, via Belfast to NY in 1811 on the Perseverance. [NWI.2.235]

DONALDSON, WILLIAM, born in 1838, son of Alexander Donaldson a butcher in Aberdeen, died in NY aboard the Edwin Forrest on 6 Apr. 1854. [AJ:7.6.1854]

DOUGLAS, AGNES, or SUTHERLAND, in NY on 9 Aug. 1866. [NAS.RS.Edinburgh#90/20]

DOUGLAS, ANNIE, in Jersey City, married William Chalmers, enginer of RMS Tarifa, in Jersey City on 31 Mar. 1870. [AO]

DOUGLAS, ARCHIBALD, born in Stirling, died at 315 Dean St., Brooklyn, NY, on 15 Feb.1863. [S#2450]

DOUGLAS, DANIEL, born in 1785, a laborer from Craganfearn, Logerait, Perthshire, from Greenock on 4 Sep. 1817 bound for NY on the William of New York arrived in NY on 17 Oct. 1817.[NYMunicipal Archives][NY Comm. Advertiser, 18.10.1817]

DOUGLAS, ESTHER, daughter of Peter Douglas a merchant in Edinburgh, wife of Walter Stampa, died in N.Y. 10 April 1870. [S#8356]

DOUGLAS, GEORGE, born in Castle Douglas, son of John Douglas and Mary Heron, a merchant in NY, died in Peerskill, NY, on 9 Oct. 1799. [ANY#1.163]

DOUGLAS, HUGH, third son of Reverend Hugh Douglas in Lockerbie,Dumfriesshire, died in NY on 14 Sep. 1875. [S#10050] [EC#28400][AO]

DOUGLAS, JAMES, a merchant in NY, 1782, 1788. [NAS.GD185.29.5][NAS.CS17.1.7,238]

DOUGLAS, JOHN, born in Dumfriesshire, during 1780, a brewer, distiller and storekeeper, settled in Whitestown, Oneida County, NY, naturalised 2 May 1821 and 11 Oct. 1830 in NY. [Court of Common PleasRecords][Superior Court Records]

DOUGLAS, MARGARET, in NY, 1829. [NAS.RD5.384.752]

DOUGLAS, PETER, naturalised, Court of Common Pleas, Philadelphia, 11 October 1823.

DOUGLAS, ROBERT, born in Bowmore, Isle of Islay, Argyllshire, during 1794, a cartman, to America via Belfast, naturalised in NY on 31 Mar. 1821. [N.Y.Court of Common Pleas Records]

DOUGLAS, ROBERT, MD Glasgow University, born in 1814, son of William Douglas, [1785-1853], and Janet Walker, [1788-

1868], a physician in NY, died on 25 July 1861 at 10 Bleecker Street, NY.[Johnstone g/s,][S#1923]

DOUGLAS, THOMAS, born in 1765, married Rebecca Myers in NJ on 13 July 1790, died on 2 June 1822. [Sgen#9.81]

DOUGLAS, WILLIAM, merchant in NY, 1788. [NAS.CS17.1.7, 238]

DOUGLAS, WILLIAM, naturalised, Court of Quarter Sessions, Philadelphia, 9 October 1826.

DOUGLAS, WILLIAM, born in Dunfermline, Fife, to USA before 1834, a linen merchant in NY, who was drowned on 8 Jan. 1839. [DJ:22.6.1905][ANY2.151]

DOUGLAS, WILLIAM, on the Draper of NY from Castle Douglas, Kirkcudbrightshire, married Isabella Vivers, daughter of Captain John Vivers of the Ann of Annan, late of NJ, in Jersey City on 20 July 1865. [AO]

DOUGLAS, WILLIAM, born in 1864, son of Daniel Douglas [1822-1890], died in Philadelphia on 21 Aug. 1888. [Stair g/s, Ayrshire]

DOW, JOHN, born in 1792, an apprentice surgeon from Perth, from Greenock to NY on the Pitt on 14 Sep.1803. [NLS.MS#1053]

DOW, JOHN, naturalised, Court of Quarter Sessions, Philadelphia, 20 September 1808.

DOWNIE, GEORGE HART, son of John Mackay Downie in Edinburgh, married Agnes Rankin Wilson, daughter of William Wilson in Kilmarnock, Ayrshire, in NY on 25 Dec. 1854. [EEC#22687]

DOWNIE, JAMES, naturalised, Court of Quarter Sessions, Philadelphia, 3 October 1828.

DOWNIE, WALTER, naturalised, Court of Quarter Sessions, Philadelphia, 7 April 1828.

DOWNIE, WILLIAM, born in 1796, from Knockneen, Kirkcolm, Wigtownshire, died in Philadelphia on 27 Mar. 1847. [DGH:27.5.1847]

DRUMMOND, JAMES, NY, died 21 Feb. 1801, cnf 23 Apr. 1806. [NAS.CC8.8.136]

DRUMMOND, JAMES, born 1790, a laborer from Quoig, Comrie, Perthshire, from Greenock on 4 Sep. 1817 bound for NY on the William of New York arrived in NY on 17Oct.1817. [NYMunicipal Archives][NY Commercial Advertiser,18.10.1817]

DRUMMOND, JOHN, born in 1773, laborer from Methven, Perthshire, via Greenock to NY on the Pitt on 14 Sep. 1803. [NLS.MS#1053]

DRUMMOND, ROBERT, in Oneida County, NY, cnf 1869 Edinburgh. [NAS.SC70.1.143/1215]

DRYBURGH, ANDREW, a horticulturalist in Philadelphia from around 1840, died there in Aug. 1885. [AP#257]

DUDGEON, WILLIAM, from Edinburgh, married Fanny Ellsworth Greeman, only daughter of James Le Valle Greeman of Buffalo, there on 27 Sep. 1879.[EC#29656][S#11,308]

DUFF, ALEXANDER, born in 1773, a laborer from Methven, Perthshire, from Greenock to NY on the Pitt on 14 Sep. 1803. [NLS.MS#1053]

DUFF, ANTHONY D., born in Dundee 1781, son of Robert Duff, to NY 1806, wine merchant there, died 20 Feb.1825. [ANY#1.392]

DUFF, Mrs HELEN, relict of Captain Duff from Kenziels, Annan, Dumfries-shire, died in NY on 25 Feb. 1864. [AO]

DUFF, JAMES, from Abernethy, Perthshire, died in NY State before Mar.1815. [NAS.CS17.1.34/317]

DUFF, JANE, born 1837, daughter of James Duff and Janet Kinnear, wife of Thomas McKnaught, died in NY on 18 Oct. 1865. [Whithorn g/s, Wigtownshire]

DUFF, MARY, from Dumfries-shire, married Andrew H. Rome a printer from Dumfries-shire, in Brooklyn on 6 Apr. 1869. [AO]

DUFFUS, or WYLLIE, JANE, from Blairgowrie, Perthshire, in Airliewight, Washington, NY, 1849. [NAS. RS.Forfar.16.18]

DUFFUS, JANE, in Princeton, NJ, died on 29 Jan. 1858, cnf 1861. [NAS.SC70.1.108]

DUGUID, WILLIAM, in Pompy, Onandago, NY, died 13 Mar. 1854, cnf 1856. [NAS.SC70.1.92; CC8.8.inv.1856]

DUMBRECK, ELIZABETH, wife of Adolphus Magnus Corn, died in Fordham, NY, 10 Dec.1861. [S#2039]

DUNCAN, ALEXANDER, born on 26 May 1805, son of Alexander Duncan of Parkhill, Arbroath, Angus, via Liverpool to NY during 1821 on the Amity, educated at Yale and Brown Universities, a lawyer in Canandaigua, NY, and in Providence, Rhode Island, naturalised in NY on 2 Mar. 1827, settled in England during 1863, died in Knossington, London, on 14 Oct. 1889. [ANY#2.298] [Montrose, Craig Inchbrioch g/s][NY Marine Court Records]

DUNCAN, CHARLES ERSKINE, son of Charles Duncan and grandson of Alexander Duncan of Ardownie, Angus, a merchant in NY, by 1795. [NAS.RD3.271.95; RD3.285.190; CS17.1.4, 299]; in NY 1817.[NAS.CS17.1.36/618]

DUNCAN, DAVID, born in Arbroath, arrived from Liverpool in NY on the Amity 14 Jan.1819, merchant in NY, died March 1842. [ANY.2.105]

DUNCAN, DAVID, a jeweller from Montrose, Angus, eldest son of William Duncan in Cupar, Fife, died in NY on 28 Sep.1877. [S#10,688]

DUNCAN, DAVID, born in Edinburgh during 1819, son of John Duncan, to America in 1830, died in NJ on 15 June 1891. [ANY#2.297]

DUNCAN, GEORGE, in Canadaigua, 18 June 1850. [NAS.RS.Edinburgh#60/105]

DUNCAN, GEORGE, son of George Duncan, Russian Warehouse, High Street, Edinburgh, died in Pittsburg, 30 October 1871. [S#8833]

DUNCAN, JAMES, born in Alyth, Perthshire, during 1827, a merchant in Dundee and NY, died in Jordanstone, Alyth, Perthshire, on 29 Jan. 1909. [ANY#2.251]

DUNCAN, JAMES, a watchmaker in PA, 25 Jan. 1874. [NAS.RS.Edinburgh#115/51]

DUNCAN, JAMES, from Glasgow, a commercial traveller, married Mary Ann Ross from Wick, Caithness, daughter of George Ross in Lowell, Massachusetts, at 785 Fifth Ave., NY, on 30 June 1876. [S#10,291]

DUNCAN, JESSY SCOTT, born in 1831, eldest daughter of Alexander Duncan in Providence, Rhode Island, died in NY on 24 Nov. 1847.   [EEC#21596]

DUNCAN, JOHN, born in Perthshire during 1790, a merchant, with his wife Jane who was born in Dundee during 1786, and children Ann born in Fife during 1816, Ellen born in Fife during 1818, David born in Fife during 1820, and daughter Jane born in NY city during 1822, naturalised in NY on 20 Feb. 1823.[Court of Common Pleas Records]

DUNCAN, JOHN, from Edinburgh, to America during 1830, a merchant in NY. [ANY#2.297]

DUNCAN, MARIA DOROTHEA, younger daughter of Rev. Dr Duncan, New College, Edinburgh, and wife of Rev. Prof. Spaeth, died in Philadelphia on 21 Dec.1878.[S#11,066]

DUNCAN, THOMAS, sutler to the Army in NY 1784.
[NAS.CS17.11.3/212]

DUNCAN, THOMAS, born 2 Sep. 1828 near Foveran,
Aberdeenshire, son of George Duncan and Elspet Webster,
married Margaret Smart on 1 May 1858, to America in 1860,
a textile manufacturer in Philadelphia, died there on 19 Jan.
1887. [AP#162]

DUNCAN, WILLIAM BUTLER, born in Edinburgh on 17 Mar.
1830, son of Alexander Duncan, educated at Edinburgh
University and at Brown University, Rhode Island, a banker
and entrepreneur in NY, married Jane Percy Sargent,
daughter of G. W. Sargent of Natchez, Mississipi, in New
Orleans during 1853, died in NY on 20 June 1912.
[EEC#22528][ANY#2.274]

DUNCAN, ..., daughter of William Butler Duncan, was born in NY
on   9 Feb. 1855. [EEC#22706]

DUNCAN, ..., daughter of William Duncan from Leith, was born
in Newark, NJ, on 4 July 1875. [S#9985]

DUNCANSON, THOMAS, born 1826, late of Glen Sciennes
Distillery, Edinburgh, died in Syracuse, on 19 March 1867.
[S#7388]

DUNDAS, JAMES, of Manor, resident in Philadelphia around
1835. [NAS.GD35.174]

DUNN, GEORGE W., naturalised, US District Court, Philadelphia,
21 October 1817, and US Circuit Court, 24 April 1823.

DUNN, JAMES H., naturalised, Court of Common Pleas,
Philadelphia, 17 June 1818, and 6 October 1823.

DUNN, JOHN, naturalised, Court of Common Pleas, Philadelphia,
31 May 1825.

DUNN, JOHN, born 1836, a builder from Edinburgh, died in
Brooklyn, NY, on 18 April 1874. [S#9606]

DURIE, ANDREW, born in 1802, from Dunfermline, Fife, died in
Jersey City, NJ, on 13 Feb. 1888. [DJ]

DURIE, JAMES, a skipper in Brooklyn, son of James Durie, a
baker in Leith, who died 25 Mar.1875. [NAS.SH.11.4.1896]

DURNO, GEORGE, a brassfounder from Aberdeen, died in
Tremont, Westchester County, NY, on 12 Mar. 1865.
[AJ:5.4.1865]

DURNO, JAMES, a watchmaker, son of James Durno in New
Deer, Aberdeenshire, died in Philadelphia on 2 May 1835.
[AJ#4575]

DUSTAN, JOHN FALCONER, born 1831, importer in NY, later in Boston, died there 13 Feb.1903. [ANY.2.256]

DYER, WILLIAM, naturalised, Supreme Court of PA, 17 June 1799.

DYKES, JAMES, youngest son of James Dykes a slater and plasterer in Traquair, Peebles-shire, died in Brooklyn, NY, on 21 August 1877. [S#10,647]

DYSON, DUNBAR SMITH, born in Kirkcudbrightshire during 1806, settled in NY by 1831, died in NO on 22 Dec. 1848. [ANY#2.27/144]

DYSON, ROBERT, born in Galloway 1790 son of James Dyson and Margaret Smith, settled in NY by 1818, merchant and financier, died New Brunswick, NJ, 31 Oct.1848. [ANY.2.75]

EADIE, ANDREW STEVENSON, born at Hogganfield, Glasgow, 19 March 1819, son of James Edie a bleacher, a clerk in NY, died in Brooklyn 19 May 1897. [ANY.2.236]

EADIE, GEORGE FREDERICK, in NY, cnf 1866 Edinburgh. [NAS.SC70.1.132/219]

EARLE, MARY, wife of John Jardine an architect in NY, from Whithorn, Wigtownshire, died in East Chester, NY, on 19 May 1873. [EC#27663]

EASTON, JOHN ARNOTT, a surgeon, only son of Peter Easton and Janet Arnott, Greencroft Cottage, Ecclefechan, Dumfries, died in NY on 3 Oct. 1875. [AO][S#10063]

EDGAR, ROBERT, from Dumfries-shire, died in Yonkers, NY, on 21 Aug. 1873. [AO]

EDMISTON, JOHN, born in Glasgow 2 March 1828, merchant at 3 Bowling Green, NY, died Bloomfield, NJ, 28 Jan.1895. [ANY.2.284]

EDWARDS, ALEXANDER, born in Edinburgh on 11 Apr. 1814, a granite importer in NY, died Brooklyn 6 June 1871. [ANY#2.298]

EDWARD, JAMES, from Natchez, married Charlotte Bruen, daughter of James Farrand, NY, there on 2 Sep. 1839. [EEC#19963]

ELDER, ALEXANDER, born in Milnathort, Kinross-shire, on 27 June 1804, son of William Elder and Christiana Mailer, educated at Glasgow University in 1830, a physician who settled in NY, died in NJ on 3 Feb. 1875. [ANY#2.276]

ELDER, WILLIAM, married Christiana Mailer before 1804 in Milnathort,Kinross-shire, to NY in 1828, settled on West Farms, Schenectady County, NY. [ANY#2.276]

ELLIOT, SAMUEL M., from Inverness, naturalised in NY on 12 Sep.1837. [Superior Court Records]

ELLIS, CHARLES, born in Netherton, Fife, during 1824, to America in 1859, a foreman dyer on Long Island and on Staten Island, died on Staten Island, NY, on 19 Oct. 1897. [DJ: 19.10.1897]

ELLIS, JAMES, born in Dunfermline, Fife, on 28 Jan. 1826, married Mary Cram in 1848, to America, a gardener on Long Island for 15 years, later a farmer in Minnesota, died in 1905. [DJ,28.10.1905]

ELLIS, WILLIAM, of Netherton, born in 1780, from Dunfermline to NY in 1857, died on Staten Island 10 June 1869. [PJ]

ELMSLIE, GEORGE, born in 1835, son of George Elmslie, Foot O'Hill, Gartly, Aberdeenshire, died at his brother's house in Brooklyn on 16 Dec.1875. [AJ:22.12.1875]

ERSKINE, WILLIAM, born in 1843, from Netherton, Dunfermline, Fife, died in Bayside, NY, on 20 July 1875. [DJ]

EWART, AGNES, born on 25 Sep. 1755, daughter of Reverend John Ewart and Mary Corrie, married John Carson, a merchant in Philadelphia, on 4 Aug. 1784.   [F#2.303]

EWART, JOHN, son of ..... Ewart and Isabella Lanford in Berwick-on-Tweed, settled in Albany, pro. May 1825 PCC

EWART, RICHARD J. W., born in Ruthwell, Dumfries-shire, during 1816, brother of William Ewart a surgeon in Annan, settled in West Brighton, NY, in 1849, died 23 Apr. 1873. [AO]

EWING, ROBERT, born in 1828, son of James Ewing [1803-1854] a forester, died in Buffalo on 24 Nov. 1893. [Galston g/s, Ayrshire]

FAILE, EDWARD G., a merchant in Eastchester, NY, by 1803. [ANY.2.207]

FAIRBAIRN, EDWARD, son of James Fairbairn a clothier in Hawick, Roxburghshire, married Nellie M. Fitzgerald, in Buffalo, NY, on 16 Jan.1879. [S#11,103]

FAIRBAIRN, JEAN KAY, daughter of William and Alison Fairbairn from Duns, Berwickshire, died at 391 State Street, Brooklyn, on 6 November 1868. [S#7900]

FAIRFOWL, JAMES, naturalised, Court of Quarter Sessions, Philadelphia, 10 March 1820.

FALCONER, PATRICK, born in 1775, son of William Falconer a farmer in Kinnermony (1720-1793) and Anna Rose (1743-

1821), settled in NY during 1794 a merchant in NY, residing at 13 Broadway, died in 1837. [Inveraven g/s, Banffshire] [ANY#2.15][1812]

FALCONER, ROBERT, born in 1782, son of William Falconer (1720-1793) a farmer in Kinnermony and Anna Rose (1742-1821), a merchant in NY, died in 1851. [Inveraven g/s, Banffshire]

FALCONER, WILLIAM, born in 1763, son of William Falconer (1720-1793) a farmer in Kinnermony and Anna Rose (1742-1821), a merchant in NY died in 1818. [Inveraven g/s, Banffshire]

FALL, JOHN, born in Roxburghshire during 1777, a carpenter, via London to America, naturalised in NY on 16 June 1825.[Court of Common Pleas]

FARQUHAR, ELIZABETH CURZON, only daughter of James Farquhar in NY, died at 65 Harley St., London, on 10 December 1860. [S#1711]

FARQUHARSON, CHARLOTTE, wife of David Andrew, died in Carbonvale, PA., 9 May 1868. [S#7751]

FARRIES, Mrs E. C., relict of William C. Farries an ironmonger in Lockerbie, died in Providence, PA, on 23 Nov. 1873. [AO]

FERGUSON, Mrs AGNES, born in Glasgow during 1810, wife of William Ferguson, died on 14 Oct. 1844. [Mount Ida Cemetery, Troy, NY]

FERGUSON, DAVID, a merchant in NY, 1793. [NAS.CS17.1.12/200]

FERGUSON, HENRY HUGH, late of Philadelphia, now in Kilmarnock, Ayrshire, 1787. Loyalist. [NAS.CS17.1.6,164][PRO.AO12.38.04]

FERGUSON, JAMES, born in 1804 son of Andrew Ferguson, a surgeon in Aberdeen, and Margaret Ramage, educated at King's College, Aberdeen, from 1816 to 1820, Rector of Rutgers College, N ew Jersey, and Superintendent of Public Schools in Lockport, NY. [KCA#2.427]

FERGUSON, JOHN, born 1782, from Greenock to NY on the Frances in 1810, married Janet McNeish in 1833, an insurance company executive in NY, died 25 July 1846. [ANY.2.158]

FERGUSON, WILLIAM GLASS, born 1863, son of David Ferguson an ironmoulder, and grandson of William Glass a painter in Adam Street, Edinburgh, died in Paterson, NJ, on 8 March 1877. [S#10,513]

FERGUSON, WILLIAM, in Beverley, Burlington County, NJ, cnf 1884. [NAS.SC70.1.230]

FERNIE, PETER, born in Perthshire during 1793, an accountant who emigrated via Belfast to America, naturalised in NY on 2 Apr. 1821.

FINLAY, JAMES, son of James Finlay a merchant in Kirkintilloch, now a weaver in Princeton, NJ, grandson of Robert Angus a merchant in Kirkintilloch, 1790. [NAS.RS.Dunbarton#514]

FINDLAY, ..., son of Alexander Findlay, was born at 291 Smith St., Brooklyn, N.Y., on 8 May 1870. [S#8368]

FINDLAY, ..., son of Alexander Findlay, was born at 468 Sackett St., Brooklyn, N.Y., on 1 January 1872. [S#8886]

FINDLAY, ..., daughter of Alexander Findlay, was born at 387 Degraw Street, Brooklyn, NY, on 10 April 1874. [S#9594]

FINDLAY, ..., son of Alexander Findlay, was born at 387 Degraw Street, Brooklyn, NY, on 3 September 1875. [S#10032]

FINNIE, MARY ANN, born in Scotland during 1781, with 4 children, arrived in NY on the <u>Camillus</u> in 1821. [USNA.par]

FISHER, Dr HENRY, married Mary Anne Roach, second daughter of Honora Roach, in NY on 3 Jan. 1854. [EEC#22534]

FLEMING, HELEN CAMPBELL, eldest daughter of William Fleming in Muselburgh, married Alexander Bennet a machinist, at 158th St., NY, 4 Oct. 1872. [S#9128]

FLEMING, JANET B., from Dunfermline, Fife, married John McPherson in Brooklyn, NY, on 28 Nov. 1866. [FA]

FLEMING, JOHN B., born 1787, settled in America around 1805 with his wife and two children, a merchant at 77 Broad Street, NY, in 1812; in NY on 6 Aug. 1830. [1812] [NAS.SC37.59.7/156]

FLEMING, MARY H., from Dunfermline, Fife, married William H. Duncan of Brooklyn, in Brooklyn, NY, on 20 Apr. 1867. [FH]

FLINT, ALEXANDER, naturalised,Supreme Court of Pennsylvania, 15 February 1798

FORBES, DAVID, born in New Mills, Banffshire, died in NY on 8 March 1856. [AJ:9.4.1856]

FORBES, Mrs MARY, second daughter of John Hood in Edinburgh, died in NY on 23 September 1877. [S#10,681]

FORBES, WILLIAM, deceased, late of Treemont, Westchester County, NY, his relict Ann Jerard, died at 59 Thistle St., Edinburgh, on 27 June 1862. [S#2196]

FORDYCE, MARGARET, born 1844, from Edinburgh, wife of Robert Martin, died at 85 Belleville Avenue, Newark, NJ, on 19 April 1873. [S#9294]

FORREST, DAVID, born 1827, son of John Forrest (1792-1865) a merchant in Alloa and Agnes Hay (1799-1874), died in NY 27 Oct. 1859. [East Preston Street cemetery, Edinburgh]

FORREST, GEORGE, from Auchneive, Tarves, Aberdeenshire, latterly of Aberdeen, drowned on his passage from NY to Glasgow in 1869. [AJ:7.7.1869]

FORREST, JAMES, a minister in Fairmount, West Farm, NY, died on 18 Feb. 1858, cnf 1858. [NAS.SC70.1.268]

FORREST, JAMES, born in 1796, died in NY on 24 Jan. 1867, his wife Grace Scott, born 1799, died on 3 Mar. 1877. [Bathgate g/s]

FORREST, JAMES, Greenwich Street, NY, eldest son of the late William Forrest in Ludquhairn, 1809. [NAS.CS17.1.28.443]

FORREST, JAMES, born 1796 in Bathgate, died in NY 24 Jan.1867.[S#7341]

FORREST, JOHN, born in Annan, Dumfries-shire, son of James and Agnes Forrest, died in Brooklyn on 18 Feb. 1866. [AO]

FORREST, ROBERT, born in Dunbar, East Lothian, around 1768, a minister who was ordained in Saltcoats, Ayrshire, on 27 Feb. 1798, via Greenock to NY on the Recovery on 8 Oct. 1802, settled in Montreal and NY from 1804 to 1808, and in Stafford, Delaware County, NY, during 1810, died there on 17 Mar. 1846. [ANY#1.385][1812][UPC#2.309]

FORRESTER, ARCHIBALD, Port Officer of NY 1818. [NAS.CS17.1.38/103]

FORRESTER, WILLIAM, naturalised, Supreme Court of Pennsylvania, 20 Feb.1798.

FORSYTH, EBENEZER, naturalised, Court of Quarter Sessions, Philadelphia, 20 Sept.1828, and Court of Common Pleas, Philadelphia, 28 Sept.1828.

FORSYTH, JAMES, naturalised, Court of Quarter Sessions, Philadelphia, 20 October 1829.

FORSYTH, JOHN, born on 19 Sep. 1784, son of John Forsyth in Newhills, Aberdeenshire, settled in Newburgh, NY, married Jane Currie on 11 Jan. 1810. [American Armory and Blue Book]

FOWLER, Dr REEVES, born in Paisley, Health Officer for New Providence, Bahamas, died in the Marine Hospital,

Staten Island, on 14 Nov. 1809. [Bahamas Royal Gazette, 20.12.1809]

FRAME, ANDREW, born in 1795, a merchant from Glasgow, from Greenock on 4 Sep. 1817 bound for NY on the William of NewYork, arrived in NY on 17 Oct. 1817.[NYMunicipal Archives] [NY Commercial Advertiser, 18.10.1817]

FRANK, WILLIAM BOUGH, born in 1735, son of James Frank of Boughbridge, Colonel and Collector of NY, died in 1810. [Eccles g/s, Berwickshire]

FRASER, ANDREW, naturalised, Court of Common Pleas, Philadelphia, 17 Sept. 1813.

FRASER, ANDREW, jr., naturalised, Court of Common Pleas, Philadelphia, 17 Sept. 1813.

FRASER, ANDREW, married Janet Briengan Sinclair, eldest daughter of John Sinclair in Dollar, Clackmannanshire, in NY on 31 December 1874. [S#9835]

FRASER, DANIEL, a commission agent and merchant in NY, second son of Robert Fraser of Kilcoy in Berbice, formerly a merchant in Inverness, died in Thompsonville, Connecticut on 22 August 1869. [S#8150]

FRASER, DOUGLAS, a barrister in Buffalo, NY, cnf 1868 Edinburgh. [NAS.SC70.1.137/1071]

FRASER, Mrs ELIZABETH, born 1820, from Drummond St., Edinburgh, died at 79 Cranberry St., Brooklyn, on 2 July 1872. [S#9048]

FRASER, GEORGE, a baker in Chicago, late of Munichyne, Ross-shire, married Catherine Ross, daughter of David Ross in Invergordon, in Hoboken, NY, on 6 December 1867. [S#7617]

FRASER, GILBERTA A., daughter of Rev. Daniel Fraser of Helmsdale, married Alexander Dallas, MD, in Westfield, NJ, on 23 Jan.1878. [S#10,782]

FRASER, JAMES, born in Edinburgh on 25 Jan. 1826, son of Andrew Fraser and Isabella Smith, settled in NY during 1842 as a leather merchant, died on 15 Dec. 1897. [ANY#2.237]

FRASER, JAMES FYFE, born in Coupar Angus, Perthshire, during 1827, son of John Fraser and Cecilia Fyfe, later a merchant in NY, died in Perth on 20 Aug. 1856. [ANY#2.231]

FRASER, JANE HELEN, in NY, niece of Eliza Fraser in Peterhead, Aberdeenshire, who died 13 July 1885. [NAS.SH.18.10.1887]

FRASER, JESSIE, daughter of Simon Fraser, and wife of Douglas Fraser, died in Buffalo on 27 February 1863. [S#2427]

FRASER, JOHN, naturalised, Court of Quarter Sessions, Philadelphia, 28 August 1821.

FRASER, JOHN JAMES, born 1840, a tenor, died in Philadelphia on 18 June 1863. [S#2526]

FRASER, THOMAS, naturalised, Court of Quarter Sessions, Philadelphia, 14 June 1813, and Court of common Please, Philadelphia, on 14 September 1813.

FRASER, THOMAS, born in Musselburgh, Midlothian, son of Andrew Fraser, leather merchant in NY, died 1 Feb. 1863. [ANY#2.195][S#2395]

FRASER, WALTER, from Falshope, Selkirkshire, a tailor in NY, married Jemima Carter 1784, died in May 1793. [ANY#1.703]

FRASER, WILLIAM, born in Inverness on 13 Mar. 1753, died in Troy, NY, on 25 Apr. 1826. [Old Troy g/s]

FRASER, WILLIAM, born in Petty, Inverness-shire, on 26 Mar. 1775, son of Donald Fraser and Mary Ann Smith, to Caledonia, NY, in 1804, married Janet Christie (1785-1807) during 1807, died on 16 July 1843. ['Genealogy of Miller & Tillotson', Scottsville, NY]

FRASER, WILLIAM, born in 1777, a farmer in Lannwelig, Almy, Inverness-shire, with his wife Janet born 1782, and children Thomas born 1804 and Ann born 1806, to NY on the George of New York, on 12 Aug. 1807. [PRO.PC1.3790]

FREELAND, JOHN, a merchant, married Isabella Rankin, daughter of Henry Rankin, a merchant, in NY on 31 July 1839. [SG#803]

FRENCH, ANNE, widow of James Todd in NY, niece of Dr Witherspoon of Princeton College, died in Villafield, Glasgow, 16 July 1840. [W#54]

FRENCH, WILLIAM, clerk at Verreville Glassworks, Glasgow, settled in NY before Dec. 1809. [NAS.CS17.1.29/108]

FULLARTON, HENRY, born in 1831, son of A. Fullarton, Castle Douglas, Kirkcudbrightshire, died in Astoria, Long Island, NY, on 16 Nov. 1857. [DGH:25.12.1857]

FULLARTON, JOHN, born in 1787, a laborer from Buttergask, Cargill, Perthshire, from Greenock on 4 Sep. 1817 bound for NY on the <u>William of New York</u>, arrived in NY on 17 Oct. 1817. [NYMunicipal Archives][NY Comm. Advertiser, 18.10.1817]

FULTON, GEORGE, naturalised, US Circuit Court, Philadelphia, 6 May 1813.

FULTON, MARK, naturalised, Supreme Court of Pennsylvania, 4 **February 1798.**

FYFFE, GABRIEL, born at Loch Fannich, Ross and Cromarty, to America in 1783, settled in Albany, NY. [BLG#2865]

FYFFE, JAMES, a journeyman millwright in PA, died on 21 Dec.1856, cnf 1858. [NAS.SC70.1.98]

GALL, ALEXANDER, born in Aberdeen around 1833, died at 79 State Street, Rochester, NY, on 2 Aug. 1879. [AJ:17.9.1879]

GALLETLY, JANET, in NY, cnf 1883. [NAS.SC70.1.225]

GALLITLY, JAMES, born in 1792, a laborer from Pittensorn, Little Dunkeld, Perthshire, from Greenock on 4 Sep. 1817 bound for NY on the <u>William of New York</u>, arrived there on 17 Oct. 1817.[NYMunicipal Archives][NY Commercial Advertiser,18.10.1817]

GALLOWAY, ALEXANDER, eldest son of James Galloway a house factor in Leith, drowned with the loss of the <u>SS United Kingdom</u> from NY 19 April 1869 bound for Glasgow. [S#8107]

GALLOWAY, JOHN, born 1812, son of John Galloway and Ann Lamb, died in NY on 30 Nov. 1840. [Arbroath Abbey g/s]

GALLOWAY, JOHN, a banker in NY, died in Buchlyvie, Kippen, Stirlingshire, in Jan. 1852, cnf 1852. [NAS.SC70.1.77]

GAMBLE, JANE, born in Scotland during 1785, with children, arrived in NY on the <u>Camillus</u> during 1821. [USNA.par]

GARDEN, ROBERT, naturalised, Court of Common Pleas, Philadelphia, 12 April 1813, and Court of Quarter Sessions, Philadelphia, 25 September 1813.

GARDEN, WILLIAM R., naturalised, Court of Common Pleas, Philadelphia, 12 April 1813.

GARDINER, JAMES, naturalised, Supreme Court of Pennsylvania, 20 February 1798.

GARR, ANDREW, born during 1745 in Auchincairn, Kirkcudbrightshire, to NY in 1784, a shipbuilder there, married.... Sheffield, (2) Mary Ogden, (3) Margaret Garr,

father of Andrew and Janet, died in NY on 12 Apr. 1812.
[ANY#1.304]

GARRET, ANDREW, born 1795, from Inch, Wigtownshire, died in NY on 19 Mar. 1858. [DGH:7.5.1858]

GEDDES, ALEXANDER, in NY, 1863. [NAS.SC48.49.25.64/144]

GEDDES, DONALD, born in 1793, a merchant from Greenock on 4 Sep. 1817 bound for NY on the William of New York, arrived in NY on 17 Oct. 1817.[NYMunicipal Archives] [NY Commercial Advertiser, 18.10.1817]

GEDDES, WILLIAM, from Edinburgh, settled in Philadelphia then in Wilmington, Newcastle County, Del., by 1795, a merchant in Philadelphia 1796. [NAS.RD3.271.359; CS17.1.15/420]

GEMMELL, ..., daughter of Francis Gemmell a baker, was born in Alleghany City, PA, on 7 June 1875. [EC#28321]

GENTLE, JAMES, naturalised in NY on 30 Nov. 1840. [Superior Court Records]

GEORGE, Rev. JAMES, born 8 Nov. 1800, son of James George a farmer in Muckhart, Perthshire, educated at Glasgow University in 1823, a minister in Philadelphia, Fort Covington, NY, and in Ontario, died there on 26 Aug. 1870. [MAGU#337][UPC#678]

GEORGESON, JOHN MOUAT, in Philadelphia, before 1888, grandson of George Georgeson tenant in Forratwatt, Walls, Shetland Islands.[NAS.SH.25.8.1888]

GIBB, HELEN, daughter of James Gibb [1791-1874] and Helen Cook, settled in Elmira. [Wallacetown g/s, Ayr]

GIBB, THOMAS, son of James Gibb [1791-1874] and Helen Cook, died in Jersey City.[Wallacetown g/s, Ayr]

GIBSON, A., from Dumfries-shire, married Jennie Christie, eldest daughter of Robert Christie, from Auchterarder, Perthshire, in Philadelphia on 3 July 1873. [AO]

GIBSON, ANN M., from Dumfries, married Adam Richardson, in NY on 23 Feb. 1849. [DGH:12.4.1849]

GIBSON, ARCHIBALD, born in 1805, son of Sergeant James Gibson of the Dumfries Militia, died at 19 Street, 8th Avenue, NY, on 31 Oct.1841. [DGH:16.12.1841]

GIBSON, DUNLOP GERARD, youngest son of John Gibson, Writer to the Signet in Edinburgh, died in NY on 11 Apr. 1835. [AJ#4558]

GIBSON, GEORGE HASTIE, born in Edinburgh on 18 Jan. 1822, son of John Gibson and Margaret Petrie, a stain glass artist, died in Philadelphia on 13 Dec. 1877. [AP#172]

GIBSON, JAMES, naturalised, Court of Common Pleas, Philadelphia, 25 October 1804.

GIBSON, Reverend JAMES, ordained in Whithorn Associate Church in 1835, a minister in Dunfermline, Fife, from 1841 to 1847, to Canada in 1856, died in NY on 7 Apr. 1860. [DP]; cnf 1860. [NAS.SC70.1.106]

GIBSON, JOHN, naturalised, Supreme Court of Pennsylvania, 26 March 1814.

GIBSON, JOHN, born in Edinburgh on 4 Apr. 1813, son of John Gibson and Margaret Petrie, a painter and decorator in NY and in Philadelphia, a stain glass and leaded glass manufacturer in Philadelphia from 1850, died there on 19 Sep. 1877. [AP#173]

GIFFORD, ANDREW, born in Loanhead, Midlothian, during 1761, wife Margaret Noble, a cabinetmaker who settled NY in 1784, later a manufacturer and timber merchant in NY, died on 28 Nov. 1846. [ANY#2.299/97]

GILFILLAN, WILLIAM DUDLEY, infant son of William Gilfillan MD, died in Brooklyn on 30 July 1861. [S#1928]

GILLESPIE, ELIZA P., youngest daughter of the late David Gillespie in NY, married Alexander Anderson a colonial surgeon, in Victoria, Hong Kong, on 30 Apr. 1844. [EEC#21087]

GILLESPIE, MARGARET, daughter of Reverend Thomas Gillespie of the University of St Andrews, died in NY on 23 April 1871.[S#8670]

GILLESPIE, ROBERT, born on 30 Dec. 1778, son of Reverend John Gillespie and Dorothea McKean in Kells, Kirkcudbright, a merchant in New York, died on 20 Sep. 1830. [F#2.12]

GILLESPIE, ROBERT, son of James Gillespie a merchant in Glasgow, via Liverpool to NY on the Manhattan 1820, a merchant in NY 1820-1852, died in Glasgow 15 Dec.1852. [ANY.2.106]

GINTY, JOHN, a contractor in NY, cnf 1885. [NAS.SC70.1.239]

GIVEN, DAVID, from Gelston, Castle Douglas, Kirkcudbrightshire, died in Rochester, NY, on 28 Aug. 1849. [DGH:1.11.1849]

GIVEN, JOHN, born 22 Mar.1786, son of Robert Given a farmer from Ednam, Roxburghshire, settled Westchester County,

NY, 1795, a manufacturer, died NY 25 Dec.1842.
[ANY.2.37]

GIVEN, ROBERT, a farmer from Highrighall, now in Ednam, NY, 1815. [NAS.CS17.1.34/285]

GLENDINNING, MARGARET JANE, infant daughter of John and Barbara Glendinning, died 291 2nd Street, NJ, 11 Sep.1872. [AO]

GLENDENNING, ROBERT, born on 13 May 1805 in Kelso, Roxburghshire, educated at Edinburgh University, to America in 1832, a merchant and a banker in Philadelphia, married Elizabeth Kennedy, from Scotland, in 1834, died in Philadelphia on 4 Mar. 1878. [AP#175]

GLENDINNING, THOMAS, born in 1833, eldest son of Robert Glendinning, a former farm steward in Outertown, Warimanbie, Dumfries-shire. died in Jersey City on 6 Feb. 1871. [AO]

GLOVER, ..., son of James D. Glover from Roslin, Midlothian, was born in Alleghany City, PA, on 18 August 1872. [S#9087]

GOODLET, JANE, from Musselburgh, Midlothian, settled in NY, died on 2 Jan. 1836, cnf 1838. [NAS.SC70.1.56]

GORDON, ARCHIBALD, born 1800, son of Archibald Gordon of Halleaths, from Liverpool to NY on the Columbia in 1822, merchant in NY, died 8 Sept.1848 on Staten Island. [ANY.2.130]

GORDON, ARCHIBALD, naturalised, Court of Quarter Sessions, Philadelphia, 31 October 1827.

GORDON, CHARLOTTE, daughter of Willam Gordon, and wife of Hugh Chalmers a merchant in NY, 1798. [NAS.CS17.1.17/49]

GORDON, DAVID, a merchant in NY, second son of Sir Alexander Gordon of Culvenan, 1807, 1809. [NAS.GD51.6/1571; CS17.1.26/400]

GORDON, ELIZABETH, from Dumfries, via Belfast to NY on the Shannon on 18 Jan. 1816. [PI]

GORDON, FRANCIS, born in 1782, from Huntly, Aberdeenshire, died in NY on 1 Dec. 1862. [AJ:24.12.1862]

GORDON, Dr GEORGE, eldest son of Reverend Adam Gordon, was washed overboard from S.S.Victoria when bound for NY on 1 Janaury 1874. [S#9501]

GORDON, HANNAH, daughter of Francis Gordon in NY, from Huntly, Aberdeenshire, died in St Kitts on 8 Sep. 1862. [AJ:29.9.1862]

GORDON, JEAN, daughter of Francis Gordon of Huntly, Aberdeenshire, died in NY City on 24 Apr. 1872. [AJ:22.5.1872]

GORDON, JOHN, from Dumfries, via Belfast to NY on the Shannon on 18 Jan. 1816. [PI]

GORDON, PETER, commission agent in South St., NY, around 1810. [ANY.2.8]

GORDON, ROBERT, born in Dumfries 17 Nov.1829, son of William Gordon and Sarah Walker, a merchant in NY 1846-1884, died in England 16 May 1918. [ANY.2.257]

GORDON, SADIE, younger daughter of T. S. Gordon in NY, married Frederick, second son of J. D. Link of London, in NY on 3 June 1879. [EC#29544]

GORRIE, JOHN, born in 1780, a merchant from Moneddy, Perthshire, from Greenock on 4 Sep. 1817 bound for NY on the William of New York arrived in NY on 17 Oct. 1817.[NYMunicipal Archives][NY Commercial Advertiser, 18.10.1817]

GOURLAY, ALEXANDER, son of John Gourlay and Janet Stark in Burntisland, Fife, naturalised in King's County, Brooklyn, on 25 Oct. 1860, died on 27 June 1865, husband of Grace Henery, father of Grace born NY on 28 Feb. 1855, John born Brooklyn on 16 Nov. 1856, Robert born Brooklyn on 19 Nov. 1858, Henry born in Brooklyn 19 Sep. 1861, and Janet born Brooklyn on 23 Feb. 1864. [GRH#159]

GOURLAY, GEORGINA, born 1848, wife of Thomas S. Nelson late of the National Bank of Scotland in Edinburgh, step-daughter of J.A.Butts, 7 Queen Street, [Edinburgh?], died at 295 Smith Street, Brooklyn, on 24 March 1871. [S#8640]

GOURLAY, LILLY ANN, born 1836, wife of George W. Murray, from Edinburgh, died at 150 West 17th Street, NY, in 1860. [S#1545]

GOURLIE, ROBERT, from Motherwell, Lanarkshire, a watchmaker in Maiden Lane, NY, from 1803. [ANY.2.258]

GOW, ALEXANDER, from Leith, died Pittsburgh 1852. [S.12.1.1853]

GOW, JOHN, born 1850 in Perthshire, died in Buffalo, NY, 26 April 1872. [S#8990]

GOW, PETER M., born 1832, a merchant in NY, died 25 July 1865. [ANY.2.298]

GOW, WILLIAM M., married Nicholas Arbuthnott Dun Beattie, youngest daughter of William Beattie in Edinburgh, in NY 18 June 1869. [S#8088]

GOW,...., daughter of William M. Gow, ws born at 2210 3rd Avenue, N.Y., on 28 April 1870. [S#8358]

GRACIE, GEORGE, in NY 1796, eldest son of the late William Gracie a shipmaster.[NAS.CS17.1.15/434]

GRAHAM, ALEXANDER, probably from Glasgow, via Liverpool to NY on the New York 1826, merchant in NY 1826. [ANY.2.106]

GRAHAM, ANDREW, born in 1769, a physician from Glasgow, via Ireland to NY on the Eagle of New York on 27 Aug. 1803. [BM]

GRAHAM, JOHN, born in 1777, son of Thomas Graham, a farmer, and his wife Christain Halliday, in Burnswark, Ecclesfechan, Dumfries-shire, to NY in 1792, a merchant there, married Ann McQueen in 1804, died in NY on 18 Jan. 1843. [ANY#1.378][NAS.CS17.1.40/313]

GRAHAM, PETER, born near Ecclesfechan, Dumfries-shire, in 1773, son of Thomas Graham of Burnswark and Christian Halliday, to America in 1798, a merchant in NY and Philadelphia, died on 10 June 1849 at The Grange,Dunduff, Susquehanna County, PA. [AP#181][NAS.CS17.1.40/313]

GRAHAM, PETER, naturalised, Supreme Court of Pennsylvania, 2 November 1813.

GRAHAM, SIMON, from Dumfries-shire, via Greenock to NY on the Maria of New York on 27 Mar. 1795. [NAS.SC15.55.2]; from Gretna Green, then in NY, 1816. [NAS.CS17.1.35/169]

GRAHAM, WALTER, a baker in NY, 1809. [NAS.CS17.1.28/443]

GRAHAM, W., late of Philadelphia, now of Glasgow 1811. [NAS.CS17.1.31/191]

GRAHAM, WILLIAM, naturalised, Supreme Court of Pennsylvania, 21 December 1804.

GRANT, FRANCIS ROBERT, born 1849, a shipbroker, eldest son of John Grant a banker in Inverkeithing, Fife, sailed from Inverkeithing on the Swiftsure bound for NY on 3 Sep.1870, lost at sea. [S#8605]

GRANT, JAMES, born 1783, to NY 1800, a tinplate worker in Broadway, NY, died 1 December 1851. [ANY.2.131]

GRANT, JAMES W., born 1846, son of James Grant a coach proprietor and hotelkeeper in Stirling, died on Broadway, NY, 8 April 1869. [S#8029]

GRANT, JOHN, a merchant from Glasgow, now in NY, 1808. [NAS.CS17.1.28/70]

GRANT, JOHN L., born in Scotland around 1799, ordained by the Presbytery of Philadelphia in 1829, pastor of the Eleventh Presbyterian Church in Philadelphia until 1849, died in Camden, NJ, on 28 July 1874. [AP#183]

GRANT, JOHN, a merchant from Elgin, Morayshire, then in NY, died on a voyage from NY to Charleston, SC, on 7 Mar. 1839. [AJ#4766]

GRANT, ROBERT, naturalised, Court of Common Pleas, Philadelphia, 29 November 1803.

GRAY, DAVID, late clerk of the British Linen Company in Edinburgh, then in NY, 1845. [NAS.GD81.307]

GRAY, JAMES, naturalised, US District Court, Philadelphia, 4 Oct. 1805.

GRAY, JOHN, naturalised, Court of Common Pleas, Philadelphia, 5 April 1811 and 8 October 1823.

GRAY, WILLIAM, born at Inchture, Perthshire, on 10 Nov. 1818, son of William Gray [1762-1827] and Elspeth Wynd [1779-1854], married Margaret McBryde on 4 Oct. 1844, a weaver and a mason, to America in 1850, settled in Philadelphia, died there 31 July1891. [AP#186][Inchture g/s, Perthshire]

GREAVES, ALEXANDER, naturalised, Court of Common Pleas, Philadelphia, 17 September 1828.

GREEN, SAMUEL NICHOLSON, from Penang, died in 5th Ave. Hotel, NY, 30 Oct.1860.[S#1693]

GREENLEES, ROBERT D., from London, married Ella P. Bosworth of Adams, New York, there on 28 Jan. 1879. [EC#29449]

GREENSHIELDS, JOHN, naturalised, Supreme Court of Pennsylvania, 20 February 1798.

GREGORY, MARY, born 19 Dec. 1791, in Kilmarnock, daughter of William Gregory a merchant and Elizabeth Smith, died in Rosebank, Paterson, NJ, on 14 Nov.1880. [Kilmarnock OPR]

GREIG, ANNIE T., wife of R. W. Tullis from Edinburgh, died at 123 Eleventh St., South Brooklyn, NY, 6May 1878. [S#10,870]

GREIG, DAVID, born on 21 Nov. 1810, eldest son of Alexander Greig a Writer to the Signet, [1776-1857] and Jane Whittet [1785-1862], an attorney and solicitor in NY, died there on 10 Sep. 1847. [EEC#21560][St Cuthbert's g/s, Edinburgh]

GREIG, JAMES, born in Edinburgh during 1767, a baker and confectioner in New York from 1796, died there on 20 Dec. 1804. [ANY#1.362]

GREIG, JAMES, an engineer in Paterson near NY, son of Simon Greig in East Wemyss, Fife, 1853. [NAS.SC20.34.29.275/278]

GREIG, JOHN, born 1781, settled in NY 1799, died in Canandaigua, NY, 1 Apr. 1858.[GM.NS2.4.682]

GREIG, MITCHELL (sic), born 1791, widow of John Steedman, from Kilmarnock, Ayrshire, died in NY on 18 Dec. 1878. [EC#299401]

GRIEVE, CHARLES, born 1812 in Edinburgh, died in NY on the USS Minnesota 19 Oct.1877. [S#10,703]

GRIEVE, WILLIAM SOMMERVILLE, from Edinburgh, married Maggy Maxwell, eldest daughter of William Maxwell, from Liverpool, in NY on 3 Sept.1873. [S#9396]

GRIEVES, ARCHIBALD, born around 1818, from Dumfries, died at 150 Chambers Street, NY, on 7 July 1856. [DGC:29.7.1856]

GRINDALL, HENRY, born around 1813, son of Henry Grindall, Locharbridge, Dumfries-shire, died in NY on 11 Oct. 1835. [DGC:16.12.1835]

GRUBB, JAMES, born in 1815, a shipmaster, died in Philadelphia on 21 May 1849. [Ferry-Port-on-Craig, Fife, g/s]

GRUBB, Mrs JANET, born in Fife during 1788, wife of George Grubb, and their son John Thornton Melville Dow born 1813, who to America via Leith,were naturalised in NY on 20 May 1828.[N.Y.Court of Common Pleas Records]

GOULD, JAMES, born in Crieff, Perthshire, during 1799, son of John Gould and Mary Bruce, settled in Little Falls, Herkimer County, NY, a stonecutter, married Anna Eva Garter on 9 Feb. 1837, probate 31 Oct. 1845.[Herkimer County Wills Vol.H, fo.115]

GUILD, ALEXANDER, born in Dundee 28 April 1826, son of John Guild, a linen merchant in NY, died Hotel Vendome 5 November 1893. [ANY.2.237]

HADDEN, ANN, born in 1785, wife of David Hadden, died in NY on 3 Sep. 1845. [AJ#5100]

HADDEN, DAVID, born in Aberdeen on 13 Oct. 1773, son of Alexander Hadden and Elspet Young, arrived in NY on 18 Nov. 1806 on the packet boat New Guide, a merchant in NY, died on 3 June 1856. [ANY#2.17]

HAGGART, ALEXANDER, born in 1787, a laborer in Barony, Glasgow, to NY on the George of New York on 12 Aug. 1807.[PRO.PC1.3790]

HAIG, ROBERT, naturalised, Court of Common Pleas, Philadelphia, 21 September 1819 and 26 September 1826.

HALDANE, JOHN, died in NY on 12 June 1849. [EEC#21825]

HALL, ADAM, born in July 1787, arrived in America on 11 June 1801, a blacksmith in Utica, Oneida County, NY, in 1812. [1812]

HALL, ELSPETH, born in Caerlaverock, Dumfries-shire, wife of James Burgess, an upholsterer from Dumfries, died in Hope Street, Kensington, Philadelphia, on 13 Jan. 1877. [AO]

HALL, G., a brewer from Hawick, Roxburghshire, with wife Elizabeth Oliver, settled in Philadelphia by 1811. [NAS.CS17.1.30/538]

HALL, GEORGE, born at Clockmill, Scotland, on 24 Nov. 1796, to America, married Margaret D. Sturgis, father of George W. Hall born in Philadelphia on 18 May 1829. [AP#190]

HALL, JAMES, naturalised, Court of Common Pleas, Philadelphia, 31 July 1821 and 20 October 1836.

HALL, JANET, daughter of Alexander Hall, married Andrew Arthur a shipbuilder in NY, in Paisley, , on 28 Mar. 1848. [SG#1740]

HALL, JOHN, second son of Alexander Hall a wood merchant in Fisherrow, Edinburgh, died in NY on 31 Jan. 1845. [EEC#21219]

HALL, ROBERT, born on 13 July 1826 possibly in Edinburgh, a merchant in New York, died on 28 Mar. 1889. [ANY#2.245]

HALL, ..., daughter of Robert Hall, was born in the Mansion House, Brooklyn, NY, on 11 March 1863. [S#2429]

HALLIDAY, GAVIN, a merchant in NY, 1800, 1801. [NAS.CS17.1.18/437]

HALLIDAY, ROBERT, a merchant in NY in 1829. [NAS.RD5.384.752]

HALLIDAY, ROBERT, a merchant from Dumfries, died in NY on 18 Apr. 1840. [DGH:29.5.1840]

HALYBURTON, FREDERICK, coach joiner, died in Philadelphia 1854. [S.28.10.1854]

HALYBURTON, HANNAH, born 1778, relict of Frederick John Halyburton, died in Philadelphia on 30 January 1870. [S#8291]

HAMILTON, ALEXANDER JAMES, only son of James Hamilton of Ballincrieff, Linlithgow, West Lothian, settled in NY by 1800. [NAS.RD2.297.400];in NY, 1808. [NAS.CS17.1.27/371; CS17.1.28/74]

HAMILTON, ALEXANDER, in NY, 1806. [NAS.CS17.1.25/456]

HAMILTON, JOHN ROBERT, in NY, died 21Sept.1874, cnf 10 July 1876. [NAS.SC70.1.179]

HAMILTON, JAMES, naturalised, Court of Quarter Sessions, Philadelphia, 24 May 1813.

HAMILTON, WILLIAM, naturalised, Supreme Court of Pennsylvania, 17 June 1799.

HAMILTON, WILLIAM, in NY, cnf 1825. [NAS.SC70.1.33]

HAMPTON, DAVID, naturalised, Supreme Court of Pennsylvania, 16 February 1798.

HARDIE, ALEXANDER MCGRUER, born in 1848, son of William Hardie, Knaps, Ellon, Aberdeenshire, died in Brooklyn on 23 Apr. 1872.[AJ:15.5.1872]

HARDIE, JOHN, eldest son of Robert Hardie in Mileend, Glasgow, died in Camden, NJ, on 3 Aug. 1873. [EC#27732]

HARDIN, ELIZABETH, in Brooklyn, NY, cnf 1882. [NAS.SC70.1.215]

HARDGRAVE, FLORENCE, born 1849, youngest daughter of Alexander Hardgrave and his wife Mary Anne Bell from Ruthwell, Dumfries-shire, died in NY on 27 Oct. 1864. [AO]

HARKINS, Reverend JOHN, from Ecclefechan, Dumfries-shire, died in Jersey City, NJ, on 4 July 1878. [AO]

HARLEY, JOHN, a moulder in Jersey City, died on 11 Nov. 1848, cnf 1849. [NAS.SC70.1.150]

HARPER, ALEXANDER, from Glasgow, died in NY 1 Sept.1861. [S#1951]

HARPER, JAMES, born in 1802, son of John Harper a merchant in Glasgow, educated at Glasgow University, a minister of the Secession Church, died in Shippenburg, PA, on 13 May 1876. [MAGU#319][UPC#677]

HARPER, THOMAS, a wood merchant from Moniave, Dumfries-shire, settled in NY by 1855. [DGC:15.1.1856]

HARRISON, RICHARD, counsellor at law in NY, graduated
Doctor of Law from Edinburgh University on 27 Sep. 1792.
[CEG]

HARDIE, ROBERT, born on 18 Feb. 1727, married Martha Cogill,
died in Philadelphia on 23 Dec. 1798. [AP#203]

HARKNESS, ADAM, naturalised, Supreme Court of
Pennsylvania, 20 February 1790.

HARKNESS, ALEXANDER, late a teacher of the Free Middle
Church School in Paisley, died in Philadelphia on 6 Oct.
1849. [SG#1870]

HART, GEORGE HOPE, born in Edinburgh 28 January 1807, son
of George Hart, merchant in NY, died at 312 State St.,
Brooklyn, 27 April 1880. [ANY.2.173]

HART, ROBERT HOPE, born in Edinburgh, son of George Hart in
Kincardine, merchant in NY, died 10 June 1865.
[ANY.2.208]

HASELBAUR, AGUSTAUS, eldest son of A. Haselbaur, a glass
engraver, late of Edinburgh, died in Corning, NY, on 14
March 1872. [S#8959]

HASWELL, ELLIOT, from Glasgow, wife of Julius L. Pollock in
Brooklyn, died there on 11 Feb. 1871. [S#8612]

HATTRICK, PETER, born around 1755, a merchant from
Greenock, in NY 1795, died in there on 11 June 1832.
[DGC:31.7.1832][NAS.RS54.PR36/1231]

HAY, ALLAN, born in Kelso, Roxburghshire, during Aug. 1813,
settled in NY during 1834, died there on 9 Sep. 1900.
[ANY#2.238]

HAY, JAMES, naturalised, US District Court, Philadelphia, 22
May 1798.

HAY, JAMES, born in Lerwick, Shetland Islands, on 22 May
1791, third son of James Hay of Laxfirth (1750-1830), via
New Brunswick, a merchant in NY by 1817, naturalised in
NY on 27 Apr.1825, died in Pelhamville, NY, on 5 May
1854. [ANY#2.69][EEC#22515/22601][Court of Common
Pleas]

HAY, JANET, daughter of David Hay in Darnchester, Coldstream,
Berwickshire, married George Muir a blacksmith, in Jane
Street, NY, 6 July 1870. [S#8472]

HAY, JANET, STEWART, born 1857, third daughter of Peter
Hay, a farina manufacturer in Glen Eden House, Fife,
married Patrick William Stephen, in NY on 2 November

1876; died in Philadelphia on 28 December 1876.
[S#10,390/10,451]

HAY, JOHN, naturalised, Court of Quarter Sessions, Philadelphia. 7 October 1818.

HAY, Mrs MARGERY, born in 1810, daughter of John Innes a merchant tailor in Aberdeen, died in Watertown, Jefferson County, NY, on 9 June 1848. [AJ:12.7.1848]

HAY, ROBERT, naturalised, Supreme Court of Pennsylvania, 20 February 1798.

HAY, ROBERT, born in 1841, from Nether Boreland, Dryfesdale, Dumfries-shire, died in NY on 25 Nov. 1870. [AO]

HAY, THOMAS, born in Kelso 1821, tallow chandler in NY, died 316 West 84th Street, NY, 17 July 1896. [ANY.2.299]

HELME, WILLIAM, born in Dumfries on 25 Apr. 1824, as a child to America, a gas engineer in Trenton, NJ, and in Philadelphia, died in Philadelphia on 12 June 1888. [AP#205]

HENDERSON, ANN, wife of ... Walker, in NY 1806. [NAS.CS17.1.25/457]

HENDERSON, DAVID, born in Annan, settled in NY by 1828, founder of the Arinondack Iron and Steel Company, died in Jersey City, NJ, on 3 Sep. 1845. [DGH:2.10.1845][ANY.2.174]

HENDERSON, JOHN, in Brooklyn, NY, 14 May 1856. [NAS.RS.Edinburgh#68/131]

HENDERSON, MATTHEW, born on 25 Apr. 1735, son of Matthew Henderson in Orwell, Kinross-shire, a minister, in 1758, settled in Del. and in Charteris, PA, died in Pittsburgh, Washington County, PA on 2 Oct. 1795. [UPC#654][GM#65/1112]

HENDERSON, ROBERT, in Alleghany City, PA, cnf 1888. [NAS.SC70.1.264]

HENDERSON, THOMAS, born in Thornhill, Dumfries-shire, during 1835, died in NY on 19 Dec. 1862. [AO]

HENDERSON, ..., son of John Henderson from Annan, was born at 39 Cumberland Street, Brooklyn, on 12 Apr. 1878. [AO]

HENDRIE, DANIEL, born in Dunbartonshire on 17 June 1835, to America in 1851, a merchant in Philadelphia, died there on 13 Dec. 1892.[AP#206]

HENRY, JOHN, born in Galashiels in 1798, son of Robert Henry, a merchant in NY and in Mobile, died in Cranbury, NJ, 4 August 1856. [ANY.2.238]

HENRY, ROBERT, from Galashiels, died in Cranbury, NJ, in June 1856. [ANY.2.238]

HEPBURN, WILLIAM, born in 1782, a merchant in Hailes, Preston Kirk, East Lothian, to NY on the George of New York on 12 Aug. 1807. [PRO.PC1.3790]

HERON, AGNES, born in Dumfries-shire during 1797, widow of James Savage, died at 328 South 2nd Street, NJ, on 4 July 1865. [AO]

HETHERINGTON, MARY SCOTT, born in 1794, widow of John Dixon, sister of Richard Hetherington in Searig, Dalton, Dumfries-shire, died in Preble, Cortland County, NY, on 30 Sep. 1868. [AO]

HEWITT, JOHN, a merchant in Philadelphia then in Hamburg 1819.[NAS.CS17.1.38/626]

HEWITT, WILLIAM, a merchant in Philadelphia then in Hamburg 1819. [NAS.CS17.1.38/626]

HILL, BARBARA, youngest dau. of George Hill in Edinburgh, married David Currie from Edinburgh, in NY 6 Dec.1870. [S#8550]

HILL, GEORGE, naturalised, US District Court, Philadelphia, 10 May 1796.

HILL, THOMAS, a carpenter in Corona, NY, son of William Peat Hill a ships carpenter in St Andrews who died 23 Nov.1850.[NAS,SH.5.5.1888]

HOGG, ANDREW, in Jersey City, NJ, brother of Jean Hogg who died 7 May 1879 wife of John Miller in Highland Falls, NY. [NAS.SH.13.10.1899]

HOGG, GEORGE, naturalised, Court of Common Pleas, Philadelphia, 28 October 1816, and Court of Quarter Sessions, Philadelphia, 11 October 1830.

HOGG, JOHN, son of James Hogg a draper in Dumfries, [1768-1833], & Anne Stewart, died in NY aged 33. [Dumfries g/s]

HOGG, JOHN, naturalised, Court of Quarter Sessions, Philadelphia, 11 October 1802.

HOGG, ROBERT, a brass-finisher in NY, eldest son of Kenneth Hogg a shoemaker in Cromarty and grandson of Robert Hogg, a seaman in Cromarty, 1854. [NAS.GD1.478.5-7]

HOLIDAY, JANET, born in 1813, from Raeburncleugh, Eskdale, Dumfries-shire, wife of Thomas Beattie from Ruthwell,

Dumfries-shire, died in Truxton, Cortland, NY, on 4 June 1870. [AO]

HOLLINGWORTH, JANET, born in 1836, daughter of Charles Hollingworth from Haddington, East Lothian, married George Allan, a currier from Anstruther, Fife, in Newark, NJ, on 2 Nov. 1858, she died on 6 Oct. 1867. [EFR][S#7560]

HOLMES, ALEXANDER, in Albany, NY, 1848. [NAS.SC48.49.47B/219]

HOLMES, ISABELLA, in Albany, NY, 1848. [NAS.SC48.49.47B/219]

HOME, BARBARA, born 1815, wife of John L. Donaldson, late of 40 Princes St., Edinburgh, died in Newton, Long Island, 10 Nov. 1870. [S#8532]

HOOD, JAMES, born in Scotland during 1787, a farmer, arrived in NY on the Camillus in 1821. [USNA.par]

HOOD, PETER, born in Scotland during 1793, a farmer, arrived in NY on the Camillus in 1821. [USNA.par]

HOOD, WILLIAM, naturalised, Court of Common Pleas, Philadelphia, 2 December 1819 and 24 January 1823.

HORSBURGH, JANET, wife of James Turnbull formerly a miller at Junction Flour Mills, Leith, died in Oneida on 10 February 1874. [S#9558]

HORSEBURGH, JOHN, naturalised, Court of Common Pleas, Philadelphia, 28 October 1796.

HORSEMAN, ROBERT, from Burghmuirhead, settled in Poppleton, NY, died on 21 Aug. 1799, cnf 5 Aug. 1802. [NAS.CC8.8.133]

HORTON, ..., daughter of Cleveland Kemble Horton was born in Buffalo, NY, on 21 July 1875. [EC#28361]

HOSSACK, SIMON, born in Avoch, Ross-shire, a minister, educated at Aberdeen University in 1779, to NY, married Catherine Carr (1767-1795) in Goshen, NY, settled in Johnstown, NY, during 1790. ["Some Pioneer Women of Johnstown", Johnstown, 1937]

HOWISON, EDWARD, a Quaker in Edinburgh, settled in NY during 1803.   [NAS.CH10.1.65]

HULL, RUTH, from Dundee, settled in NJ, cnf 1893. [NAS.SC70.1.316]

HUNT, CHARLES A., naturalised, Court of Common Pleas, Philadelphia, 25 August 1820.

HUNTER, AGNES, from Dumfries, wife of Dr John Carson, died in Philadelphia on 28 July 1826. [DGC:8.8.1826]

HUNTER, GEORGE, born in Aberdeen during 1829, died at Broadway, NY, on 7 Dec. 1874. [AJ:30.12.1874]

HUNTER, JAMES, naturalised, Court of Quarter Sessions, Philadelphia, 4 October 1808.

HUNTER, ROBERT, born in Galloway during 1759, via England to America, naturalised in NY city on 19 Nov. 1804. [NYPL.MS]

HUTCHEON, JOHN, born in 1835, son of William Hutcheon from Aberdeen, died in S.Brooklyn, NY, on 19 Aug. 1851. [AJ#5408]

HUTCHINSON, HENRY, naturalised, Supreme Court of Pennsylvania, 29 November 1804.

HUTCHISON, ROBERT, born during 1783, in St Ninians, Stirlingshire, naturalised in NY city on 2 Nov. 1811. [NYPL.MS]; born 1783, to America in 1808, a merchant at 143 Pearl Street, NY.[1812]

HUTCHISON, WILLIAM, son of Rev. Patrick Hutchison in Paisley, settled in NY 1818, merchant, died 8 Jan.1875.[ANY.2.89]; cnf 1875 Edinburgh. [NAS.SC70.1.173/731]

HUTTON, ALEXANDER, born 25 January 1821, youngest son of James Hutton, Greenside Place, St Andrews, Fife, a merchant in NY, died at 59 Morton St., NY, on 5 June 1863. [S#2503][ANY.2.228]

HUTTON, JOHN, born 1808 in St Andrews, settled in NY 1827, merchant in NY, died 13 July 1874 at West 34th Street. [ANY.2.160]

HYATT, ..., daughter of Edgar Smith Hyatt, was born in New Brunswick, NJ, on 22 Feb.1878. [S#10,797]

HYSLOP, MAXWELL, son of the late William Hyslop of Lochend, a merchant in NY, later in Kingston, Jamaica, 1809. [NAS.CS17.1.28/400]

HYSLOP, WELLWOOD, son of the late William Hyslop of Lochend, a merchant in NY, later in Kingston, Jamaica, 1809. [NAS.CS17.1.28/400]; a merchant in NY 1816. [NAS.CS17.1.35/198]

INCHES, THOMAS, naturalised, Court of Quarter Sessions, Philadelphia, 25 march 1813, and the Supreme Court of Pennsylvania, 2 December 1813.

INGLIS, ARCHIBALD, from Montreal, third son of Archibald Inglis MD FRCS Edinburgh, married Charlotte Douglas Gordon, daughter of William Gordon in Madeira, in NY on 27 July 1874. [EC#28036][S#9688]

INGLIS, DAVID, born in 1780, a power loom manufacturer from Dunfermline, Fife, died in Paterson, NJ, on 14 May 1868, his wife died there on 1 Aug. 1868, and James, their youngest son, died there on 9 Aug. 1860. [DP][S#7751]

INGLIS, FRANCES ERSKINE, third daughter of William Inglis a Writer to the Signet, married Chevalier Calderon de la Barca the Spanish Minister in Washington, in NY on 24 Sep. 1838. [AJ#4738]

INGLIS, JOHN, born 1805, son of William Inglis (1775-1833) supervisor of excise in Teviotdale and his wife Janet Tweedie (1771-1850), surgeon in NY, died 1849. [Greyfriars g/s, Edinburgh]

INGLIS, WILLIAM, a merchant in NY 1849. [NAS.SC48.49.25.48/175]

INGRAM, ..., daughter of W. J. Ingram, was born in NY on 30 Oct. 1875.[EC#28300]

INNES, JOHN, born 1828 in Leith, died in Jersey City on 5 April 1871. [S#8667]

INNES, JOSEPH, naturalised, Court of Common Pleas, Philadelphia, 9 June 1798.

INNES, MARGERY, daughter of John Innes a merchant tailor in Aberdeen, and wife of Alexander Hay, died in Watertown, Jefferson County, NY, on 9 June 1848.[AJ#5244]

INNES, ..., daughter of Alexander Innes a printer from Edinburgh, was born at 355 West 39th Street, NY, on 28 Dec.1871. [S#8884]

INNES, ..., daughter of Alexander Innes a printer from Edinburgh, was born at 467 West 46th Street, NY, 12 Sept. 1876. [S#10,354]

INNES, JOHN KERR LILLIE, son of Alexander Innes a printer from Edinburgh, was born at 467 West 46th Street, NY, 18 Oct. 1877, died there on 16 April 1878. [S#10,697/10,852]

IRONSIDE, GEORGE EDMUND, born Aberdeen around 1766, graduated King's College there in 1781, wife (1) Helen, (2) Mary McKay, teacher in NY 1808-, died 7 May 1827 in Washington. [ANY.2.10]

IRVINE, ALEXANDER ECCLESTONE, a saddler in Philadelphia, son of James Irvine a merchant in Lossiemouth who died 25 Dec.1883.[NAS.SH.21.1.1889]

IRVINE, PETER, born in 1772, brother of Washington Irvine and Mrs Van Wart inBirmingham, died in NY during 1838. [AJ#4728]

IRVINE, ROBERT, naturalised, Court of Quarter Sessions, Philadelphia, 9 April 1829.

IRVIN, RICHARD, born in 1799, son of William Irvin a merchant in Glasgow, educated at Glasgow University around 1810, a merchant in NY, died at Oyster Bay, Long Island, on 27 June 1858. [MAGU#253][ANY.2.98]

IRVING, ELIZABETH, daughter of G. F. Irving in NY, and niece of Washington Irving, married Thomas Wilnslow, late of the 72nd Highlanders, son of Rev. Octavius Winslaw, 25 April 1868. [S#7733]

IRVING, HELEN, born in Dumfries-shire during 1796, wife of Gilbert Dickson, died in Bovina, Del. County, NY, on 11 Apr. 1879. [AO]

IRVING, JONAH N., third son of William Irving a farmer in Townfoot, Mousewald, Dumfries-shire, died in Buffalo, NY, on 27 Apr. 1874. [AO]

IRVING, JOHN, born in 1868, only son of John Irving a builder, died at 864 Atlantic Avenue, Brooklyn, in 1874. [AO]

IRVING, MAGGIE, infant daughter of John Irving a builder, died at 20 Rochester Avenue, Brooklyn, on 12 Nov. 1872. [AO]

IRVING, MARY, daughter of John Irving, a mason from Annan, Dumfries-shire, married Colin M. Rome, in Brooklyn on 16 May 1870. [AO]

IRVING, WILLIAM SKIDMORE, born in 1854, son of Reverend David Irving, died in Morriston, NJ, on 14 June 1864. [AO]

IRVING, ..., daughter of John Irving a mason, was born at 864 Atlantic Avenue, Brooklyn, on 23 Mar. 1876. [AO]

IRVING, ..., daughter of John Irving a builder, was born at 496 Atlantic Avenue, Brooklyn, on 10 Apr. 1879. [AO]

JACK, CHARLES, naturalised, Court of Quarter Sessions, Philadelphia, 6 December 1822.

JACK, WILLIAM, born in 1782, a laborer from Bellshill, Lanarkshire, to NY on the George of New York on 12 Aug. 1807. [PRO.PC1.3790]

JACKSON, GEORGE, born in 1811, partner of Jackson and Robins in NY, "he travelled for several years for Messrs Raimes and Co. in Edinburgh", died in Brooklyn on 26 Nov. 1851. [FJ#990]

JACKSON, HENRY, eldest son of ..... Jackson in Musselburgh, Midlothian, died in NY on 2 Feb. 1849. [EEC#21825][SG#1829]

JAFFRAY, JANE, born on 29 May 1773, daughter of Reverend Andrew Jaffrey and Agnes Armstrong in Ruthwell, Dumfriesshire, married ..... Renwick in NY during 1794, died 1850. [F#2.214]

JAFFREY, ROBERT, born 1779 in Kilmarnock son of Rev. Robert Jaffrey, educated Glasgow University ca.1792, a merchant in NY, died 11 June 1845. [ANY.2.100]

JAMES, JANE DALTON, born in 1851, second daughter of Reverend John James, died at 91 Lancaster Street, Albany, NY, on 31 Mar. 1876. [EC#28564]

JAMIE, DAVID, naturalised, Supreme Court of Pennsylvania, 8 April 1813.

JAMIESON, CATHERINE,born 1820, daughter of George Jamieson and Isabella George, died on Long Island, NY, 22 Dec. 1851. [East Preston Street cemetery, Edinburgh]

JAMIESON, JOHN, from Thornhill, Dumfries-shire, a minister in Bathgate, West Lothian, from 1776 to 1783, to America, a minister in Newville, PA, from 1784 to 1792, and in Hannastown, PA, from 1792 to 1797, died on 1 July 1821. [UPC#1.599]

JAMIESON, ROBERT, naturalised, Supreme Court of Pennsylvania, 27 July 1819.

JARDINE, ANDREW, born in 1850, son of John Jardine of Rigg, Gretna, Dumfries-shire, then in Rochelle, NY, died on 19 Feb. 1875.   [AO]

JARDINE, THOMAS, born in Lochmaben, Dumfries-shire, during 1808, died in Pelham, Westchester County, NY, on 13 Jan. 1863. [AO]

JEFFREY, ISABELLA, youngest daughter of John Jeffrey a writer in Edinburgh, married Reverend B. C. Hill, from York, Upper Canada, at the house of John McConnel, Markbroom, Canandalgua, NY, on 8 Nov. 1841. [AJ#4902]

JEFFREY, JOHN, late minister of the Reformed Church in Quarelwood, Kirkmahoe,Dumfries-shire, died in NY on 25 Dec. 1831. [AJ#4387]

JENKINSON, THOMAS, in Trenton, NJ, brother of John Jenkinson who died in Edinburgh 8 Nov.1884. [NAS.SH.25.6.1888]

JENKINSON, ..., daughter of M. Jenkinson from Edinburgh, was born in Geneva, Ontario County, NY, on 23 October 1875. [S#10078]

JENKINSON, BESSIE, infant daughter of M. and E.Jenkinson, died in Geneva, NY, on 17 Nov.1878. [S#11,046]

JENKINSON, GRACIE, born 1875, daughter of M. and E. Jenkinson, died in Geneva, NY, on 21 Oct.1878. [S#11,046]

JOHNSON, MATTHEW, naturalised, Court of Common Pleas, Philadelphia, 12 October 1829.

JOHNSON, THOMAS, naturalised, Court of Quarter Sessions, Philadelphia, 7 October 1826

JOHNSTON, ALEXANDER, born 14 June 1810 at Barnboard Mill, Nalmaghie, Kirkcudbright, son of John Johnston and Margaret Rae, emigrated to SC 1835, later in NY, died in Scotland 13 December 1845. [ANY.2.186]

JOHNSTONE, ALICE, born during 1786, wife of Reverend John Johnstone late of Glasgow,died in Jersey City, NY, on 26 July 1849. [SG#1847]

JOHNSTON, ANDREW, youngest son of Michael Johnston a merchant in Glasgow, died at 236 West 48th Street, NY, on 26 April 1873. [S#9285]

JOHNSTON, FRANK, born in 1827, eldest son of George Johnston of Newington Lodge, Annan, Dumfries-shire, died in NY on 15 June 1857. [AO]

JOHNSTON, GEORGE, born in Kirkcudbright around 1782 son of William Johnston, settled in NY 1804, in NY around 1813.[ANY.2.167] [DGA#GGD.92/1]

JOHNSTONE, JAMES, born in Sep. 1777, son of James Johnstone and Anne Fraser in Croy, Inverness-shire, a farmer who with his wife Mary born in 1777 and son James born in 1806, to NY on the George of New York on 12 Aug. 1807. [PRO.PC1.3790]

JOHNSTON, JANET, daughter of John Johnston, Newton, Closeburn, Dumfries-shire, married John Beck, a merchant in NY 4 January 1853, died in May 1882. [ANY.2.221]

JOHNSTON, JEREMIAH, in NY 1809. [NAS.CS17.1.28/482]

JOHNSTON, JOHN, born 22 Jan.1781, son of John Johnston, miller at the Haugh of Urr, Kirkcudbrightshire, [1750-1841] and Dorothea Proudfoot, [1758-1794], died in Patterson, NJ, on 13 Dec. 1846. [Balmaghie g/s, Kirkcudbrightshire] - possibly the John Johnston who to NY in 1804, husband of Margaret Taylor father of John Taylor Johnston. [HOJ]; to NY 1804, a merchant. [ANY.2.32]

JOHNSTON, JOSEPH, born in Duns, distiller in NY in 1830s, died at 454 Hudson St., NY, on 23 July 1841. [ANY.2.169]

JOHNSTONE, MARGARET, born in 1737, a spinster in Croy, Inverness-shire, to NY on the George of New York on 12 Aug. 1807. [PRO.PC1.3790]

JOHNSTONE, MARGARET, born in 1767, a spinster in Croy, Inverness-shire, to NY on the George of New York on 12 Aug. 1807. [PRO.PC1.3790]

JOHNSTON, MARY, daughter of Robert Johnston a joiner in Ruthwell, Dumfries-shire, wife of Walter Barton from Ruthwell, died in Jersey City on 3 Aug. 1863. [AO]

JOHNSTON, ROBERT, born in Kirkcudbrightshire during 1804, via Liverpool to America, an accountant who was naturalised in NY on 29 Oct. 1821.[Court of Common Pleas Records][ANY.2.176]

JOHNSTON, ROBERT, born 1803, son of David Johnston, Mayfield, Leslie, Fife, died in West Hoboken, NJ, 4 Sept.1873. [S#9428]

JOHNSTON, THOMAS S., from Rochester, NY, married Mary Ann White, from Stromness, Orkney, in Glasgow on 24 Dec. 1877. [EC#29092]

JOHNSTON, WILLIAM, a merchant from Glasgow, in NY 1804. [NAS.CS17.1.23/472]

JOHNSTON, WILLIAM JOHN, born in Dumfries around 1775, via Cork to America, arrived in NY during Nov. 1802, naturalised there on 21 Dec. 1805. [Court of Common Pleas Records]

JOHNSTON, WILLIAM, born in Kirkcudbrightshire during 1800, via Greenock to America, a merchant who was naturalised in NY on 27 Oct. 1821.[Court of Common Pleas Records]

JOHNSTONE, WILLIAM, third son of James Johnstone a tanner in Glasgow, died in NY during 1817. [S.1.34]

JOHNSTON, WILLIAM, born in Scotland during 1791, arrived in NY with 5 children on the Camillus during 1821. [USNA.par]

JOHNSTON, WILLIAM, from Annan, Dumfries-shire, married Mary Scott in Jersey City on 27 Jan. 1863. [AO]

JOHNSTON, WILLIAM, born in 1835, a mariner, son of James Johnston a carrier in Annan, Dumfries-shire, died in Jersey City on 21 Apr. 1873. [AO]

JOHNSTON, ..., brother of John Johnston, a spirit dealer in Dumfries, settled in NY during 1807. [NAS.CS235.SB.J2]

JOHNSTON, ..., son of Thomas Johnston a compositor, was born at 269 Pearl Street, Brooklyn, NY, on 11 August 1876. [S#10,325]

JUST, JOHN, from Perthshire, settled in NY by 1868, died there on 14 Sep. 1893. [ANY#2.267]

KAY, THOMAS JAMES, only son of Henry R. Kay, 34 Alva Street, Edinburgh, drowned in the North River, NY, 22 June 1874. [S#9659]

KEDDIE, JOHN, Edinburgh, married Catherine Leckie, youngest dau. of John Kelly in Lochwinnoch, at the home of David Cant, her brother in law, 297 10th Avenue, NY, on 14 Nov. 1867. [S#7603]

KEILLER, GEORGE THOMSON, born in Stirling during 1847, died in East Moriches, Long Island, NY, on 19 Aug. 1873. [EC#27750]

KEIR, ALEXANDER, late a merchant in NY, in Halifax 1801. [NAS.CS17.1.9/84]

KEIR, ALEXANDER, from Newton Stewart, via Londonderry to NY on the Barkley on 14 Aug. 1816. [NWI#2.358]

KEIR, ANNIE, late from London, married Rev. Frederick Busch, pastor of the   German Reformed Church of NY, there in 1850. [W#1097]

KEIR, JEAN, in Philadelphia, cnf 1831. [NAS.SC70.1.44]

KELLY, ANN, in Paterson, NJ, cnf 1891. [NAS.SC70.1.291]

KELLY, JOAN, born 1863, daughter of Alexander Kelly an ironmonger from Edinburgh, died in NY on 23 July 1873. [Dean g/s, Edinburgh][S#9372]

KEMP or PATISON, ELIZABETH, NY, 1849. [NAS.SC48.49.48/208]

KEMP, HENRY, born in Musselburgh, Midlothian, on 10 Dec. 1814, settled in NY 1840s, died on 16 May 1898. [ANY#2.232]

KEMP, MARGARET, daughter of Henry Kemp from Edinburgh, married Frank Watt of Lockport, Niagara, in Peekskill, N.Y., on 21 December 1869. [S#8255]

KEMPT, JOHN, son of John Kempt in Coull, Aberdeenshire, educated at Marischal College, Aberdeen, from 1779 to 1783, graduated MA, graduated LL.D. from King's College, Aberdeen, in 1787, later Professor of Mathematics in NY.[MCA#2.355]

KENNEDY, DAVID, born in 1773, son of Thomas Kennedy and Ann Gibb in Falkland, Fife, a merchant in Philadelphia, died in Germantown, PA, during 1798. [Falkland g/s, Fife]

KENNEDY, DAVID SPROAT, born in Kirkcudbright 1791 son of Capt. John Kennedy and Mary Lenox, a merchant in NY 1807-1825. [ANY.2.55]

KENNEDY, HUGH, son of Daniel Kennedy in Glasgow, died in Philadelphia 1802.   [GkAd#75][GM.73.86]

KENNEDY, JAMES LENOX, born in Kirkcudbright, son of Captain John Kennedy and Mary Lenox, arrived in the Glenthorn in 1815, a merchant in NY, 1818, merchant and US Consul in Mazatlan, Mexico, died there 1838.[ANY.2.83] [NAS.CS17.1.38/195]

KENNEDY, JAMES, MD, born 1799, to NY 1800, surgeon and physician in NY, died 361 West 51st Street, 29 March 1884. [ANY.2.299]

KENNEDY, JOHN, from Kirkcudbright, died on his passage from NY on 5 Jan. 1797. [GM#67.165]

KENNEDY, JOHN, in Beaver Falls, PA, cnf 1885. [NAS.SC70.1.244]

KENT, Mrs JANET, born in 1822, second dau. of Marion Scott from Annan, Dumfries, died in W. Philadelphia on 27 Aug. 1857. [AO]

KENT, WILLIAM, a compositor from Edinburgh, died in NY on 20 June 1862. [S#2208]

KERR, AGNES ANNE, spouse of William Wilson, NY, 1821. [NAS.CS17.1.40/216]

KERR, JEAN, eldest dau. of Robert Kerr, from Millbank, widow of John Thompson barrackmaster at Eyemouth lately British Vice Consul in Baltimore, died in York, PA., 1 Sept.1860. [S#1643]

KERR, JOHN, born in Glasgow in 1800, to America via Greenock,naturalised in NY on 27 Jan. 1827. [Court of Common Pleas]

KERR, THOMAS, from Aberdeen, married Sarah Jane Jacox, youngest daughter of Thomas Jacox, in Saltspringville, Montgomery County, NY, on 1 Oct. 1845. [AJ#5105]

KEVAN, ANDREW, born Kirkcudbright 1757, a shoemaker in NY, married Jean Dill 22 June 1806, died 25 Apr. 1827. [ANY#1.363]

KEVAN, SAMUEL, born Kirkcudbrightshire, a master slater in NY by 1827, married Mary Tannahill in Schenectady 1831. [ANY#1.117]

KEVAN, WILLIAM, born in Kirkcudbright during 1765, a leather and shoe merchant in NY by 1808, died there 7 Dec. 1847. [ANY#2.7]

KEY, JAMES, a printer, late in Philadelphia now in Edinburgh, 1800. [NAS.CS17.1.19/33]

KIGGINS, JAMES, from Pollockshaws, Glasgow, to USA in July 1845, settled in PA. [Boston Pilot, 8.11.1845]

KING, CHARLES, born in Dumfriesshire during 1800, a slater, with his wife Mary born in Galloway in 1798, and daughter Mary born in Dumfries during 1825, via Port Patrick and Belfast to America, naturalised in NY 20 Oct. 1826.[Court of Common Pleas Records]

KING, JAMES, a merchant in NY, dead by 1789. [NAS.CS17.1.8,24]

KING, JAMES, jr., merchant in NY, deceased, son of James King of Drums, 1800. [NAS.CS18.712.10]

KING, JANE, born in 1833, youngest daughter of William King late of Edinburgh, died in Canandaigua on 6 Dec. 1849. [W#1071]

KINNIER, ..., daughter of Rev. James Kinneir, was born at the First Presbyterian Parsonage, Cedarville, NJ, 24 Feb.1876. [S#10,181]

KIRK, ELIZA, born 1857, wife of James Wightman, died in Brooklyn, on 18 May 1885. [Auchenleck g/s, Ayrshire]

KIRKPATRICK, MAGGIE EMILY OLDER, widow of William Kirkpatrick of Ellisland, Dumfries-shire, married Peter Haining of Susquehanna, PA, in Hoboken on 10 June 1867. [AO]

KIRKPATRICK, SAMUEL, naturalised, Court of Quarter Sessions, Philadelphia, 7 June 1826.

KIRKWOOD, WILLIAM, born 1786, a merchant from Girvan, via Greenock on 4 Sep. 1817 bound for NY on the William of New York arrived in NY on 17 Oct. 1817.[NYMunicipal Archives][NY Comml Adv, 18.10.1817]

KNOX, ALEXANDER, born in Paisley 1786 son of Alexander Knox a weaver, died in Jane St., NY, 22 Dec.1851. [ANY.2.108]

KNOX, ALEXANDER, naturalised, Supreme Court of Pennsylvania, 17 June 1799.

KNOX, JOHN, born in Edinburgh, a merchant in NY, died there on 18 July 1810. [ANY#1.305]

KNOX, JOHN, in Fishkill, NY, cnf 1852. [NAS.SC70.1.77]

KNOX, MARY, a widow, born in Paisley 1769, to America via Greenock, naturalised in NY on 22 Dec. 1830.[Court of Common Pleas Records]

KNOX, WILLIAM, born in 1781, son of William Knox a glazier in Edinburgh, [1743-1804] and Janet Howden [1751-1822], died in Philadelphia during 1806. [St Cuthbert's g/s, Edinburgh]

LAIDLAW, JOHN, born 5 April 1794 son of Thomas and Ann Laidlaw, merchant in NY by 1816, died in Brooklyn 1 April 1863. [ANY.2.153]

LAIDLAW, JOHN, born in Roxburghshire during 1794, a teacher, with his wife Agnes, born in Edinburgh during 1794, also a teacher, via Leith to America, settled in Brooklyn, naturalised in NY on 24 July 1820. [Court of Common Pleas]

LAIDLAW, JOHN, born 1850, a sailor, son of William Laidlaw a tailor in Edinburgh, died in Rochester Hospital, NY,8 July 1874. [S#9681]

LAING, JOHN C., a stonecutter from Aberdeen, died in Albany, NY, on 16 June 1871. [AJ:12.7.1871]

LAING, ROBERT, from Abernethy, a minister in Duns, Berwickshire, then a pastor in Buffalo, Washington County, PA, in 1791, in South Argyle 1805, in Bovina, Delaware County, NY, in 1814, died on 29 May 1839. [UPC#1.339]

LAING, ..., son of James Laing in Berbice, was born in NY on 25 Aug. 1848. [SG#1752]

LAIRD, SAMUEL, born in Scotland during 1801, a laborer, arrived in NY on the Camillas, Captain Peck, during 1821. [USNA.par]

LAMB, MARIA ANN, born in Edinburgh during 1798, wife of John Lamb, to America via London, naturalised in NY on 24 Dec. 1824. [Court of Common Pleas Records]

LAMB, ROBERT, a manufacturer from Glasgow, in America by 1808. [NAS.CS17.1.27/344]

LAMB, ROBERT, a clerk in NY, son of Robert Lamb, a merchant in Elgin, Morayshire, who died on 6 Feb.1857. [NAS.SH.24.9.1897]

LAMB, ROBERT, born in Langholm, Dumfries-shire, to USA in 1848, died in Watertown, NY, on 10 Feb. 1872. [AO]

LAMONT, DUNCAN, born in Greenock 31 Oct.1792, a merchant in NY, died in Brooklyn 13 Feb.1865. [ANY.2.259]

LAMONT, PATRICK B., born Aberdeen 1787, painter in NY 1818, died 7 May 1828. [ANY.2.69]

LANG, WILLIAM, born in Glasgow 1771, settled Portsmouth, NH, married Maria Bailey in NY 3 Jan.1796, a merchant in NY until 1844, died in Wyoming, Mass., 27 August 1849. [ANY.2.101]

LANGWILL, JESSIE, in Ingraham, Clinton County, NY, cnf 1899. [NAS.SC70.1.385]

LATOU, ROBERT, born 10 July 1799 in Cupar, Fife, son of Peter Latou and Janet Henderson, a shipbuilder, emigrated to Montreal in 1816, settled in NY by 1851, died 12 January 1869. [Leuchars g/s, Fife][ANY.2.229]

LAUDER, JOHN, from Lochmaben, Dumfries-shire, died at Lake George on 9 Mar. 1870. [AO]

LAUDER, WILLIAM, from Lauder, Berwickshire, general superintendent of the Kemble Coal and Iron Company in Fiddlesburg, married Mary, eldest daughter of Charles Ashcom of Hopewell, PA, there on 29 July 1874. [S#9674]

LAURENCE, ALEXANDER, born in Peterhead, Aberdeenshire, in 1789, son of Charles Laurence and Margaret Yule, a stonecutter in NY, died at 17 Wooster St., NY, on 3 March 1853. [ANY.2.171]

LAURIE, JOHN, born Musselburgh 1784, to America in 1805, merchant in NY, died in London 28 Dec.1870. [ANY.2.23]

LAW, ANDREW, naturalised, Court of Common Pleas, Philadelphia, 8 October 1827.

LAWRENCE, MARGARET, wife of William Wood, died at West 18th Street, NY, 21 March 1871. [S#8642]

LAWRENCE, SARAH JANE, on Long Island, NY, cnf 1893. [NAS.SC70.1.318]

LAWSON, ALEXANDER, naturalised, Court of Common Pleas, Philadelphia, 9 June 1804.

LAWSON, JAMES, born on 9 Nov. 1799, son of James Lawson a merchant in Glasgow, educated at Glasgow University in 1812, a merchant in USA from 1815 to 1826, then a journalist and insurance broker in NY, died in Yonkers, NY, on 20 March 1880. [MAGU#266][ANY.2.77]

LAWSON, OSCAR, born in Lanark 1772, a line engraver, died in Philadelphia 22 August 1846. [AP#217]

LAWSON, WILLIAM, born in Dundee during 1808, later a merchant in NY, died in Brooklyn on 15 Oct. 1852. [ANY#2.245]

LECKIE, CATHERINE, wife of John Keddie from Edinburgh, died at 455 West 44th Street, NY, 16 November 1868. [S#7912]

LECKIE, GEORGE, from Edinburgh, settled in NY before 1841. [ANY#2.181]

LECKIE, JOHN, eldest son of Reverend Thomas Leckie in Peebles, educated at Edinburgh University, a teacher at NY University Grammar School, died in NY on 22 Aug. 1841. [AJ#4889][ANY#2.181]

LECKIE, ROBERT MARSHALL, son of Reverend Thomas Leckie in Peebles, died in NY on 4 Aug. 1860. [DC#23530][S#1618]

LEE, ALLAN, born in Paisley, during 1777, a gardener, to America via Greenock, naturalised in NY on 18 Feb. 1817.[Court of Common Pleas Records]

LEE, ALLAN, born in 1776, a laborer, arrived in NY on the Camillas during 1821. [USNA.par]

LEE, JAMES, born in St Andrews, Fife, settled in NY, married Mary Crookshank, father of James, died in NY on 9 Oct. 1795.   [ANY#2.83]

LEGGAT, ANDREW, born in 1805, son of Andrew Leggat, a whip manufacturer, and Helen Hume, died in NY on 1 June 1827.[Greyfriars g/s, Edinburgh]

LEGGAT, GEORGE, in NY, cnf 1872 Edinburgh. [NAS.SC70.1.158/15]

LEGGAT, WALTER, born in Hawick, Roxburghshire, in 1785, a merchant in NY by 1827, died there on 30 Sep. 1850. [ANY#2.24/118]

LEGGET, WILLIAM, born 1781, died in Albany, USA, 1 Apr.1832. [Perth g/s]

LEGGAT, WILLIAM, born in Hawick 1790, settled in NY 1818, merchant and insurance company director, died 26 June 1868. [ANY.2.160]

LEITH, ROBERT, a former baillie of Pittenweem, Fife, settled in Philadelphia before 1851. [NAS.SC16.1.85]

LENNOX, JANE, daughter of Robert Lennox [1850-1927] and Jane Lennox [1847-1920], died in Braddock, Alleghany County, PA, 16 July 1897.[Patna g/s, Ayrshire]

LENNOX, ROBERT, from Port Mary, Renwick, Stewartry of Kirkcudbright, a merchant in NY before 1829. NAS.RD5.387.745]

LEONARD, HUGH, in Pittsburgh, son of Patrick Leonard [died 1843] and Ann Dawson [died 1893]. [Kilmarnock Laigh g/s]

LESSELS, WILLIAM, younger son of John Lessels, 21 Herriot Place, Edinburgh, died in NY on 15 July 1874. [EC#28027]

LESLY, DAVID, son of David Lesly and Jane Kinnear, a ship - master who settled in NY before 1826. [Monimail g/s, Fife]

LESLIE, GEORGE, a former magistrate and corn merchant of Edinburgh, a shopkeeper in Schenectady, NY, 1796, 1797. [NAS.CS17.1.15/403; GD51.6/1218, 1257]

LESLIE, JOHN, a builder in NY, 1883. [NAS.RS.Burntisland.11.263]

LESSELS, WILLIAM, youngest son of John Lessels, 21 Herriot Row, Edinburgh, died in NY on 15 July 1874. [S#9679]

LEYDEN, MARGARET OGLE, born 1800, relict of William Notman Hawick, grand-daughter of Rev. William Burn in Minto, died in Cohoes, Albany, NY, 26 July 1873. [S#9379]

LIDGERWOOD, JOHN, born in Longside, Aberdeenshire, during 1795, a mason then a merchant, to America via Liverpool, naturalised in NY during 1829. [Court of Common Pleas Records]

LILLIE, Reverend JOHN, born in Kelso, Roxburghshire, on 18 Oct. 1812, educated at Edinburgh University around 1833, a minister and schoolmaster in NY, died in Kingston, NY, on 23 Feb. 1867. [ANY#2.239][S#7369]

LILLIE, SUSAN, from Scotland, married Adam Pearson from Scotland, in NY on 6 May 1840. [EEC#20061]

LILLIE, SUSAN PEARSON, daughter of Rev. John Lillie, Kingston, NY, married Rev. John Hutchins, in NY on 10 Dec.1879. [S#11,366]

LILLIE, WILLIAM, born in Kelso, Roxburghshire, on 4 Feb. 1802, to NY in 1835, a leather merchant there, died in Edinburgh on 16 Jan.1863.[ANY#2.239]

LINDORES, Mrs JANE, born 1838, wife of Robert Lindores, died in Alleghany City, PA, 9 March 1877. [S#10,516]

LINDSAY, JAMES, born in 1815, son of Robert Lindsay [1783-1864] and Jean Lindsay [1788-1852], died in NY on 18 Aug. 1848.[Kirriemuir g/s, Angus]

LINDSAY, JAMES, of Bruce and Lindsay typrefounders in NY, son of Robert Lindsay a typefounder in Edinburgh, died in Brooklyn, NY, on 2 Sept.1879. [S#11,275]

LINDSAY, JOHN, born in 1801, son of John Lindsay and Margaret Jackson, a joiner, died in NY on 22 May 1855. [Falkland g/s, Fife]

LINDSAY, NINA, eldest daughter of John Lindsay a typefounder from Seton Place, Grange, died in Brooklyn, NY, on 14 November 1875. [S#10096]

LINDSAY,...., daughter of John Bruce Lindsay, was born at 695 President Street, Brooklyn, on 30 January 1878. [S#10,786]

LISTER, ISABELLA RAITT, daughter of John Lister a Draper of NY and manufacturer in Pathhead, Fife, wife of David Fowler sometime traveller in Glasgow, then in Arnot, Bloomsbury, PA, 1890. [NAS.SC20.4.47.135-138]

LISTON, JOHN, born 1813, merchant in NY 1837, died in Fishkill, NY, 6 October 1850, cnf 1852. [NAS.SC70.1.77][ANY.2.181]

LITHGOW, JOHN, naturalised, Supreme Court of Pennsylvania, 19 February 1798.

LITTLEJOHN, AGNES, wife of Captain James Alexander, died in NY 16 Aug.1871. [S#8772]

LITTLEJOHN, DAVID, died in NY 1 May 1869. [S#8051]

LIVINGSTON, JOHN, born in Nov. 1771, a spinner from near Glasgow, with his wife and two children, arrived in America on 1 May 1811, settled in Whitestown, Oneida County, NY. [1812]

LIVINGSTONE, WILLIAM HARDIE, in Jersey City, cnf 1892. [NAS.SC70.1.314]

LOCHEAD, WILLIAM, son of William Lochead a craftsman in Bridgeton, Glasgow, educated at Glasgow University in 1816, a theological student from 1821 to 1824, settled in Kingston, Canada, moved to Albany, NY. [MAGU#289]

LOCKERBIE, GEORGE, naturalised, Court of Common Pleas, Philadelphia, 1 June 1812.

LOCKHART, ALEXANDER, a veterinary surgeon in NY, cnf 1899. [NAS.SC70.1.377]

LOCKHART, WILLIAM, a veterinary surgeon, third son of John Lockhart a cattle salesman in Glasgow, died at 137 East 53rd Street, NY on 27 April 1874. [S#9609]

LOGAN, ADAM, born in Ayr, wife Margaret McNeil, settled in NY, father of Adam David Logan born there 1804. [ANY.2.131]

LOGAN, JOAN, born 1836, fourth daughter of William Logan, wife of Joseph Winkle, died in Pittsburgh, PA, 12 October 1869. [S#8202]

LOGAN, JOHN, naturalised, US District Court, Philadelphia, 5 March 1799.

LOGAN, JOHN, born during 1791 in Ayrshire, via Liverpool and Nova Scotia to Philadelphia in Dec. 1816, declaration to naturalise on 24 June 1818, naturalised 5 June 1824. [DC District Court Records]

LOGAN, JOHN, sr., born in 1811, from Lettermill, Killearn, Stirlingshire, died in Farmington, Warren County, PA, on 8 Mar. 1879. [EC#29491]

LOGGAT, JOHN, a shipmaster in Philadelphia, cnf 15 June 1785. [NAS.CC8.8.126]

LORIMER, WILLIAM H., a dyer from Port Eglinton, died in Raritan, NJ, on 27 Feb. 1874. [EC#27912]

LOTHIAN, PATRICK, a mariner in NY, died on 23 May 1793, cnf 24 Dec. 1824 Commisariat of Edinburgh, [NAS.CC8.8.150]

LOTTIMER, WILLIAM, born in Glasgow 1815, settled in NY 1844, a merchant, died at Fishkill, NY, 7 October 1876. [ANY.2.222]

LOUDON, ..., daughter of William Loudon, was born at 329 West 21st Street, NewYork, on 29 July 1877. [AO]

LOUDON, ..., twin sons of William Loudon, were born at 315 West 218th Street, NY, on 10 Dec. 1874. [AO]

LOVE, ALEXANDER, naturalised, Court of Quarter Sessions, Philadelphia, 30 September 1822.

LOVE, JOHN, naturalised, Court of Quarter Session, Philadelphia, 20 October 1802.

LOWE, Rev. JAMES MILLER, born 1830 in Perthshire, a minister in Thornton, Fife, died in Philadelphia 20 Oct.1872. [S#9150]

LOWSON, JAMES, a wheelwright from Westhaven, Angus, with 4 or 5 children, from Dundee on the <u>Providence of Perth</u>, master Robert Nicoll, to New York in May 1819. [NAS.CE70.1.15]

LUNDY, Rev. Dr., born 1814, died in Newburg, NY, 7 April 1868. [S#7721]

LUSK, JOHN, from Greenock, settled in NY, cnf 1889. [NAS.SC70.1.276]

LYON, JAMES, naturalised, Supreme Court of Pennsylvania, 20 February 1798.

LYON, JOHN, naturalised, Supreme Court of Pennsylvania, 14 February 1798.

LYON, PATRICK, naturalised, Court of Common Pleas, Philadelphia, 26 May 1797.

LYON, JEAN, born 1800, wife of Thomas Hamilton, died 21 Nov.1883, buried in Greenwood, NY. [Newmilns g/s, Ayr]

MCADAM, JOHN, a merchant in NY, 1804. [NAS.CS17.1.23/284]

MCADAM, QUINTIN, son of Alexander McAdam of Grimont, Ayrshire, died in Candidaigua 1853. [S.12.11.1853]

MCALESTER, CHARLES, born in Campbeltown, Argyll, on 5 Apr. 1765, a mariner, married Ann Simpson a Scotswoman in Baltimore during Oct. 1786, a ship-master and merchant in Philadelphia, died in Willow Grove, Montgomery County, PA, on 29 Aug. 1832. [AP#254]

MCALLISTER, JAMES, born in Scotland during 1801, a laborer, arrived in NY on the Camillas during 1821. [USNA.par]

MCALLISTER, JOHN, naturalised, Court of Common Pleas, Philadelphia, 20 September 1813.

MCALISTER, JOHN, in Pennsylvania, cnf 1866 Edinburgh. [NAS.SC70.1.131/770]

MCALPIN, ANDREW, naturalised, US Circuit Court, Philadelphia, 13 October 1806

MCALPIN, JAMES, naturalised, Supreme Court of Pennsylvania, 20 February 1798.

MCALPIN, JAMES, born in Glasgow during Aug. 1761, to VA, later a tailor in Philadelphia, died there on 20 July 1847. [AP#236]

MCALPINE, ..., son of Robert McAlpine, was born in Trenton, N.J., in 1870. [S#8332]

MCARDLE, DUNCAN, born in 1782, a laborer from Dalvrack, Monzievaird, Perthshire, from Greenock on 4 Sep. 1817 bound for NY on the William of New York arrived in NY on 17 Oct. 1817.[NYMunicipal Archives][NY Commercial Adv., 18.10.1817]

MCARTHUR, DANIEL, naturalised, US District Court, Philadelphia, 29 June 1798.

MCARTHUR, DONALD, a shoemaker from Lochgoilhead, Argyll, with his family to America in 1812, settled as a farmer in PA. ['History of Cowal', Greenock, 1908]

MCARTHUR, JAMES, a manufacturer in NY, 1858. [NAS.SC58.59.24.22]

MCARTHUR, JOHN, naturalised, Court of Common Pleas, Philadelphia, 27 September 1815.

MCARTHUR, PETER, naturalised, Court of Common Pleas, Philadelphia, 13 October 1828.

MCBEAN, JANE ANN, third daughter of Lieutenant McBean, Auchenblair, Strathspey, married Alexander Paterson, divisional engineer, Equality, Kentucky, at 306 Fulton Avenue, Brooklyn, 9 Jan.1871. [S#8586]

MCBEATH, ALEXANDER, naturalised, Supreme Court of Pennsylvania, 17 February 1798.

MCBEATH, FRANCIS, an indentured servant who emigrated from Glasgow on the Friendship, Captain McAdam, to Philadelphia in 1784, absconded from Edward Pole, Market St., Philadelphia, 7 August 1785. [Pa. Gaz.#2295]

MCCAIG, LIZZIE, born in Paisley in 1846, married William Allan in Bloomfield, NJ, on 18 Feb. 1869, died in Brooklyn on 19 Sep. 1888. [EFR]

MCCALL, JOHN, from Glasgow, arrived in NY from Liverpool on the Roscoe in 1833, a merchant in NY 1833-1851, returned to Glasgow. [ANY.2.187]

MCCALLUM, ARCHIBALD, born in 1796, a mariner, his wife Elizabeth born in 1800, and son Dugal born in 1823, via Greenock to America, intent to naturalise 23 Aug. 1833, naturalised 10 Apr. 1834.[Superior Court Records, NY]

MCCALLUM, DANIEL CRAIG, born in Johnstone, during 1815, with his parents to Rochester, NY, an engineer, died in 1878.

MCCALLUM, M., in NY, cnf 1876. [NAS.SC70.1.180]

MCCANDLISH, WILLIAM, naturalised, Supreme Court of Pennsylvania, 4 April 1798.

MCCAUSLAND, ALEXANDER, naturalised, Court of Common Pleas, Philadelphia, 28 September 1806.

MCCAUSLAND, JOHN, naturalised, Court of Common Pleas, Philadelphia, 28 September 1806.

MCCLELLAR, WILLIAM, from Glasgow, in NY City, probate 28 November 1788 NY

MCCALL, Rev. ALEXANDER, from Berwick on Tweed, died in Philadelphia on 16 November 1872. [S#9159]

MCCOLL, HUGH, 29 Broadway, NY, died 21 Aug.1870 in Bellevue Hospital, cnf 17 May 1876. [NAS.SC70.1.178/86]

MCCOMB, ARCHIBALD, a smith in Glasserton, Wigtownshire, then in NY state during 1796. [NAS.RS.Wigtown#481]

MCCONNELL, Mrs HARRIET HACCAU or, wife of advocate John McConnell, died in Markbroom, Canandagua, NY, on 29 July 1833. [SG#173]

MCCOSH, JAMES, born 1 Apr.1811 in Carskeoch, minister and professor, died in Princeton, NJ, 16 Nov.1894.[Straiton g/s]

MCCRACKEN, JAMES E., born in 1853, from 10 Carrington Street, Great Western Road, Glasgow, died at Mount Holly, NJ, on 16 Sep. 1875. [EC#28393]

MCCREE, HUGH, merchant in NY, 1784.[NAS.CS17.1.3/324]

MCCREERY, JOHN, born in 1822, from Aberdeen, died in NY on 1 Feb. 1860. [AJ:29.2.1860]

MCCRINDELL, THOMAS, born in Aberdeen around 1794, son of George McCrindell and Margaret Cruickshank, via London to NY aboard the Venus on 27 Apr. 1827, a merchant in NY from 1822 to 1837. [ANY#2.85]

MCCULLOCH, HAWTHORN, born in Glasserton, Wigtownshire, during 1772, son of Andrew McCulloch, via Greenock to America in 1802, settled in NY during 1803. [BLG#2806]; born in Scotland during 1772, a mariner, wife Christiana born in Scotland during 1782, settled in Clinton, Rennsselaer County, NY. [C]

MCCULLOCH, HUGH, in Yonkers, Westchester County, cnf Edinburgh 1888.[NAS.SC70.1.264]

MCCULLOCH, Mrs MARY, or Easton, formerly of 7 Hill Street, Edinburgh, died at Haledon, Paterson, NJ, 4 Dec.1875. [S#10,132]

MCCULLOCH, ROBERT, naturalised, Supreme Court of Pennsylvania, 20 February 1798.

MCDERMETT, WILLIAM, naturalised, Supreme Court of Pennsylvania, 20 February 1798.

MCDONALD, ALEXANDER, son of Reverend John McDonald in Albany, educated at Marischal College, Aberdeen, from 1795 to 1799, graduated MA. [MCA#2/378]

MCDONALD, ALLAN, naturalised, Court of Common Pleas, Philadelphia, 9 May 1815 and 8 May 1824.

MCDONALD, ARCHIBALD, former British Army surgeon, settled in White Plains, West Chester County, NY, husband of Flora McDonald, pro. Feb. 1817 PCC

MACDONALD, FRANCIS, born 1824, of Henderson Bros. in NY, died Roseneath Cottage, Staten Island, on 7 Nov. 1878. [S#11,016]

MCDONALD, JAMES, born in Edinburgh, a turner, via Greenock to America in May 1820, naturalised in NY on 9 Apr. 1834.[Superior Court Records]

MCDONALD, JOHN, son of Alexander McDonald of Steveston and Janet Cowan, settled in Williamsport, Lycoming County, PA, before 1829. [NAS.NRAS.2522/CA41.80]

MCDONALD, JOHN, born 1847, son of Sergeant McDonald, 1 forth St., Edinburgh, died on the City of Paris on way home from NY, 4 July 1871. [S#8724]

MCDONALD, THOMAS R., from Dunfermline, died in NY on 4 June 1862. [DP]

MCDONALD, WILLIAM, naturalised Supreme Court of Philadelphia, 20 February 1798.

MCDONALD, ..., daughter of William McDonald a bookbinder from Edinburgh, died at 286 North 2nd Street, Brooklyn, on 19 November 1874. [S#9789]

MCDOUGAL, DUNCAN, a weaver from Glasgow, then in NY 1809.[NAS.CS17.1.28/477]

MCDOUGAL, JOHN, naturalised, Supreme Court of Pennsylvania, 28 March 1798.

MCDOUGALL, PETER, born in Inveraray, Argyll, a merchant in NY from 1782 onwards, married Helen Robertson in 1791, died on 19 Sep. 1798.[ANY#1.175] [NAS.CS17.1.6/51]

MCDOWALL, JAMES, settled in NY, died in Dunfermline, Fife, cnf 1888.[NAS.SC70.1.266]

MCDOWALL, PATE, born in Paisley around 1789, a weaver, his sons Matthew, born in Glasgow during 1814, and William, born in Glasgow during 1815, to America via Greenock, naturalised in NY on 23 Apr. 1828. [Court of Common Pleas Records]

MCELROY, JANET, in NY, cnf 1872 Edinburgh. [NAS.SC70.1.158/502]

MCEWEN, EWEN, son of Alexander McEwen, a farmer in Keprannich, [1715-1797] and Janet McVichie, [1736-1794], settled in NY, died in Newtown, Killin, Perthshire, on 21 Sep. 1811. [Kenmore Ardtainaig g/s, Perthshire]

MCEWEN, ..., son of John McEwen, was born in NY on 2 Oct. 1867. [AO]

MCEWEN, ..., daughter of John McEwen, was born at 143 Meadow Street, NJ, on 1 Jan. 1869. [AO]

MCEWEN, ..., daughter of John McEwen, was born in Hudson City, NY,on 25 Feb. 1871. [AO]

MCEWEN, ..., son of John McEwen, was born in Laidlaw Avenue, Jersey Heights on 11 Apr. 1873. [AO]

MCFARLAND, DUNCAN, naturalised, Court of Common Pleas, Philadelphia. 22 September 1813

MACFARLANE, ANDREW, born in Milngavie, Stirlingshire, around 1790, a merchant in NY by 1826, died at the Belmont Hotel 3 January 1873. [ANY.2.210]

MCFARLANE, FREDERICK, a minister in Montrose, Angus from 1787 to 1795, then settled on Long Island, USA. [UPC#1.69]

MCFARLANE, FREDERICK, junior, born in 1795, via Leith to NY, a painter and glazier, naturalised in NY on 27 June 1827. [NY Marine Court]

MCFARLANE, JOHN, born in 1791, a teacher, his wife Catherine born 1795, to America via Glasgow, naturalised in NY on 15 Mar. 1831. [Southern District Court Records]

MCFARLANE, RODERICK, born in 1810, late in St Kitts and in NY, died in Tain, Ross and Cromarty, on 10 Sep. 1835. [AJ#4577]

MCFARLANE, THOMAS, born in 1795, via Leith to NY, a painter and glazier, naturalised in NY on 27 June 1827. [NYMarine Court Records]

MCFARQUHAR. COLIN, born in Killearnan during 1733, a minister educated at Marischal College and at King's College, Aberdeen, from 1749 to 1753, a minister in Applecross,Wester Ross, from 1761 to 1775, married Betty Jeffrey in 1764, father of Ninian, Mary, Anne, Janet and Betty, settled in PA.
[MCA#320][KCA#2.320][F#7.144]

MCFEAT, JAMES, late of NY, died in Westmuir, Glasgow, on 3 Oct. 1873. [EC#27771]

MCGLASHAN, WILLIAM, in Syracuse, NY, 1856.
[NAS.SC48.49.25.57/134]

MCGAW, ALEXANDER, born near Stranraer, Wigtownshire, in May 1831, to Canada in 1851, settled in Philadelphia during 1873 as a bridgebuilder, died there on 29 Jan. 1905. [AP#243]

MCGEOCH, GRACE, from Glen Luce, Wigtownshire, via Belfast to NY on the Lorenzo on 2 May 1816. [NWI#2.361]

MCGEOCH, SAMUEL, from Glen Luce, Wigtownshire, via Belfast to NY on the Lorenzo on 2 May 1816. [NWI#2.361]

MCGIBBON, CHARLES, eldest son of John S. McGibbon a builder in Edinburgh, died in NY 10 January 1872. [S#8891]

MCGLASHAN, PETER, born 1831, from Stockbridge, Edinburgh, died in McKeesport, Alleghany County, PA., 1874.[S#9814]

MCGOUN, LACHLAN CAMPBELL, second son of Duncan McGoun a merchant in Glasgow, educated at Glasgow University 1831, resident of NY to 1850. [ANY.2.229]

MACGOWAN, BERNARD, from Newton Stewart, Wigtownshire, via Newry to NY on the Leda in 1815. [NWI#2.361]

MCGOWAN, JOHN, naturalised, Supreme Court of Pennsylvania, 19 February 1798.

MCGREGOR, DANIEL B., naturalised, Court of Common Pleas, Philadelphia, 20 February 1798.

MCGREGOR, JOHN, naturalised, Court of Common Pleas, Philadelphia, in August 1811, and 9 October 1817.

MCGREGOR, JOHN C., naturalised, Supreme Court of Pennsylvania, 20 February 1798.

MCGREGOR, JOHN, naturalised, Supreme Court of Pennsylvania, 20 November 1805.

MCGREGOR, MALCOLM, born in 1797, a laborer from the House of Burn, Monyvaird, Perthshire, from Greenock on 4 Sep. 1817 bound for NY on the William of New York arrived in NY on 17 Oct. 1817.[NYMunicipal Archives][NY Comm Adv, 18.10.1817]

MCGREGOR, PETER, born in Greenock during 1788, naturalised in NY on 7 Apr. 1811.

MCGREGOR, WILLIAM, a merchant in NY, 17 May 1877. [NAS.RS.Nairn, 11/124]

MCGUIRE, LAUCHLANE MCQUARY, a shipmaster from Campbeltown, Argyll, settled in NY, husband of Katherine ...., died in Jan. 1783, cnf 1785. [NAS.CC8.8.126]

MCILVAINE, Reverend CHARLES, born in 1839, son of C. P. McIlvaine, died in Towanda, PA, on 28 Feb. 1876. [EC#28519]

MCILWRAITH, JOHN, born 1808, drowned NY 12 Aug.1845. [Barr, Ayrshire, g/s]

MCINNES, DUNCAN, naturalised, Supreme Court of Pennsylvania, 16 February 1798.

MCINNES, JOHN T., born in Paisley 24 March 1828, son of John McInnes and Martha Hunter, settled in Philadelphia 1840, a quarry owner, died in Philadelphia 5 March 1886. [AP#244]

MCINNES, ..., son of John McInnes, was born in Palisade Avenue, Jersey City Heights, NJ, on 9 Aug. 1873. [EC#27738]

MCINTOSH, JAMES, born in 1805, from Croy, Inverness-shire, to NY on the George of New York on 12 Aug.1807. [PRO.PC1.3790]

MCINTYRE, DANIEL, born in around 1814, a chemical manufacturer in Philadelphia, died on 30 Aug. 1870. [AP#245]

MCINTYRE, DAVID, a schoolmaster in Albany, NY,a witness in 1786. [NAS.RD2.241/2.776]

MACIVER, DONALD, born at Lochalsh, Wester Ross, on 1 Nov. 1778, son of Reverend Murdoch MacIver and Mary McKenzie, later a merchant in NY, died in Bermuda. [F#7.155]

MCIVOR, JOHN, in GA and NY, cnf 1824. [NAS.SC70.1.31]

MACKAY, JOHN, born 1837, died in NY 1876. [S#10,168]

MCKAY, JOHN, born in Maxwelltown, Dumfries-shire, during 1815, died in NY on 31 Dec. 1878. [AO]

MACKAY, JOHN, born Ross-shire 1826, tea merchant in NY, died Hudson County 3 April 1885. [ANY.II.260]

MACKAY, MARY. second daughter of Donald Mackay in Thurso, Caithness, married Robert M. Easdale, Morrison, Whiteside County, Illinois, in Brooklyn on 17 October 1874. [S#9769]

MACKAY, ROBERT BROWN, late in Calcutta, died NY 20 Oct. 1870. [S#8498]

MACKAY, SOPHIA, wife of Peter MacKay from Aberdeen, died in NY on 9 Jan. 1858. [AJ:3.2.1858]

MACKAY, WILLIAM, son of Hugh MacKay a tailor in Aberdeen, died in Yonkers, NY, on 21 Feb. 1875. [AJ:7.4.1875]

MCKEAN, ..., daughter of William McKean, was born in NY 10 July 1863. [S#2531]

MCKENZIE, ALEXANDER, sometime Ensign of the 2nd Battalion of the King's Royal Regiment of NY, afterwards tacksman of Elgin in Assynt, deceased, and his relict Isabella, 1799. [NAS.CS17.1.18/194]

MCKENZIE, ALEXANDER, born Strathpeffer, Ross-shire, 1818, to NY 1840, a plumber, died Vermont 25 Aug.1874. [ANY.II.260]

MCKENZIE, ALEXANDER, of the Pittsburgh Railway, married Maggie, only daughter of Angus McKellar Reid, agent at

Ratho Station for the Edinburgh and Glasgow Railway, in Boston 15 September 1871. [S#8794]

MCKENZIE, ALEXANDER, from NY, married Anna Maria Thompson, eldest daughter of Laurence Thompson in Montrose, Angus, in St Andrews, Fife, on 15 July 1873. [EC#27703]

MCKENZIE, ANGUS, born in Kylestrome, Sutherland, a banker in St John, New Brunswick, during the 1820s, settled in NY in 1836. [ANY#2.253]

MCKENZIE, BARBARA, born 1804, wife of James Muir sr. from Edinburgh, died in Newark, NJ, 1875. [S#10,134]

MCKENZIE, DONALD, son of William McKenzie born 1748 schoolmaster at Leys died 7 July 1838 and Janet Chisholm born 1754 died 1815, settled in Caledonia, Livingstone County, NY. [Dunlichty g/s, Inverness-shire]

MACKENZIE, EDWARD, a merchant from Glasgow, married Margaret, second daughter of William Welch a merchant in NY on 27 Oct. 1823. [DPCA#1110]

MCKENZIE, HECTOR, in Bath, Steuben County, NY, later by 1796 in Philadelphia. [NAS.RD4.263.834]

MACKENZIE, JAMES, in Newark, NJ, late of Edinburgh, married Kate, daughter of William Donald, in NY 18 March 1868. [S#7703]

MCKENZIE, JOHN, naturalised, US District Court, Philadelphia, 28 February 1797.

MACKENZIE, JOHN, born in 1777, a farmer from Baluich, Daviot, Inverness-shire, to NY on the <u>George of NY</u>, 12 Aug.1807. [PRO.PC1.3790]

MCKENZIE, JOHN, in Philadelphia, cnf 1809. [NAS.SC70.1.1]

MCKENZIE, JOHN, a baker in Port Glasgow then in NY, 1824. [NAS.RS4.1933]

MCKENZIE, KATY, wife of James McKenzie from Edinburgh, died in Newark, NJ, 16 December 1871. [S#8875]

MCKENZIE, KENNETH, born in Ross-shire, a painter and glazier in NYby 1797, died in Bloomingdale, NY, Oct. 1803. [ANY#1.363]

MCKENZIE, MAGGIE STEEL, born 1869, daughter of James Mackenzie from Edinburgh, died at 506 West 20th Street, NY, on 20 October 1875. [S#10079]

MACKENZIE, PETER, born in Perth on 24 Mar. 1809, a horticulturalist in Philadelphia from 1827, died there on 25

Mar. 1868 and was buried in Mount Vernon Cemetery there. [AP#257]

MCKENZIE, SIMON, son of William McKenzie born 1748 schoolmaster at Leys died 7 July 1838 and Janet Chisholm born 1754 died 1815, settled in Caledonia, Livingstone County, NY. [Dunlichty g/s, Inverness-shire]

MCKENZIE, WILLIAM, an engineer from Leith, married Alice, daughter of Simon Fraser in Leith, at 334 West 55th Street, NY, on 8 June 1874. [S#9647]

MCKENZIE, ..., son of William McKenzie an engineer from Leith, was born at 211 York Street, Brooklyn, on 30 July 1875. [S#10002]

MCKENZIE, ..., daughter of William McKenzie, was born at 211 York St., Brooklyn, NY, on 11 May 1877. [S#10,560]

MACKERGO, WILLIAM TAYLOR, born in Kilmarnock, Ayrshire, on 23 Oct. 1829, graduated MA from Glasgow University in 1849, a minister in NY from 1872 to 1895, graduated DD from Yale in 1872, LL.D. from Princeton in 1883, DD from Amherst in 1872, died in Feb. 1895. [MAGU#602]

MACKERSIE, ANDREW, from Auchtermuchty, Fife, of the Bank of the Republic in NY, died in Whitestone, Long Island, on 1 Sept. 1863. [S#2577]

MCKEUN, ARCHIBALD, born in Scotland during 1787, a laborer, arrived in New York on the Camillas during 1821. [USNA.par]

MACKIE, WILLIAM, born in 1816, a music seller from Aberdeen, died in Rochester, NY, on 20 July 1866. [AJ: 15.8.1866]

MCKINLAY, DAVID, a carpenter in NY, 1826. [NAS.RS.Kirkcaldy.4.20]

MCKINLAY, JOHN, married Antoinette Sterling, daughter of James Sterling, Sterlingville, NY, in London on Easter Day 1875. [EC#28234]

MCKINLAY, JOHN STEWART, born in Airdrie on 17 Apr. 1850, with his parents to Brown County, Ohio, in 1852, settled in Philadelphia in 1869, a lawyer there, died 31 May 1892. [AP#247]

MCKINLEY, WALTER DOUGLAS, from Aberdeen, married Ruth Anna Van Deusen of Hudson, NY, in NY on 7 Mar. 1877. [EC#28853]

MCKINLEY, WILLIAM, in Elizabeth, NJ, son of Alexander McKinley, a wright in Dalmellington who died 5 Oct. 1829. [NAS.SH.18.6.1885]

MCKINNELL, JOHN, in NY, shipmaster of the <u>Fame of New York</u> cnf 16 July 1784. [NAS.CC8.8.126]

MCKNAUGHT, THOMAS, born in 1834, son of Thomas McKnaught {1839-1867}, died NY 14 Nov. 1869. [Wigtown g/s]

MCLACHLAN, ALEXANDER, in NY, 1809. [NAS.SC48.49.25.1/26]

MCLACHLAN, ROBERT, in NY, son of Robert McLachlan a china merchant in Sinclairtown, Kirkcaldy, who died 8 Sep.1883. [NAS.SH.12.12.1889]

MCLACHLAN, WILLIAM, born in 1749, a farmer from Baluich, Dores, Inverness-shire, with his wife Margaret Fraser born 1756, and children Catherine born 1779, Alexander born 1787, Andrew born 1790, Donald born 1795, Lachlan born 1797, Isabel born 1799, and James born 1803, to NY on the <u>George of New York</u>, on 12 Aug. 1807. [PRO.PC1.3790]

MCLAINE, JOHN, in NY, 1784. [NAS.GD174.1361]

MCLANBURGH, JOHN, naturalised, Supreme Court of Pennsylvania, 4 May 1798.

MCLAREN, DUNCAN, a merchant in Albany, NY, a deed witness in 1786.[NAS.RD2.241/2.776]

MCLAREN, DUNCAN, son of Donald McLaren and Margaret McGregor, settled in NY during 1783, died there on 17 Aug. 1825, buried in Greenwood Cemetery. [Comrie g/s, Perthshire]

MCLAREN, HUGH, formerly an accountant with the North British Railway, died in Philadelphia 24 January 1869. [S#7975]

MCLAREN, JOHN, a weaver, and his wife Elizabeth Crawford, from Bridgeton, Glasgow, settled in Philadelphia by Nov. 1814. [NAS.CS17.1.34/26]

MCLAREN, M., in NY, cnf 1876. [NAS.SC70.1.180]

MCLAUGHLAN, DAVID, naturalised, US Circuit Court, Philadelphia, 20 April 1799.

MCLAUGHLAN, STEWART, born in 1802, son of John MacLaughlan a mason in Perth, [1758-1824], and Margaret Kidd, [1771-1842], died in NY on 18 June 1855. [Greyfriars g/s, Perth]

MCLAURIN, ALEXANDER, naturalised, US Circuit Court, Philadelphia, 13 October 1796.

MCLAWS, WILLIAM, a saddler, husband of Beatrix Sharp, settled in Philadelphia, parents of Elizabeth born there on 27 Aug. 1796, William born there on 6 Dec. 1798, and Beatrix born there on 15 Dec. 1800. [Glasgow OPR]; William McLaws, naturalised, US Circuit Court, Philadelphia, 13 October 1796.

MACLAY, MARY, daughter of William Brown a seedsman in Glasgow, and wife of Reverend Archibald MacLay, died in NY on 20 Sep. 1848. [SG#1765]

MACLEAN, DANIEL, married Mary Frances Balmain, eldest daughter of George Balmain, in Philadelphia on 19 Dec. 1867. [S#7632]

MCLEAN, EWAN, in NY, cnf 1877. [NAS.SC70.1.181/718]

MCLEAN, FANNY, born 1841, daughter of William McLean in Edinburgh, wife of William K. Scoullar from Dollar, Clackmannanshire, died in NY on 26 Oct.1863. [S#2638]

MACLEAN, JOHN, born in Glasgow on 1 Mar. 1771 son of John MacLean and Agnes Lang, a surgeon and chemist educated in Glasgow, Edinburgh and Paris, to America in 1795, Professor of Chemistry and Natural Philosophy at Princeton,husband of Phoebe Bainbridge, died in Princeton, NJ, on 17 Feb.1814. [MB#31][MAGU#137]

MCLEAN, NORMAN, born in 1813, son of Charles McLean in Gavinston, died in NY on 12 Feb. 1851. [Langton g/s]

MCLEAN, SAMUEL, born in Kirkcudbright in 1820 son of Thomas McClune (sic), a merchant in NY, died 10 January 1893. [ANY.2.218]

MCLEAN, WILLIAM, born in Ruthwell, Dumfries-shire, sexton of St Thomas in NY, died there on 4 Nov. 1862. [AO]

MCLELLAND, JOHN GOURLIE, born in Glasgow on 10 May 1850, son of John McLelland and Elizabeth Ann Gourlie, settled in NY, father of Mary Ann McLelland born there in 1869. [MG#2/329]

MCLEOD, ALEXANDER, born in Kilfinichen, Mull, Argyll, on 12 June 1774, son of Reverend Neil McLeod and Margaret McLean, a minister of the Reformed Presbyterian Church in NY, married Mary Ann Agnew on 16 Sep.1805. [F#4.113][MB#33]

MCLEOD, DONALD, a Quaker from Edinburgh, settled in NY during 1818.[NAS.CH10.1.65]

MCLEOD, HECTOR, master in the Royal Navy, resident in Newburgh, Orange County, NY, probate Aug. 1822 PCC

MCLERAN, JAMES, naturalised, Court of Common Pleas, Philadelphia, 13 Dec.1813, and 20 Sep.1823.

MCMILLAN, ALEXANDER, in Pittstown, Luzern, PA, died on

4 Nov. 1859, cnf 1860. [NAS.SC70.1.106]

MCMURTRIE, WILLIAM, born 1792, a brewer in NY, died 18 January 1838. [ANY.2.171]

MCNAB, FRANCIS FREDERICK, youngest son of Archibald McNab of Holm, Dumfries-shire, died in NY 26 Sept.1840. [W#83]

MCNAB,......, son of William McNab a basket maker, was born in Philadelphia on 29 Mar. 1875. [S#9900]

MCNAUGHT, CHARLES HENRY, in PA, cnf 1866. [NAS.SC70.1.132/161]

MCNEIL, GORDON, born in Hawthornden on 5 Feb. 1830, to America in 1850, a carpenter, died in Germantown, Philadelphia, on 2 June 1876, buried in Ivy Hill Cemetery. [AP#252]

MCNEIL, JOHN, a cabinetmaker in NY, 1794. [NAS.CS17.1.14,23]

MCNEIL, JOHN, naturalised, Supreme Court of Pennsylvania, 14 Mar. 1798

MCNEILLEDGE, ALEXANDER, naturalised Court of Common Pleas, Philadelphia, 14 Apr. 1813, and Supreme Court of Pennsylvania 23 July 1816.

MCNEISH, JOHN, born in Largo, Fife, during 1785, a merchant who from Falkirk to America, his wife Janet born in Glendevon, Perthshire, in 1777, and their children Jane born 1808, Elizabeth born 1810, Janet born 1812,and James born 1816, all in Falkirk, , naturalised in NY on 5

MCNERAN, MALCOLM, from Rosneath, Dunbartonshire, settled in Philadelphia, naturalied in the Court of Common Pleas, Philadelphia on 14 Oct.1808, died on 18 Mar. 1806, cnf 1842 Edinburgh. [NAS.SC70.1.61; SC53.56.2]

MCNICOLL, PETER, naturalised, Supreme Court of Pennsylvania, 20 Feb.1798.

MCOWEN, PETER, born in Scotland during 1795, a laborer, arrived in NY on the <u>Camillas</u> during 1821. [USNA.par]

MACPHERSON, ANGUS, born in 1789, a farmer from Balmvoich, Dores, Inverness-shire, to NY on the <u>George of New York</u> on 12 Aug. 1807. [PRO.PC1.3790]

MACPHERSON, ANGUS NEILSON, born in Cluny, Inverness-shire, on 12 July 1812, son of Angus MacPherson and Margaret Neilson, settled in Philadelphia as a mechanic, died in Fieldsboro, NJ, on 31 July 1876. [AP#258]

MCPHERSON, DUNCAN, son of John McPherson (died in 1873) and Mary Russell (died in 1847), settled in NY. [Kilmore g/s]

MCPHERSON, JOHN, naturalised, Supreme Court of Pennsylvania, 16 Feb.1798.

MCPHERSON, MELVILLE, in NY city, husband of Margaret ..., probate Feb. 1839 PCC

MCPHERSON, ..., son of Duncan McPherson, was born at 101 East 40th Street, NY, on 22 Dec. 1874. [AO]

MCQUEEN, JAMES, born in 1795, a laborer from Dalverack, Monyvair, Perthshire, from Greenock on 4 Sep. 1817 bound for NY on the William of New York arrived in NY on 17Oct. 1817.[NYMunicipal Archives] [NY Commercial Advertiser, 18.10.1817]

MCQUISTON, JOHN, born in 1777, a merchant, with his wife Jane born in 1777, and children Mary born 1802, Arabella born 1813, Charles born 1808, and Myrtilla born 1815, from Greenock on 4 Sep. 1817 to NY on the William, arrived on 17 Oct. 1817.[NYMunicipal Archives] [NY Commercial Advertiser, 18.10.1817]

MCREADY, F. R., commissioned in the 51st Infantry Regiment of the NY Volunteers as a 1st Lieutenant on 14 Apr. 1864, and as a Captain on 12 Oct. 1864. [DU.lib.MS29/2/10]

MCWILLIAM, GEORGE, son of Donald McWilliam, a farmer from Buchromb, Mortlach, Banffshire, died in Brooklyn, NY, on 5 Nov. 1868.[AJ:2.12.1868]

MAIN, JESSIE, eldest daughter of James Main in Glasgow, married Henry A.Hart MD from New Brunswick, in NY on 22 July 1837. [AJ#4679]

MAIN, MARGARET, eldest daughter of James Main in Glasgow, married Le Baron Batsford MD of New Brunswick, in NY on 22 July 1837. [AJ#4679]

MAIR, HUGH, born on 16 July 1797, son of Archibald Mair a gentleman in Newmilns, Ayrshire, educated at Glasgow University from 1811 to 1818, a minister at Fort Miller, Northumberland County, NY, in 1825, at Johnstown, NY, from 1830 to 1843, and in Waterloo, Canada, from 1847 until his death on 1 Nov. 1854. [MAGU#256]

MAITLAND, DAVID, born in Kirkcudbright during 1802, via Liverpool to America, a merchant who was naturalised in NYon 15 Mar. 1821.[Court of Common Pleas Records]

MAITLAND, JAMES WILLIAM, youngest son of Lord Dundrennan, died on Staten Island, NY, 25 June 1860. [GM.NS2.9.213][S#1577]

MAITLAND, JOSEPH, born in Kirkcudbright during 1801, a merchant, to America to settle in Norfolk, Virginia, naturalised in NY on 15 Dec. 1823. [Court of Common Pleas Records]

MAITLAND, MARY, daughter of Lieutenant Colonel Alexander Maitland of Chipparkyle, and relict of Robert Lenox Maitland, died in NY on 27 Oct. 1877. [EC#29055]

MAITLAND, STUART CAIRNS, born in Kirkcudbright 27 August 1816, son of Thomas Maitland, Lord Dundrennan, and Isabella Graham, merchant in NY, 1830s-1850, died Dresden, Germany, 4 December 1861. [ANY.2.178]

MAITLAND, ..., son of James William Maitland, born NY 4 April 1860.[S#1511]

MALCOLM, THOMAS, born 1845, eldest son of Thomas and Mary Malcolm from Edinburgh, died in N.Y. on 20 March 1870. [S#8332]

MALCOLM, WILLIAM, born in 1800, a schoolmaster in Echt, Aberdeenshire, for 53 years, died in the Grand Central Hotel, NY, on 27 Aug. 1871. [AJ:20.9.1871][S#8780]

MALTMAN, JAMES, a stonecutter in NY 1827. [NAS.SC48.49.25.23/112]

MANN. FLORENCE MARY FORTUNE, infant dau. of David G. R. Mann, born 24 Sept. 1870, died at Greenpoint, Long Island, on 8 Oct.1870. [S#8508]

MANSON, GEORGE, eldest son of George Manson in Calder, Caithness, married Maggie, eldest daughter of David Manson, Ham Cottage, Dunnet, Caithness, in Hudson City, NJ, 8 June 1869. [S#8080]

MAR, JAMES, born in Edinburgh, settled in Boston, died in NY on 19 Nov. 1841. [EEC#20297]

MARSHALL, WILLIAM, son of William Marshall a craftsman in Glasgow, educated at Glasgow University in 1811, a minister in Colinsburgh, Fife, from 1823 to 1829, then in Pickersgill, NY, from 1832 to 1843, died in 1864. [MAGU#250]

MARTIN, ALEXANDER, born in Forfar, Angus, on 29 Feb. 1796, a stonecutter who via Halifax, Nova Scotia, to NY city, naturalised there on 2 May 1829.

MARTIN, DAVID, in Brooklyn, son of Alexander Martin surveyor in Cupar, Fife, died in Torquay on 30 Oct. 1847. [EEC#21574]

MARTIN, EDWARD, naturalised, Supreme Court of Pennsylvania, 20 February 1798.

MARTIN, FANNY, daughter of John Martin of Bombay and of Penicuik, Midlothian, married Joseph R. Thomson, at 113 Bedford Street, NY, on 16 April 1875. [S#9915]

MARTIN, WILLIAM, merchant in NY, died in Edinburgh 4 May 1844. [ANY.2.181]

MARTIN, WILLIAM, born in Dunfermline, Fife, 1810, died in Paterson,NJ, on 28 Mar. 1872. [PJ]

MASON, JANE SUSANNAH, daughter of Mr Mason formerly of the Theatre Royal in Edinburgh, niece of the late John Kemble and Mrs Siddons, married Henry Hillyard, artist of the Park Theatre, in NY on 23 Nov. 1839. [S#24/2090]

MASON, JANET, widow of Robert Copley a laborer, settled in NY, died on 27 Nov. 1850. [NAS.SC70.1.83; CC8.8.inv.1854]

MASON, WILLIAM, in NY, died on 14 Aug. 1849, cnf 1854. [NAS.SC70.1.83]

MATHEWSON, JOHN, born in 1813, died in NY on 26 Sep. 1878. [EC#29340]

MATHIESON, AGNES, born in 1849, third daughter of A. Mathieson inStonywood, Aberdeen, died at sea on passage to NY on 19 Dec. 1872. [EC#27547]

MATHESON, DAVID, a merchant in NY, 1792. [NAS.RD2.260.214]

MATTHEW, AMELIA, born in 1774, wife of James Cameron formerly a merchant and banker in Dunkeld, Perthshire, died in NY on 23 Jan. 1840. [EEC#20040]

MATTHEWSON, JOHN, son of George Matthewson and Elizabeth Melville, settled in NY before 1854. [Dunnikier g/s, Fife]

MATHER, JOHN, naturalised, Supreme Court of Pennsylvania, 19 December 1796.

MAXWELL, MARGARET F., wife of William Somerville Grieve, died in Valley Forge, PA, 3 Oct. 1874. [EC#28095][S#9747]

MEIKLE, JAMES, born in Linlithgow 8 March 1760 son of Archibald Meikle and Margaret Johnston, settled in Orange County, NY, 1790. [ANY.2.223]

MEIKLE, THOMAS, late in NY, now in Leith, 1822.
[NAS.CS17.1.42]
MEIKLEHAM, DAVID SCOTT, MD, born Glasgow 6 January
1804, son of Prof. William Meikleham, educated at Glasgow
and Oxford universities, a physician in Paris, Havana, and
NY, settled in NY 1844, died in NY on 20 Nov. 1849.
[EEC#21903] [AJ#5328] [SG#1882]
[GM.NS.33.342][ANY.2.218]
MEIKLEHAM, ROBERT, second son of Rev. William Meikleham
in Tollcross, died in Cohose, Albany, on 7 June 1873.
[EC#27688]
MEIN, ROBERT, in Brooklyn, cnf 1888. [NAS.SC70.1.265]
MELDRUM, ALEXANDER, a brewer in NY, 1818, husband of
Agnes Sim, possibly from Aberdeenshire.
[NAS.CS17.1.38/347]
MELDRUM, JOHN BALFOUR, born in 1810, son of James
Meldrum, died in Paterson, NJ, in Mar. 1883. [Leuchars, g/s]
MELLIS, Mrs JAMES, late of Edinburgh, died at Grove Terrace,
Peckham Park,Philadelphia, in 1840. [AJ#4856]
MELLIS, WILLIAM, born in 1812, from Huntly, Aberdeenshire,
died in NY on 20 Sep. 1864. [AJ:26.10.1864]
MELROSE, ELIZABETH, born Inverness-shire 1832, wife of
Joseph Campbell, died at 20 North Oxford St., Brooklyn, 23
June 1871. [S#8733]
MENZIES, Captain JOHN, born in Scotland during 1777, a watch
and clockmaker in Philadelphia, died in 1860. [AP#272]
MENZIES, ROBERT, born during 1781, a farmer, with Christian
born in 1786, arrived in NY on the 1821. [USNA.par]
METCALFE, ROBERT FULTON, eldest son of Major Metcalfe of
the 79th Highlanders, died in NY on 8 June 1873.
[EC#27690]
MIDDLEMAS, JOSEPH, from Yetholm, a divinity student in 1825,
a minister in Bethlehem, Albany County, NY. [UPC#678]
MILL, GEORGE, a baker from Kilmarnock, with his wife Ann and
son James, settled in Albany by 1810. [NAS.CS17.1.30/67]
MILLER, ALEXANDER, an ironmonger from Dundee, then a
planter at Fort Niagara, NY, 1809. [NAS.CS17.1.28/329]
MILLER, AMELIA, born 1789, relict of Thomas Anderson in
Galashiels, Roxburghshire, died in Skowhegan, Maine, on
28 March 1878. [S#10,839]
MILLER, ARTHUR, naturalised, Supreme Court of Pennsylvania,
19 Feb.1798.

MILLER, CHARLES, naturalised, Supreme Court of Pennsylvania, 30 June 1807.

MILLER, JAMES F., son of Thomas Miller a skipper in Dundee [died in 1809] and Elizabeth Gardiner [died in 1818], settled in NY. [Howff g/s, Dundee]

MILLER, Mrs JANET, widow of Robert Miller late of Anderston, Glasgow, died in West Galway, Fulton County, NY, on 24 Apr. 1856. [CM#20793]

MILLER, JOHN, born in Edinburgh on 27 July 1760, son of Professor John Miller of Glasgow University, educated at Glasgow University in 1774, an advocate in 1783, died in PA during 1796. [MAGU#107][CM#11736;19.11.1796]

MILLAR, JOHN, in Brighton, Munroe, NY, 1 June 1824. [NAS.SC371/59/5/156]

MILLER, JOHN, son of James Miller [1731-1818] a glover, died in Philadelphia 11 May 1836. [Canongate g/s, Edinburgh]

MILLER, JOHN, naturalised in NY on 3 Nov. 1844. [Superior Court Records]

MILLER, ROBERT, naturalised, Court of Common Pleas, Philadelphia, 31 Dec.1823 and 9 Nov.1827.

MILLER, ROBERT, born Edinburgh 1839, an engraver, died in NY 28 Dec.1871. [S#8883]

MILLER, WILLIAM J., son of James Miller a glover in Edinburgh, died in Woodside, Philadelphia, 20 Sep.1839. [EEC#19964]

MILLER, WILLIAM, born in Scotland during 1820, a stonemason who settled in Ohio, Alleghany County, PA, by 1850. [C]

MILLIGAN, ROBERT, son of Thomas Milligan a plumber in Dumfries, [1785-1857] and Allison Wight Anderson, died in NY aged 37. [Dumfries g/s]

MILLIGAN, ROBERT, in Wilmington, Delaware, 1808. [NAS.CS17.1.28/76]

MILLS, FRANK, born 1806, third son of Thomas Mills a farmer in Greenend, died in Roway, NY, 9 April 1872. [S#8970]

MILNE, Mr .., born in Fochabers, Moray, died in Philadelphia 2 Jan. 1845. [GM.NS.23.223]

MILLS, THOMAS, born in Melrose, Roxburghshire, on 11 May 1839, tool maker in Philadelphia by 1864, died 9 May 1905. [AP#280]

MILNE, Mrs ANN, widow of George Milne a brewer and baker in Riccardtonholm, then in Albany with her son James, 1809. [NAS.CS17.1.29/535]

MILNE, DAVID, born in Aberdeen on 26 Dec. 1787 son of James Milne and Agnes Copeland, educated at King's College, Aberdeen, shipowner, to America in 1827, settled in Cincinatti, Ohio, and by 1829 in Philadelphia, a merchant and manufacturer, died there on 30 July 1873 and buried at North Laurel cemetery. [AP#281]

MILNE, HARRY, infant son of Alexander Milne from Aberdeen, died in NY City on 6 June 1869. [AJ:30.6.1869]

MILNE, JAMES, born in Aberdeen son of David Milne and Helen Forbes, emigrated to USA 1826, a textile manufacturer in Philadelphia, died there 9 December 1865. [AP#282]

MILNE, ROBERT, born in 1801, son of Hugh Milne a gardener at Woodend Cottage, Banchory Ternan, Kincardineshire, died in Jersey City in 1872.[AJ:4.9.1872]

MILNE, THOMAS, son of William Milne of the New Inn, Alford, Aberdeenshire, died in NY on 9 Jan. 1851. [AJ:15.2.1851]

MILNE, WILLIAM, born in Scotland during 1796, a merchant, arrived in NY on the Amity during 1821. [USNA.par]

MILNE, Mr ..., born in Fochabers, Moray, died in Philadelphia on 2 January 1845. [GM.ns23/223]

MINTO, ARCHIBALD BUTTER, youngest son of John Minto, M.D., in Edinburgh, died in N.Y. on 11 December 1869. [S#8250]

MIRRIE, ROBERT, naturalised, Supreme Court of Pennsylvania, 20 Feb.1798.

MITCHELL, ANNIE J., infant daughter of John and Eliza Mitchell from Annan, Dumfries-shire, died in Brooklyn, 9 Apr. 1870. [AO]

MITCHELL, DAVID, born in Glasgow during 1835, son of John Mitchell a merchant in Glasgow, educated at Glasgow University, a minister in Glasgow and in Forfar from 1858 to 1866, then a minister of the Scots Church in NJ, died there 1905. [F#5.287]

MITCHELL, JAMES, born in Kilmarnock, Ayrshire, during 1800, a carpet weaver, to America via Greenock, naturalised in NY on 18 Mar. 1822.[Court of Common Pleas Records]

MITCHELL, JOHN, born in Annan, Dumfries-shire, during 1834, died in Brooklyn on 5 Sep. 1874. [AO]

MITCHELL, MONCRIEFF, born in Glasgow 2 January 1818 son of Rev. John Mitchell, merchant in NY, died in Sea Girt, NJ, 10 August 1889. [ANY.2.219]

MITCHELL, WILLIAM, naturalised, Supreme Court of Pennsylvania, 10 Sep.1796.

MITCHELL, WILLIAM, a merchant from Glasgow, then in Philadelphia, 1804. [NAS.CS17.1.23/442]

MITCHELL, ..., daughter of D. Mitchell, was born in NY on 26 March 1874. [S#9582]

MITCHELL,...., son of Thomas S. Mitchell, was born at 2128 Franklin St., Philadelphia, on 17 Jan.1878. [S#10,799]

MOFFATT, DAVID, born in Musselburgh, Midlothian, during 1810, to NY in 1827, a currier, died at Cold Spring on the Hudson on 24 July 1887. [ANY#2.268]

MOFFAT, JOHN, a minister and a teacher, in 1751, settled in Wallkill, Orange County, died in Little Britain on 22 Apr. 1788. [F#7.664]

MOFFAT, THOMAS, late with A. & C. Black booksellers and compiler of the third index to the 'Edinburgh Review', died on passage to NY in 1851.[FJ#953]

MOFFAT, WILLIAM, born in Gateside, Wamphrey, Dumfries-shire, died in Syracuse, NY, on 1 Jan. 1874. [AO]

MOIR, JAMES, born on 15 Mar. 1817 in Edinburgh, son of James Moir and Margaret Stenhouse, a merchant in NY, died there on 7 Dec.1899. [ANY#2.247]

MOIR, WILLIAM, born in Aberdeen during 1826, to America in 1835,a watchmaker who died in NY on 21 Mar. 1896. [ANY#2.285]

MONACH, ANDREW, a hatter in Glasgow, then in Philadelphia, husband of Mary Wilson and father of Mary, Jane, Janet, James and Andrew, died by 1822.[NAS.RD5.245.5]

MONCREIFFE, THOMAS, in the Service of His Britannic Majesty, died in NY during Dec. 1791. [GCr#72][PRO.AO13.56.234]

MONTEITH, THOMAS LOGHLAN, in Canadaiglia, NY, cnf 1872. [NAS.SC70.1.159/982]

MONTGOMERY, ANNIE AGNES, wife of George Greenfield, died in Brooklyn,NY, on 19 Feb. 1842. [AJ#4916]

MONTGOMERY, JAMES, born in 1800, a milkman, to America via Greenock, naturalised in NY on 10 June 1828. [Southern District Court Records]

MONTGOMERY, JOHN, farmer in Downsville, Delaware, 1875. [NAS.SC48.49.25.75/26, 59]

MONTGOMERY, LAURENCE, eldest son of George Montgomery manager of the Glasgow Paper Mill, died in Newburgh, NY, on 4 Feb. 1877.[EC#28836]

MOON, WILLIAM, born in 1776, a laborer, to NY on the
George of New York on 12 Aug. 1807.[PRO.PC1.3790]

MOORE, MARTHA, born in Scotland during 1781, arrived in NY
on the Camillas during 1821. [USNA.par]

MORRIS, GEORGE, naturalised, Supreme Court of PA, 11
Jan.1810

MORRIS, GEORGE, from Glasgow, a divinity student in 1827,
then a minister in Silverspring, PA. [UPC#679]

MORRISON, FRANCIS, from Edinburgh, intent to naturalise 13
Mar. 1833, naturalised in NY on 5 Apr. 1838. [Superior
Court Records]

MORRISON, JOHN, born in Lanark 29 July 1805, emigrated to
Boston in 1819, settled in NY 1820, a haberdasher in NY,
died there 23 November 1876. [ANY.2.211]

MORISON, JOHN, born in 1829, son of Reverend Joseph
Morison, Millseat, King Edward, Aberdeenshire, died in
Rochester, NY, on 15 Aug. 1854.[AJ:13.9.1854]

MORRISON, MARY, born 1806, wife of David Pringle a carver
and gilder from Edinburgh, died in NY 8 April 1869.
[S#8032]

MORRISON,........, daughter of James Morrison, was born in New
Brunswick, NJ, on 17 January 1877. [S#10,468]

MORROW, WILLIAM, naturalised, Supreme Court of PA, 26
Sep.1799.

MORTON, JOHN, born in Kelso 1798, settled in Boston 1817,
moved to NY 1821, merchant, died West 4th St., NY, 15 May
1891. [ANY.2.182]

MORTON, JOHN, jr., engineer, Newark, by 1888. [NAS.SH.1888]

MORTON, PETER, formerly of Hunter, Rainey and Morton in
Glasgow, died in Pittsburgh, PA, on 1 Oct. 1837. [SG#762]

MORTON, ROBERT, born in 1793, a laborer from Glasgow, from
Greenock on 4 Sep. 1817 bound for NY on the William of
NewYork, arrived in NY on 17 Oct. 1817.[NYMunicipal
Archives][NY Commercial Advertiser, 18.10.1817]

MORTON, THOMAS CAMPBELL, born in 1772, a merchant in
NY from 1793, died there on 30 Apr. 1833. [ANY#1.341]

MORTON, WALTER, born in Kelso, Roxburghshire, later a
haberdasher in NY,died there on 15 Apr. 1891. [ANY#2.302]

MOSSMAN, WILLIAM, a watchmaker from Edinburgh, died in
Brooklyn 4 July 1872. [S#9054]

MOWAT, GEORGE, probably from Logie-Pert, Angus, settled in
NY city, probate 17 Mar. 1796 NY

MOWAT, JOHN, formerly a carpet manufacturer in Glasgow, then in NY, 1829.[NAS.CS17.1.4.236]

MOXEY, LOUIS WHITE, son of John Gray Moxey from Edinburgh, died in Philadelphia on 18 Aug. 1841. [EEC#20268]

MUIR, ALLAN, Edmiston, Oswego County, NY, dead by 1802. [NAS.CS17.1.21/368]

MUIR, JAMES, born 1794, from Edinburgh, died in Newark, NJ, in 1876. [S#10,162]

MUIR, JOSEPH, born in Kelso, Roxburghshire, 1812, a merchant tailor in NY, died in Glen Ridge, NJ, 31 May 1902. [ANY.2.211]

MUIRHEAD, ALEXANDER, naturalised, Court of Common Pleas, Philadelphia, 4 Sep.1817.

MUNN, ALEXANDER, merchant in NY, 1784. [NAS.CS17.1.3/324]

MUNRO, JOHN, from Glasgow, an ironmoulder in NY, cnf 1884. [NAS.SC70.1.238]

MUNRO, JOHN, born in 1819, son of Alexander Munro a miller in Kilmachalmaig, died in NY 11 May 1864. [Kincardine Ardgay g/s]

MURDOCH, ANDREW, possibly from Morayshire, in Philadelphia, 1785. [NAS.GD248.box 354, bundle 4]

MURRAY, DAVID, born in 1851, from Aberdeen, died in Brooklyn on 22 Oct. 1873. [AJ:19.11.1873]

MURRAY, GEORGE, an engraver, settled in Philadelphia around 1800, died there on 2 July 1822. [AP#297]

MURRAY, HENRY, naturalised, Court of Quarter Sessions, Philadelphia, 9 Oct.1826 and 11 Oct.1828.

MURRAY, JAMES, and his son William, in Newark, NJ, 1805. [NAS.CS17.1.24/42]

MURRAY, Professor A. JAMES, married Lizzie Owen, in Lockport, NY, 16 Feb.1868. [S#7687]

MURRAY, JOHN, a merchant in NY, 1786. [NAS.RD3.245.1215; CS17.1.6, 251]

MURRAY, JOHN J., late of Staten Island, then in Glasgow, 1805. [NAS.CS17.1.24/164][NAS.RD4.277.37]

MURRAY, JOHN, born in Sutherland during 1797, a carpenter who emigrated via Greenock to USA, naturalised in NY on 29 Mar. 1827. [Court of Common Pleas Records]

MURRAY, JOHN, a flax dresser who from Aberdeen to America before 1824, intent to naturalise on 6 July 1824, naturalised in NY on 12 Sep. 1840.[Southern District Court Records]

MURRAY, Mrs MARGARET, relict of John Murray late of Paterson Court, Old Broughton, Edinburgh, died in NY 14 April 1872. [S#8676]

MURRAY, PATRICK, son of Patrick Murray a writer in Glasgow, drowned in the Passaic River, NJ, on 4 July 1874. [EC#28020][S#9670]

MURRAY, ROBERT, a merchant in NY, 1786. [NAS.RD3.245.1215; CS17.1.6]

MURRAY, ROBERT, a merchant in NY, died in England in 1807. [DPCA#275]

MURRAY, SARAH, from Middleton, Midlothian, settled in NY. cnf 1886.[NAS.SC70.1.364]

MURRAY, THOMAS, born in Scotland during 1788, a merchant, with his wife born inScotland during 1795, arrived in NY on the Catherine, a brig, during 1821. [USNA.par]

NAISMITH, WILLIAM, born 1826, second son of William Naismith, 2 Causewayside, Edinburgh, died in Brooklyn 27 Aug.1861. [S#1981]

NAPIER, JOHN, naturalised, Supreme Court of PA., 17 Feb.1798.

NAPIER, JOHN, born on 3 Nov. 1788 in Bervie, Kincardineshire, to America in 1815, a merchant in NY from 1817 to 1859, died in Brooklyn on 23 June 1879. [ANY#2.73]

NEILSON, ISABELLA, wife of Allan Hay, died in NY 1853. [S.13.4.1853]

NEILSON, CATHERINE, born in 1850, daughter of Benjamin Park, shipcarpenter, died in Brooklyn on 11 June 1875. [AO]

NEILSON, ELIZABETH, daughter of James Neilson, grocer, and Elizabeth Kyle in Glasgow, in NY, 1798. [NAS.CS17.1.17/31]

NEILSON, ISABELLA, daughter of Benjamin Neilson a ship carpenter in Annan Dumfries, wife of Robert Hogg, died Jersey City on 12 Mar. 1872.[AO]

NEILSON, JAMES, son of James Neilson grocer and Elizabeth Kyle in Glasgow, to NY 1793, died in August 1795.[NAS.CS18.712.18]

NEILSON, JANET, daughter of James Neilson grocer in Glasgow and Elizabeth Kyle, in NY, 1798. [NAS.CS17.1.17/31]

NEILSON, JOHN, in NY 1789, son of William Neilson, a shipmaster in Glasgow.[NAS.CS17.1.8,45]

NEILSON, SAMUEL, in NY 1789, son of William Neilson, a shipmaster in Glasgow. [NAS.CS17.1.8,45]

NEILSON, WILLIAM, in NY 1789, son of William Neilson, a shipmaster in Glasgow. [NAS.CS17.1.8,45]

NEILSON, WILLIAM, born 1781, a merchant, with two children, arrived in NY on Camillas in 1821. [USNA.par]

NELSON, MARGARET, eldest daughter of Benjamin Nelson, a ship carpenter in Annan, Dumfries-shire, married James Colville a plasterer, in Jersey City, during 1857. [AO]

NELSON, ROBERT, naturalised in NY on 10 Mar. 1837. [Superior Court Records]

NELSON, ..., son of Thomas S. Nelson late of the National Bank of Scotland in Edinburgh, was born at 295 South Street, Brooklyn, on 17 March 1871. [S#8633]

NEWLAND, ALEXANDER, son of John Newland in Edinburgh, probate 4 Dec.1809 NJ. [NJSA#10593G]

NEWLAND, ANTHONY, born in Edinburgh during 1769, a merchant in NY 1808, died in Newark, NJ, on 29 Nov. 1809. [ANY#1.394]

NEWLANDS, JESSIE, born 1858, daughter of John Newlands, died in NY 11 May 1861. [S#1866]

NICHOL, ALEXANDER, born Scotland 1793, a carpenter, wife Margaret born Scotland 1794, settled in Philadelphia by 1850. [C]

NICHOL, THOMAS, a compositor from Dumfries-shire, married Elizabeth Brown from Dumfries-shire, in Brooklyn on 24 Feb. 1870. [AO]

NICOL, GEORGE, naturalised, Court of Common Pleas, Philadelphia, 20 Oct.1813.

NICOL, JAMES, born in Paisley 1798, a weaver, via Greenock to America, naturalised in NY on 27 Nov. 1822. [Court of Common Pleas Records]

NICOLL, ROBERT, naturalised, Court of Common Pleas, Philadelphia, 20 Sep.1823 and 2 Oct.1826.

NICOL, ..., daughter of William Nicol, born 8 August 1860 in 159 Oxford Street, Brooklyn, NY; a son born 13 Dec.1861.[S#1615/2038]

NISBET, ALEXANDER, naturalised, Supreme Court of PA, 16 Feb.1798.

NISBIT, CHARLES, born on 21 Jan. 1736, son of William Nisbit schoolmaster in Long Yester, East Lothian, educated at Edinburgh University in 1754, a minister in Montrose, Angus, married Ann Tweedie in 1766, President of Dickenson College, Carlisle, PA, in 1786, father of Thomas, Mary, William, Alison, Ann, Elizabeth, Alexander, and Charles, died on 18 Jan. 1804.
[F#5.411][NAS.RD3.312.1689]

NISBET, WILLIAM, born in 1795, a mariner, via Kirkwall, Orkney Islands, to NY, naturalised there on 22 May 1827. [NY Marine Court Records]

NISBET, WILLIAM, an engineer, married Elizabeth Milne Cameron, eldest daughter of Charles Cameron, 10 St Patrick Square, [Edinburgh?], late a bookseller in Huntly, Aberdeenshire, in NY on 25 April 1871. [S#8670]

NIVEN, JOHN PATERSON, in Paterson, NJ, died 16 Aug. 1840, cnf 1846.[NAS.SC70.1.66]

NOBLE, JOHN, born 1825, third son of James Noble in Biggar, Lanarkshire, died in NY on 11 Sept.1879. [S#11,296]

NOON, JANE, wife of John Burnett, from Kilpatrick Fleming, Dumfries-shire, died in NY on 15 Feb. 1863. [AO]

NORMAND, JAMES, born 10 Jan.1827 in Dysart, son of James Normand a linen manufacturer, settled in NY 1850, linen merchant, died Edinburgh 26 May 1882. [ANY.II.253]

NORMAND, WILLIAM, in NY city, son of John Normand in Bank Street, Cupar, 1873. [NAS.SC20.34.40.84/87]

NORRIE, ADAM, born in Montrose, Angus, on 13 Feb.1796, settled in NY by 1827, died there on 6 June 1882. [ANY#2.24]

NOTMAN, JOHN, born in Edinburgh on 22 July 1810 son of David Notman and Mary Christie, an architect, to Philadelphia in 1831, died there on 3 Mar.1865.[AP#299]

NOTMAN, MARY JOLLY, daughter of John Notman from Edinburgh, widow of Thomas Thorp, died in Patterson, NJ, on 20 Mar. 1877. [EC#28867][S#10,519]

NOTMAN, PETER, born in Edinburgh on 14 Aug. 1820, to America in 1833, an underwriter in NY, died in Brooklyn on 26 Oct. 1893. [AP#300]

OGILVIE, ALEXANDER MILNE, son of Robert Ogilvie in Leith, died in NY on 26 Apr. 1847. [EEC#21530]

SCOTS IN THE MID-ATLANTIC STATES, 1783-1883

OGILVY, ARCHIBALD, NY, married Hannah Buchan, eldest
   daughter of James Buchan, in Springwood, Westchester,
   NY, on 14 May 1863. [S#2485]

OGILVIE, ARCHIBALD, youngest son of James Ogilvie a
   merchant in Edinburgh, died in Westchester, NY, on 13 Dec.
   1866. [S#7306]

OGILVIE, JAMES, second son of James Ogilvie a writer in
   Dundee, educated at Glasgow University, a commission
   agent in NY, died in Dundee 1836, cnf 1837 Edinburgh.
   [NAS.SC70.1.56][ANY.2.167]

OGILVIE, WILLIAM, an accountant, married Kate, fourth
   daughter of Thomas Bonnar, 77 George Street, Edinburgh,
   on Staten Island, NY, 4 Oct. 1868. [S#7870]

OLIVER, ANDREW, naturalised, Supreme Court of PA, 20
   Feb.1798

OLIVER, HELLEN, youngest daughter of Christopher Oliver in
   Haddington, married Andrew Wallace, a farmer in Springhill,
   on 17 July 1860 in Pittsburg.[S#1625]

ORD, ...,son of John Ord an architect, was born at 3240
   Sanson Street, Philadelphia, on 16 April 1879. [S#11,165]

ORMISTON, Mrs WILLIAM, a widow from Glasgow, died in NY
   on 12 May 1875. [S#9936]

ORR, GRACE ALLAN, infant daughter of John Orr and Grace
   Allan, died in Philadelphia on 27 July 1866. [New Luce g/s]

ORR, HUGH, a merchant in Albany, NY, then in Kilburnie,
   Ayrshire, died in Anderston, Glasgow, on 23 Sep. 1789,
   father of Margaret wife of James Peebles a wright in
   Kilburnie, cnf 10 Mar. 1790 Glasgow. [NAS.CC9.7.74]

ORROK, MARY LOUISA, eldest daughter of Cornelius Edgar
   Orrok, and granddaughter of Wilson Orrok of Kinghorn,
   Fife, and grandniece of William Orrok of Linktown,
   Kirkcaldy, and Overgate, Kinghorn, and greatgrandniece of
   William Rae Wilson, LL.D. of Kelvinbank, Glasgow, married
   Reverend William Colloque, MA, in NY on 17 April 1876.
   [S#10,276]

ORROCK, FERGUS EDGAR, in NY and Jersey City, cnf 1900.
   [NAS.SC70.1.394]

OSWALD, JOHN, from Edinburgh, died in West Troy, Albany
   County, NY, on 15 Nov. 1845. [EEC#21286]

OVENSTONE, ..., daughter of D. Ovenstone, was born in NY on
   2 Mar.1873. [EC#27600]

PAGE, HENRY, from Kirkcaldy, Fife, in NY by 1858.
[NAS.RS.Kirkcaldy.11.62]

PALMER, GEORGE, naturalised, Supreme Court of PA, 18
Dec.1807.

PARK, JOHN, born in Scotland during 1761, a laborer, with Letitia
born in Scotland during 1776, and six children, arrived in NY
on the <u>Camillas</u> during 1821. [USNA.par]

PARK, MARY AGNES, daughter of W. Park a Draper of NY in
Annan, Dumfries, married W. H. Crannidge of NY, in Jersey
Heights, NJ, 26 June 1875. [AO]

PARK, WALTER, from Annan, Dumfries-shire, married Mary Ann
Rogers from Annan, at Portland Avenue, Brooklyn, on 11
Sep. 1871. [AO]

PARKER, ADA, daughter of George Parker from Fairlie, Ayrshire,
married J. A. Corbett in NY 29 June 1860. [S#1582]

PARKINSON, GEORGE, to NJ around 1814, a textile
manufacturer, later by 1818 a hotel-keeper in Philadelphia.
[AP#301]

PARLAN, THOMAS, naturalised, Supreme Court of PA, 15
Feb.1798

PARLANE, WILLIAM, son of James Parlane and Mary Slack
from Bonhill, Dunbartonshire, died in Brooklyn on 8 July
1875. [EC#28333]

PATERSON, AGNES, from Cockburnspath, married. John
Lindsay from Glasgow, in NY 1860. [S#1500]

PATERSON, ALEXANDER BAIRD, a cabinetmaker in NY, cnf
1886.[NAS.SC70.1.250]

PATERSON, ELIZABETH, in NY, died on 17 Jan. 1853, cnf 1857.
[NAS.SC70.1.94]

PATTERSON, ISAAC, born in Inverness-shire during 1798, his
wife Ann ...., born in Ross-shire during 1805, via Liverpool
to America, were naturalised in NY on 30 Oct. 1823. [Court
of Common Pleas, NY]

PATERSON, JESSIE, relict of Alexander Leitch a tailor and
clothier from Edinburgh, died in Vineland, NJ, 17 June
1872.[S#9034]

PATERSON, JOHN, jr., a miner in PA, son of James Paterson
joiner in Glasgow who died 20 Dec.1868.
[NAS.SH.18.1.1888]

PATTERSON, SUSAN DRYDEN, eldest daughter of John
Patterson of the Clydesdale Bank in Penicuik, married John

Lawson Ramage, NY, in Patterson, NJ, 30 April 1868.
[S#7723]

PATTISON, GRANVILLE SHARP, FTCS London, Professor of Anatomy at the University of NY, born in Glasgow in 1791 son of John Pattison in Kelvin Grove, educated at Glasgow University, to Philadelphia 1819, died in NY on 12 Nov. 1851. [FJ#989][ANY.2.198]

PATTULLO, DAVID, a merchant in NY, cnf 1870 Edinburgh. [NAS.SC70.1.146/958]

PATTON, ALEXANDER, born in Auchtermuchty, Fife, on 13 Dec. 1779, cooper who settled in NY on 22 June 1801. [Sgen#32.3]

PATON, THOMAS, born in Freuchie, Fife, in 1806, son of David Paton, settled in NY as a merchant in 1826, died in Dobbs Ferry, NY, 19 June 1874. [ANY.2.162]

PATON, WILLIAM, born in Edinburgh during 1818, settled in NY during 1832, a merchant who died 25 Sep. 1890. [ANY#2.179]

PATRICK, ALEXANDER, naturalised, Court of Quarter Sessions, Philadelphia, 9 Oct.1823.

PATRICK, EDWARD, died in 4 Feb. 1876, Kate died 9 Feb. 1876, Minnie died 12 Feb. 1876, all of diptheria, children of James Patrick of Benmore and Kilmin, Argyll, died at Park Terrace, Brooklyn, NY.[EC#28523]

PATRICK, JOHN, second son of John Patrick of Trechorn, Beith, Ayrshire, educated at GlasgowUniversity in 1783, a merchant in NY, married Sarah Anne Stewart in NY on 6 Dec. 1801, died there on 6 Dec. 1801.[MAGU#136][GkAd#8] [NAS.CS17.1.27/416; CS17.1.25/509]

PATTISON, JOHN, a merchant in Philadelphia, 1821. [NAS.CS17.1.40/200]

PATTISON, MATHEW MONCRIEFF, a merchant in Philadelphia, 1821. [NAS.CS17.1.40/200]

PATTISON, ROBERT, naturalised, Court of Quarter Sessions, Philadelphia, 9 Oct.1823.

PATTON, ALEXANDER, born on 13 Dec. 1779, a cooper in Auchtermuchty, Fife, to NY on 22 June 1801. [SG#32.3]

PATTULLO, DAVID, a merchant in NY, cnf 1870. [NAS.SC70.1.146]

PATTILLO, THOMAS, naturalised, Court of Quarter Sessions, Philadelphia, 25 June 1828.

PAUL, JAMES, of Invercarnie, JP, Captain of the Wisconsin
Volunteers, married Angeline Adams, daughter of Samuel
Adams late of NY, in Pitch Grove, USA, on 21 June 1849.
[AJ#53001]

PAUL, JOHN ERSKINE, second son of Robert Paul a banker in
Edinburgh, died on passage from NY on 30 Jan. 1850.
[W#1083]

PEACOCK, JOHN BENNET, in Yohogany, PA., cousin of
Thomas Storie Peacock in Dalkeith who died 8 June 1884.
[NAS.SH.20.7.1885]

PEARSON, ADAM, born in Cockenzie, East Lothian, during 1817,
son of Adam Pearson and Jane Stewart, a merchant in NY,
married Susan Lillie from Scotland, in NY on 6 May 1840,
died in Edinburgh on 29 July 1889.
[EEC#20061][ANY#2.240]

PEARSON, DAVID, born in Cockenzie, East Lothian, on 10 Dec.
1821, son of Adam Pearson and Jane Stewart, a book-
keeper in NY, died on 18 Mar. 1886. [ANY#2.270]

PEARSON, WILLIAM, born in Lockerbie, Dumfries-shire, during
1835, died in Franklin, Essex County, NJ, on 28 Apr. 1870.
[AO]

PEDDIE, WILLIAM, born in Glasgow, died in Newark, NJ, on 25
Dec. 1873. [EC#27857]

PETRIE, JAMES STURROCK, born in Arbroath, Angus, on 2
Mar. 1809, son of John H. Petrie, later a merchant in NY,
died in 1860. [ANY#2.226]

PETTIGREW, ROBERT, born in East Lothian during 1783, a
laborer, with his wife Eleanor born in East Lothian during
1782, and children John born 1805, Margaret born 1807,
Jane born 1808, Ann born 1815 and Ellen born 1812, via
Leith to America, naturalised in NY on 1 Nov. 1826.[Marine
Court Records]

PHEMISTER, ALEXANDER, NY, married Isabella Kent, NY,
there 10 Apr.1866. [S#2147]

PHILLIPS, GRIZEL, in Albany, NY, 1813. [NAS.CS17.1.32/283]

PILMORE, JAMES, naturalised, Court of Common Pleas,
Philadelphia, 18 Nov.1816.

PIRIE, Rev. JOHN, fr. Edinburgh, married Fanny Maria Fraser,
youngest daughter of Rev. Alexander Garden Fraser in NY,
in Kenmore 12 June 1861. [S#1867]

PIRNIE, JOHN, born in Perthshire 22 July 1791, son of James
Pirnie and Elizabeth Herries, Moss-side, Redgorton, from

Greenock to America by 1817, naturalised in NY 3
Mar.1820, a distiller in NY by 1831, married Margaret W.
Brown on 16 July 1817, died there on 20 Feb. 1862.
[ANY#2.27][Court of Common Pleas Records]

PIRNIE, PETER, born 1792, an accountant from Perthshire, via
Greenock to America, naturalised in NY on 2 Apr. 1821.
[Court of Common Pleas Records]

PITBLADO, JAMES, jr., from Edinburgh, married Isabella, dau.
of H.E.Wells a builder, in Brooklyn 3 Nov.1870. [S#8527]

PITCAIRN, JOSEPH, born on 1 Nov. 1764, son of Reverend
James Pitcairn and Janet McCormick in Carnbee, Fife, a
merchant in NY; US Vice Consul in Paris 1795, US Consul
in Hamburg 1798, married Lady Pamela Fitzgerald in 1800;
of the house of Pitcairn, Brodie and Company in Hamburg,
died in NY on 18 June 1844. [EEC#21059][F#5.189][ACK]

POLLOCK, MARGARET AITCHISON, daughter of Reverend
John Pollock in Govan, married Reverend Horatio Potter,
rector of St Peter's, Albany, at Trinity Church, NY, on 26
Sep. 1849. [EEC#21878][SG#1867]

POPPLEWELL, JOHN, late a manufacturer in Aberdeen, died in
NY on16 Sep. 1845. [AJ#5103]

PORTEOUS, JOHN, from Muthill, Perthshire, settled in Herkimer
County, NY, probate 13 June 1799, Albany County, NY.

PORTEOUS, THOMAS, born 1798, a merchant in NY, died at
206 President St., Brooklyn, on 3 August 1874.
[ANY.2.182][S#9695]

PORTERFIELD, MARY, via Greenock to Philadelphia on board
the Alexander in Apr. 1787. [NAS.E504.15.45]

POTTS, JASON, born in 1777, a merchant from Glasgow, to NY
on the George of New York on 12 Aug. 1807.
[PRO.PC1.3790]

POTTS, JOHN THORPE, married Frances M. Reynolds, in Troy,
NY, on 21 Nov. 1872. [EC#27514]

PRENTICE, THOMAS, born in 1798, son of Archibald Prentice in
Cleghorn Mill, Lanark, naturalised, Court of common Pleas,
Philadelphia, 3 May 1813 and 17 Sep.1817, died in
Philadelphia on 28 June 1821. [Covington g/s, Lanarkshire]

PRINGLE, DAVID, jr. in Brooklyn, nephew of Alison Russell who
died 12 Sep.1886, widow of Peter Cameron in Kinghorn,
Fife.[NAS.SH.6.11.1888]

PRINGLE, Reverend FRANCIS, born in Fife during 1747, died in
NY on 2 Nov. 1833. [AJ#44990]

PRINGLE, MARGARET, daughter of William Pringle, and grand-daughter of John Pringle, 40 North Richmond Street, Edinburgh, died NY 27 September 1871. [S#8803]

PRINGLE, ROBERT, son of John Pringle of Haining, a physician who settled in Jamaica, died in Philadelphia on 13 Oct. 1775. [SM#38.53]

PORTEOUS, JOHN, a merchant in NY, 1786.
[NAS.CS17.1.5/224]; from Perthshire, pro.13 June 1799 NY

PROUDFOOT, LAURENCE, in NY, 1810.
[NAS.SC48.49.25.1/229]

PURDIE, ALEXANDER, born in 1767, died in Syracuse on 9 Oct. 1834.[Thankerton g/s, Lanarkshire]

PYOTT, JAMES, or MAITLAND, son of James Pyott a merchant from Montrose a merchant in NY, 1798.
[NAS.CS17.1.17/20]

RADCLIFFE, HENRY, born in 1820, died in Truxton, NY, on 19 Nov. 1873. [AO]

RADCLIFFE, JOAN ANN, born in 1806, from Simmerfield, Ruthwell, Dumfries-shire, died in Truxton, Cartland County, NY, on 4 Nov. 1873. [AO]

RAE, GEORGE MACAULEY, in NY, cnf 1878 Edinburgh.
[NAS.SC70.1.190/534]

RAE. ....., son of Thomas Rae, late of Symington, Lanarkshire, was born at 155 7th Avenue, NY, 29 Sept.1872. [S#9122]

RAIT, CRICHTON S., born 1844, died in Brooklyn, NY, on 25 Oct.1877.[S#10,705]

RAIT, ROBERT, born in Edinburgh during 1806, a jeweller in NY from 1833 to 1866, died on 1 Feb. 1869. [ANY#2.182]

RAMSAY, DAVID, in NY, 1804. [NAS.CS17.1.23/503]

RAMSAY, GEORGE, arrived in NY during 1794, settled in Albany by 1810. [NAS.GD23.6/469]

RAMSAY, JAMES, born in Arbroath, resident of Patterson, NJ, died on the Columbia when bound from NY to Glasgow. [S#7504]

RAMSAY, THOMAS, jr, from Edinburgh, married Helen, only daughter of Robert Mason, Lothian Road, Edinburgh, in NY on 16 September 1871. [S#8797]

RAMSAY, ..., daughter of Thomas Ramsay jr., was born in Brooklyn 23 June 1872. [S#9060]

RANKEN, ALEXANDER, born in Glasgow 7 March 1813, eldest son of Andrew Ranken a merchant, educated at Glasgow

University, to NY 1841, a merchant there, died in Guernsey 17 April 1887. [ANY.2.200]

RANKIN, ISABELLA, daughter of Henry Rankin a merchant, married John Freeland, a merchant, in NY on 31 July 1839. [SG#803]

RANKIN, JOHN, born 1788, an advocate, died in Canandaigua on 27 Sept.1861. [S#1977]

RANKIN, ROBERT, a merchant and grocer in Edinburgh from 1821 to 1834,who absconded to NY, later in Savannah and possibly Virginia.[NAS.CS46.1835]

RANKIN, WILLIAM, from Fraserburgh, Aberdeenshire, died in NY on 22 June 1853. [AJ:20.7.1853]

RANKINE, WILLIAM MCQUORN, son of John Rankine of Drumdow, Ayrshire, an advocate, died in Canandaigua, NY, 8 Sept.1872. [S#9107]

RAPHAEL, JAMES, died in Philadelphia on 10 Mar. 1844. [SG#1285]

REA, DANIEL, naturalised, US District Court, Philadelphia, 22 Nov.1811.

REED, Reverend, born in Scotland, died in Erie County, PA, 1858. [GM.NS2.4.684]

REEKIE, WILLIAM, naturalised, US District Court, Philadelphia, 16 Sep.1808.

REID, ALEXANDER M., born 1845, son of Adam F Reid, [1811-1853], died 9 Apr. 1879, buried in Philadelphia. [Dean g/s, Edinburgh]

REID, GEORGE, from Langholm, Dumfries-shire, married Catherine P. Hemming of NY, there on 3 June 1869. [AO]

REID, JOHN, a bookseller in NY, 1789. [NAS.CS17.1.8,45]

REID, JOHN, a schoolmaster in NY, then in Leith 1810. [NAS.CS17.1.30/519]

REID, JOHN, born 1826, son of Hugh Reid [1796-] and Elizabeth Wyllie [1798-1889] died in Uttica on 13 Aug. 1852, buried in Ottawa. [Kilmarnock g/s, Ayrshire]

REID, JOHN HOPE, born in 1803, a merchant, intent to settle in Savannah, naturalised in NY on 5 Oct. 1833. [Southern District Court Records]

REID, Dr LAURENCE, youngest son of Dr Peter Reid in Edinburgh, died in NY on 4 Feb. 1874. [EC#27892]

REID, ROBERT, born in Langholm, Dumfries-shire, during May 1796, a florist, died at 22 West 30th Street, NY, on 25 Jan. 1866. [AO]

REID, PETER BOSWELL, second son of Dr William Reid in Edinburgh, died in NY on 23 Jan. 1874. [EC#27882]

REID, WILLIAM, born in Langholm Dumfries-shire, during 1838, a Major of the 57th Regiment of NY Volunteers, died in Hudson City, NJ, on 9 June 1872. [AO]

RENWICK, WILLIAM, a merchant in NY, husband of Jane Jeffrey, 1803.[NAS.RD4.273.1197; RD4.279.864]

RICHARDSON, ANN, relict of James Richardson a blacksmith from Stennishill, Dumfries-shire, died at the home of William Pow, her son in law, Seneca Falls, NY, 21 Nov. 1873. [AO]

RICHARDSON, JOHN, a maltmaker from Stirling and Dunbarton, settled in NY by 1798. [NAS.GD1.660/1]

RICHARDSON, JOHN, in NY 1813. [NAS.CS17.1.33/39]

RICHARDSON, Reverend W., from St Mungo's, Dumfries, then in St Andrew's, New Brunswick, died in NY on 16 July 1878. [AO]

RIDDELL, JOHN, born 1848, second son of Robert Riddell in Dunbar, died in Stroudsburg, PA, 6 Aug.1872. [S#9073]

RIDDOCK, JAMES, naturalised, Court of Common Pleas, Philadelphia, 10 Feb.1827.

RINTOUL, AGNES, third daughter of John Rintoul of Montrose Academy, Angus, married Reverend Milo Templeton, from Troy, Miami County, Ohio, in Alleghany City, PA, on 3 Aug. 1846. [AJ#5747]

RITCHIE, JAMES, a commission agent in NY, cnf 1873 Edinburgh. [NAS.SC70.1.162/492]

RITCHIE, JOHN, a merchant in NY 1839-1842. [ANY.2.188]

RITCHIE, THOMAS, in NY, 1867. [NAS.SC48.49.25.67/242]

RITCHIE, WILLIAM, born 1807, from Kilbarchan, died at 349 West 12th Street, NY, on 11 Jan. 1884. [EC#31003]

RITCHIE, ..., son of David Stuart Barclay Ritchie, was born at The Maple, Vineland, 18 October 1869. [S#8193]

RISH, JOHN, born in 1736, a gardener from Glasgow, from London to Philadelphia on the Sally in May 1774. [PRO.T47.9/11]

RITCHIE, JAMES, a commission agent in NY, cnf 1873. [NAS.SC70.1.162]

RITCHIE, JAMES, a horticulturalist in Philadelphia around 1874. [AP#257]

RITCHIE, SAMUEL F., in Brooklyn, NY, cnf 1866. [NAS.SC70.1.132]

RITCHIE, WILLIAM, born in Aberdeenshire, an engineer who was killed on the NJ railway on 12 Mar. 1860. [AJ:11.4.1860]

ROBB, JAMES, naturalised, Supreme Court of PA, 16 Feb.1798

ROBB, JOHN, a merchant from Aberdeen, died in NY on 18 Dec. 1870. [AJ:11.1.1871]

ROBERTON, JOHN, naturalised Court of Common Pleas, Philadelphia, 21 Mar.1829 and 3 Oct.1832.

ROBERTS, Reverend JAMES, born in Montrose, Angus, on 25 Dec. 1839, with his parents to America in Aug. 1850, settled on the Brandywine near Wilmington, Delaware, a Presbyterian minister in New Jersey and in PA, died 27 Sep. 1906, buried in Oakland Cemetery, West Chester, PA. [AP#303]

ROBERTS, OWEN J., naturalised, Court of Common Pleas, Philadelphia, Oct.1810.

ROBERTS, WILLIAM ROGERS, NY, married Fannie Winant Ellis, youngest daughter of Abraham Ellis of Kreischerville, Richmond County, NY, there on 28 Nov.1872. [S#9168]

ROBERTSON, AENEAS, in NY, 1809. [NAS.CS17.1.28/192]

ROBERTSON, ALEXANDER, son of William Robertson in Aberdeen, educated at Marischal College, Aberdeen, from 1786 to 1788, later a painter in NewYork.[MCA#2.365]; born in Aberdeen during 1764, an artist and Secretary of the American Academy of Fine Arts, died in NY on 27 May 1841.[AJ#4877]

ROBERTSON, ALEXANDER, son of Archibald Robertson in NY, educated at Marischal College, Aberdeen, in 1803. [MCA#2.393]

ROBERTSON, ALEXANDER, a merchant from Fortrose, then in NY 1809.[NAS.CS17.1.29/129]

ROBERTSON, ARCHIBALD, born in Aberdeen during 1764 son of William Robertson, educated at King's College, Aberdeen, 1783, a portrait painter for 44 years in NY, died there on 6 Dec. 1835. [AJ#4593][KCA#2.361]

ROBERTSON, ARCHIBALD, born in 1834, from Woodside, Aberdeen, died in NY on 24 Aug. 1856. [AJ:17.9.1856]

ROBERTSON, DONALD, born 1843, son of John Robertson, Canonmills, Edinburgh, died in Jersey City on 28 March 1872. [S#8962]

ROBERTSON, DUNCAN AENEAS, in NY, 1794. [NAS.CS17.1.13/28;CS17.1.15/435]

ROBERTSON, ELIZABETH PARK, eldest daughter of Thomas Robertson in Musselburgh, Midlothian, married David B. Fleming a currier, at 218 42nd St., NY, on 24 September 1869. [S#8176]

ROBERTSON, GEORGE, naturalised, court of Quarter Sessions, Philadelphia, 29 Sep.1807.

ROBERTSON, HUGH, born in Perthshire during 1791, via Greenock to NY, naturalised there on 17 Apr. 1821.

ROBERTSON, JAMES, a printer and bookseller in Edinburgh, to America in 1759, a newspaper publisher in Charleston, SC, then a printer in Boston and NY, settled in Nova Scotia during 1783. [NAS.CS236.R12/3]

ROBERTSON, JAMES, in Sussex, NJ, 1796, eldest son of John Robertson a thread manufacturer in Paisley. [NAS.CS17.1.15/220]

ROBERTSON, JAMES, naturalised, Court of Quarter Sessions, Philadelphia, 9 Oct.1802 and 23 Sep.1808.

ROBERTSON, JAMES, born in Edinburgh during 1777, a confectioner, with his wife Margaret, born in Edinburgh in 1781, and children Margaret, born 1804, Jean, born 1813, James, born 1816, and John born 1819, via Greenock to America after 1819, naturalised in NY on 31 May 1823. [Court of Common Pleas]

ROBERTSON, JAMES, in NY, 1826. [NAS.RS.Dysart.2.112]

ROBERTSON, JAMES, born in Edinburgh 10 Jan. 1833, son of John Robertson, book distributor in NY, died London 30 Apr. 1920. [ANY#2.304]

ROBERTSON, JAMES, Newbigging, Lieutenant General, pro 22 Mar. 1788 NY; pro 5 Apr.1788 NJ.[NJSA, Liber.38/520] [NAS.GD172]

ROBERTSON, JESSIE MCNAB, second daughter of Thomas Robertson in Musselburgh, Midlothian, married A. W. Harris, at 218 42nd St., NY, 24 September 1869. [S#8176]

ROBERTSON, JOHN, naturalised, US District Court, Philadelphia, 16 May 1803.

ROBERTSON, ROBERT, jr., from Balgrochan, now in NY, 1821. [NAS.CS17.1.40/240]

ROBERTSON, WILLIAM, naturalised, Supreme Court of PA, 26 Aug.1805.

ROBEY, Mrs JANET, born in Perthshire around 1779, wife of George Robey a dyer, to America via Dundee, naturalised in NY on 20 Apr. 1822.[Court of Common Pleas Records]

ROBINSON, DOUGLAS, born in Orchardton, Kirkcudbrightshire, on 24 Nov. 1824, son of George Rose Robinson, to Philadelphia in 1842, later settled in Herkimmer County, NY, died at sea on the Kaiser Wilhelm III on 25 Nov. 1893. [ANY#2.235]

ROBISON, JAMES, settled as a farmer in Still Water Village, Easton County, NY, before 1830. [NAS.GD16.35/68]

ROBISON, WILLIAM, born in 1763, died in Bergen Neck, NJ, on 24 Jan.1849. [Balmaghie g/s, Kirkcudbrightshire]

ROBSON, JAMES, from Paisley, settled in NY by 1798. [NAS.CS17.1.17/12]

RODGER, LAUCHLAN, second son of Robert Rodger in Largs, Ayrshire, died in Philadelphia on 22 Dec. 1876. [EC#28480]

ROEBUCK, JOHN S., naturalised, Court of Common Pleas, Philadelphia, 28 Mar.1805.

ROGERS, AGNES, from Annan, Dumfries-shire, married Thomas H. Rome from Annan, at Portland Avenue, Brooklyn, on 11 Sep. 1871. [AO]

ROGERS, JOSEPH, born in Paisley, , during 1794, a stonecutter, to America via Greenock, naturalised in NY on 19 Feb. 1823. [Court of Common Pleas Records]

ROGERS, ..., from Annan, Dumfries-shire, married Walter Park from Annan, at Portland Avenue, Brooklyn, on 11 Sep. 1871. [AO]

ROGERS, ..., son of James Rogers, was born at 129 Summit Street, Brooklyn, NY, on 11 March 1878. [S#10,821]

ROMANIS, ROBERT, born in 1766, a merchant,, and his wife Barbara, born in 1778, to America via London, naturalised in NY on 22 May 1818.

ROME, ANDREW H., a printer from Dumfries-shire, married Mary Duff from Dumfries-shire, in Brooklyn on 6 Apr. 1869. [AO]

ROME, ANDREW, born in 1871, son of Andrew H. Rome and Mary Rome, died at 79 North Portland Ave., Brooklyn, in 1876. [AO]

ROME, COLIN M., in Brooklyn, married Mary Irving, daughter of John Irving a mason from Annan, Dumfries-shire, in Brooklyn on 16 May 1870. [AO]

ROME, ELIZA JANE MONCRIEFF, infant daughter of George and Eliza Rome, died in Montecello Avenue, South Bergen, NY, on 23 June 1867. [AO]

ROME,......,born in 1826, wife of G. D. Rome from Heathfield,
Annan, Dumfries-shire, died at 184 Devoe Street,
Williamsburgh, Long Island, on 9 July 1876. [AO]

ROME, GEORGE, born 1773, from Langlands, Dornock,
Dumfries-shire, '35 years in Trent Hills, Long Island', died in
1857. [AO]

ROME, GEORGE, from Annan, Dumfries-shire, married Margaret
Paterson,daughter of Robert Paterson from Inverness, in
Brooklyn on 15 Mar. 1870.[AO]

ROME, GEORGE S., infant son of Andrew H. Rome a printer in
Brooklyn, died in Wheatley, Long Island, on 6 Aug. 1874.
[AO]

ROME, GEORGE, publisher, died in Brooklyn, on 21 Oct.1875.
[AO]

ROME, EVERETT GEORGE, born in 1868, son of William and
Sarah Rome, died in Brooklyn on 30 Apr. 1872. [AO]

ROME, GEORGE, born in 1798, died at 79 North Portland
Avenue, Brooklyn, on 15 May 1879. [AO]

ROME, HENRY B., born in 1840, son of George Rome from
Annan, Dumfries-shire,died in Brooklyn on 13 Dec. 1872.
[AO]

ROME, HENRY, only child of Thomas Rome a printer, died at 107
North Portland Avenue, Brooklyn, on 8 Feb. 1876. [AO]

ROME, HOWARD GEORGE, in Brooklyn, married Grace
Spinning in Jersey City, NY, there on 1 Aug. 1876. [AO]

ROME, LUCY A., eldest daughter of George and Eliza Rome,
married James Jones, at 184 Devoe St, Brooklyn, on 13
Oct. 1875. [AO]

ROME, Mrs MARY ANN, born in 1804, wife of George Rome,
died in Wheatley,Long Island, on 14 Oct. 1861. [AO]

ROME, THOMAS H., from Annan, Dumfries, married Agnes
Rogers from Annan, in Portland Ave, Brooklyn,11 Sep.
1871. [AO]

ROME, WILLIAM M., from Annan, Dumfries-shire, married Sarah
J. Johnston,in Brooklyn on 25 Nov. 1865. [AO]

ROME, ..., son of Thomas Rome, was born at 107 North
Portland Avenue, Brooklyn, on 3 June 1876. [AO]

RONALDSON, JAMES, born in Gorgie, Edinburgh, during 1768,
son of William Ronaldson, [1738-1817] a baxter burgess of
Edinburgh, and Marion Cleghorn, [1734-1825], settled in
Philadelphia during 1794, naturalised, supreme Court of PA,

13 Feb.1798, a printer who died on 29 Mar. 1841.
[AP#305][OEC#28.45][NAS.RD5.338.114; RD5.367.338]

RONALDSON, JANET, from Gorgie, Edinburgh, settled in
Philadelphia, died on 16 Oct. 1834, cnf 1835.
[NAS.SC70.1.53]

RONALDSON, JOHN, second son of Archibald Ronaldson in
Leith, died in Philadelphia on 2 Jan. 1842. [EEC#20323]

RONALDSON, RICHARD, born 1772, son of William Ronaldson,
[1738-1817], baxter burgess of Edinburgh, and Marion
Cleghorn, [1734-1825], a jeweller in Edinburgh, to
Philadelphia before 1823, a typefounder in Philadelphia,died
there on 16 July 1863. [OEC#28.45][S#2517]

ROSS, ALEXANDER, born in 1756, son of Alexander Ross
[1712-1785] and Catherine Rutherford, [1713-1785], died
NY 26 Dec.1805. [Kinnoull g/s]

ROSS, ALEXANDER, from Dumfries, a draper in NY, cnf 1888.
[NAS.SC70.1.264]

ROSS, DAVID, born in 1788, son of John Ross, a cooper in
Dundee, and Jean Lindsay, [1749-1821], died in NY on 29
Jan. 1818. [Howff g/s, Dundee]

ROSS, DAVID, naturalised, Court of Common Pleas,
Philadelphia, 18 Mar.1822.

ROSS, DONALD, son of Reverend Thomas Ross and Jane
Mackenzie at Lochbroom, Wester Ross, died in NY on 8
Jan. 1853. [F#7.159]

ROSS, HUGH, born 1847, youngest son of John Ross, Ribreck,
Edderton, Ross-shire,

ROSS, JOHN, naturalised, Court of Common Pleas, Philadelphia,
11 June 1796.

ROSS, MARY ANN, from Wick, Caithness, daughter of George
Ross in Lowell, Massachusetts, married James Duncan,
from Glasgow, a commercial traveller, at 785 Fifth Ave., NY,
on 30 June 1876. [S#10,291]

ROSS, Mrs ...., and her child, from Glasgow, via Liverpool to NY
on20 June 1833. [SG#153]

ROWE, WILLIAM, born 1845, second son of William Hutton
Rowe a surgeon in Coldstream, Berwickshire, died in
Hobart, NY, in September 1868. [S#7881]

ROXBURGH, JANET, born in 1785, wife of William Ellis of
Netherton, from Dunfermline to NY in 1857, died at
Bayside, Long Island, on 18 Aug.1865. [PJ]

ROY, JAMES, of Nenthorn, Berwickshire, died in Philadelphia on 1 July 1836.[AJ#4622]

ROY, JAMES, born in 1806, died in West Troy, NY, on 9 July 1878.[EC#29262]

ROY, JANET, born in 1802, widow of James McEwan from Glasgow, died at 86 Putnam Avenue, Brooklyn, NY, on 19 Apr. 1875. [EC#28264]

RUSSELL, ARCHIBALD, third son of James Russell a Professor of Clinical Surgery in Edinburgh University, died at 21 West 10th Street, NY, on 17 April 1871. [S#8662]

RUSSELL, JAMES, a mariner in Philadelphia, 1791. [NAS.RS.Fife#2943]

RUSSELL, JAMES, naturalised, Court of Common Pleas, Philadelphia, 13 Oct.1806.

RUSSELL, MARY, spouse of William Walton in PA, 1785. [NAS.CS17.1.3/11]

RUSSELL, ROBERT, a wright from Edinburgh, then in NY 1819. [NAS.CS17.1.39/491]

RUTHERFORD, ALEXANDER, in NY, died on 9 Nov. 1834, cnf 1841.[NAS.SC70.1.60/328]

RUTHERFORD, DAVID, born in Kirkcaldy, Fife, 1812, died at 49 Horatio Street, NY, 27 August 1871. [S#8807]

RUTHERFORD, GEORGE, born in 1816, son of Thomas Rutherford, [1773-1835], and Margaret Hay, [1776-1837], died in NY on 13 July 1835.[Westruther g/s, Berwickshire]

RUTHERFORD, JAMES, born in Crieff 1819, a distiller in NY, died 14 February 1903. [ANY.2.193]

RUTHVEN, JAMES, born in Edinburgh during 1783, son of John Ruthven and Elizabeth Irvin, a horner in NY and in Bridgeport, Connecticut, died in NY on 25 Nov. 1855. [ANY#2.111]

RUTHVEN, Mrs JANE, born 1781, widow of James Ruthven, second daughter of .... Ruthven in Edinburgh, died at 144 West 23rd Street, NY in 1874. [S#9592]

SAMPSON, GEORGE LESLIE, born in Kirkcaldy 2 April 1798, son of George Sampson and Euphemia Leslie, to America 1816, iron founder in Richmond, Virginia, later in NY, died at 122 Columbia St., Brooklyn, 2 January 1866. [ANY.2.183]

SAMPSON, JOHN, naturalised, Supreme Court of PA, 19 Feb.1798, and Court of Quarter Session, Philadelphia, 11 Oct.1802.

SANDERSON, JAMES, infant son of Charles Sanderson from Edinburgh, died at 548 Hudson St., NY, 25 May 1869. [S#8082]

SANDERSON, MARIA, infant daughter of Charles Sanderson from Edinburgh, died at 548 Hudson St., NY, 2 June 1869. [S#8082]

SANDFORD, W. GRAHAM, son of Erskine Douglas Sandford, married Carrie Marion Sims, daughter of Dr Marion Sims, in NY on 22 Apr. 1875. [S#9915][EC#28263]

SANDYSON, JOHN, a mason from 11 Upper Grove Place, Edinburgh, and Turriff, Aberdeenshire, died in Philadelphia on 28 March 1875. [S#9901]

SANG, DAVID, born in 1800, married Helen Brodie, died in NY on 15 Oct. 1842. [St Andrews g/s, Fife]

SAYERS, FREDERICA, born in Scotland during 1794, sailed from NY on the Sally bound for Bermuda in Aug. 1812. [1812]

SCOON, JOHN, born in Hawick, Roxburghshire, on 27 Apr. 1771, settled in Geneva, NY, during 1820, married Margaret Renwick, father of William born in 1823, died on 26 Jan. 1861. [BLG#2904]

SCOTLAND, ANDREW GIBSON, son of William Scotland, a skipper from Greenock, and his wife Jessie Buchanan who married in London on 14 July 1860, was born aboard the Saguenay in New York on 22 September 1865. [NRH.MRB]

SCOTT, ADAM, in Waverly, Tioga County, NY, cnf 1898. [NAS.SC70.1.382]

SCOTT, DAVID, naturalised, Court of Quarter Session, Philadelphia, 9 Oct.1802.

SCOTT, DAVID, born on 17 July 1794 in Glasgow, educated at Theology Hall in1820, to America in 1829, a minister in Albany and in Rochester, NY, died in Rochester on 29 Mar. 1871. ["Relief Presbyterian Church in Scotland", p.163]

SCOTT, DAVID R., 144 Nary Street, Brooklyn, 1888. [NAS.RS.Forfar.46.191]

SCOTT, GEORGE WILLIAMSON, formerly a grain merchant from Glasgow, died in Brooklyn, NY, on 23 August 1876. [S#10,335]

SCOTT, GEORGE, in Roseboom, NY, brother of Margaret Scott in Bowden, St Boswells, who died 20 Nov.1883. [NAS.SH.18.2.1885]

SCOTT, HENRY, from Cupar, Fife, via Belfast to NY during 1811 on the Perseverance. [NWI#2.243]

SCOTT, JAMES, a merchant in NY, 1806, eldest son of George
Scott a coachmaker in Glasgow. [NAS.CS17.1.25/455, 492]

SCOTT, JAMES, a minister in Albany, died on 22 Oct. 1852, cnf
1855.[NAS.SC70.1.87]

SCOTT, JANET, from Annan, Dumfries-shire, married Andrew R.
Rome a printer in Brooklyn, in Jersey City on 18 Oct. 1864.
[AO]

SCOTT, JANET, born in Annan, Dumfries-shire, wife of A. R.
Rome, died in Brooklyn on 17 June 1865. [AO]

SCOTT, JENNETTE, widow of Samuel Cochrane a merchant in
NY, died 27 East 21st St. NY on 19 April 1876. [S#10,234]

SCOTT, JOANNA H., daughter of John Scott from Melrose,
married George B. Stote, in Yorkville, NY, in 1869. [S#8195]

SCOTT, JOHN, a mason from Dundee, in Philadelphia 1882.
[NAS.RS.Forfar.39.246]

SCOTT, MARGARET, daughter of James Scott a merchant in
Glasgow, wife of James Taylor a merchant in NY, died on
19 Nov. 1797. [AJ#2609]

SCOTT, Mrs MARION, born in 1791, widow of John Scott in
Annan, Dumfries-shire, died in Jersey City on 5 Apr. 1858.
[AO]

SCOTT, MARION, from Annan, Dumfries-shire, married George
Brown of NY, in Jersey City on 1 Sep. 1858. [AO]

SCOTT, MARY BROWNLIE, in Paterson, NJ, cnf 1891.
[NAS.SC70.1.291]

SCOTT, ROBERT, born in Edinburgh 2 Oct. 1745, to VA, an
engraver, settled in Philadelphia, died there on 3 Nov. 1823,
buried in the Friends burial ground. [AP#312]

SCOTT, ROBERT, naturalised, Court of Quarter Sessions,
Philadelphia, 4 Oct.1813.

SCOTT, WILLIAM, born in Hawick on 21 October 1789, to
America around 1812, merchant, died in 34th St., NY, 10
Feb.1867. [ANY.2.164]

SCOTT, WILLIAM DONALDSON, from Aberdeen, a banker in
NY 1841-1858, died in Aberdeen 22 August 1883.
[ANY.2.189]

SCRYMGEOUR, WILLIAM, born in Perth on 23 Feb. 1807, to NY
in 1836, died in Brooklyn on 10 June 1885. [ANY#2.286]

SELLAR, THOMAS, born in Mowick, Shetland, on 12 Jan. 1820,
a merchant in NY from 1840 to 1846, died in Cannes,
France, on 22 Oct. 1855.[ANY#2.219]

SELLARS, ADAM NORRIE, son of David P. Sellars, was born 16 November 1860 at 237 5th Ave., NY. [S#1702]; died in NY 5 October 1869. [S#8183]

SENIOR, RICHARD, son of Joshua Senior in Sandyford, Glasgow, died in NY 1854. [S.18.10.1854]

SHAND, JOHN, son of Alexander Shand a merchant in Aberdeen, died in NY on 6 Apr. 1851. [AJ:14.5.1851]

SHANKLAND, JANE, born in 1835, wife of W. B. Edgar from Lockerbie, Dumfries-shire, died in Yonkers, Westchester County, NY, on 30 Jan. 1860. [AO]

SHARP, ALEXANDER, born in 1772, a gentleman via London to America, nat. NY on 1 June 1822. [Court of Common Pleas]

SHARP, HENRY DAVID, born in 1802, a merchant, via Greenock to America, naturalised in NY on 20 Mar. 1823. [Court of Common Pleas Records]

SHARPE, JAMES, of the Union Railroad and Transport Co., married Sallie C. Machesney of Alleghany, in Pittsburg, PA., 14 october 1868. [S#7888]

SHAW, JOSEPH, born in Rattray, Perthshire, in 1778 son of James Shaw and Ann Patterson, an Associate minister educated at Edinburgh University around 1794, to Philadelphia in 1805, later a professor at Dickinson College, Carlisle, PA, and at Albany Academy, NY, naturalised in the Philadelphia Court of Quarter Sessions, 22 Mar.1813, died in Philadelphia 21Aug. 1824. [AP#313]

SHEARER, ALEXANDER, of SS Alsatia, married Elizabeth Strain, at 302 8th Ave., NY, 30 March 1879. [S#11,155]

SHEARER, THOMAS, from Edinburgh, in NY 1812. [NAS.CS17.1.31/573; 7/265] Probate July 1852 PCC]

SHEPHERD, THOMAS, born in Perth during 1792, son of John Shepherd and Ann Jamieson, a merchant in NY, died there on 7 Mar. 1854. [ANY#2.205]

SHERIFF, ROBERT, eldest son of Robert Sheriff a merchant in Glasgow, educated at Glasgow University around 1819, merchant in NY, died on Diamond Estate, St Croix, on 18 August 1847. [ANY.2.183]; cnf 1859. [NAS.SC70.1.101]

SHETKY, G., son of the late Mr Shetky, died in Philadelphia on 11 Dec.1831. [AJ#5257]

SHIELD, JAMES ARRAN, born 1 Jan. 1844, son of George Shield [1806-1899]and Mary Dickson [1816-1898], died in Buffalo, NY, on 5 May 1886.[Dean g/s, Edinburgh]

SHIELS, CHARLES, born 1807 in Earlston, Berwickshire, died in
Buffalo, NY, on 20 June 1874. [S#9659]

SIBBALD, ANNABELLA, from Grindlay Street, Edinburgh,
married Captain W. Williams, in Jersey City, NY, on 28 Nov.
1879. [EC#29713][S#11,364]

SIBLEY, GEORGE, in NJ, cnf 1876 Edinburgh.
[NAS.SC70.1.177/629]

SIM, CATHERINE, born in 1837, grand-daughter of Reverend D.
Sim in Aberdeen, died in Brooklyn, NY, in 1872.
[AJ:30.10.1872]

SIME, Reverend DAVID, in Brooklyn, USA, 1883.
[NAS.SC48.49.83/121]

SIMMONS, ..., son of J. C. Simmons, born in NY 25 April 1868.
[S#7734]

SIMPSON, ALEXANDER, born in 1780, a merchant from West
Church parish in Edinburgh, to NY on the <u>George of New
York</u> on 12 Aug. 1807. [PRO.PC1.3790]

SIMPSON, JAMES, naturalised, Court of Quarter Sessions,
Philadelphia, 25 Mar.1813.

SIMPSON, JOHN, in NY, died during Nov. 1784, cnf 26 May 1785
Commissariat of Edinburgh. [NAS.CC8.8.126]

SIMPSON, ROBERT, naturalised, Supreme Court of PA, 20
Feb.1798.

SIMPSON, ROBERT, from Rothes, Morayshire, settled in Florida,
Montgomery County, NY, by 1812. [NAS.RD5.59.545]

SIMPSON, WILLIAM, naturalised, Court of Common Pleas,
Philadelphia, 23 Apr.1813.

SINCLAIR, ANTHONY, naturalised, Court of Common Pleas,
Philadelphia, 28 Sep.1826 and 3 Oct.1828.

SINCLAIR, HENRY, at NY Mills, Oneida County, NY, 1870.
[NAS.PS3.16.454]

SINCLAIR, JAMES, naturalised, Court of Common Pleas,
Philadelphia, 9 Oct.1802 and 25 Sep.1813.

SINCLAIR, JOHN, in NY, son of Robert Sinclair a merchant in
London then in NY, 1800. [NAS.CS17.1.19/57]

SINCLAIR, MARGARET ELIZABETH, second daughter of John
Sinclair, Alfred Place, London, married Francis Voorhees, in
NY during 1847. [EEC#21481]

SINCLAIR, WILLIAM C., a locksmith from Edinburgh, died at 240
East 110th Street, NY, in 1879. [S#11,153]

SKEEN, JOHN, born in Angus 1795, a tailor, via Dundee to America, naturalised in NY on 22 Feb. 1820. [Court of Common Pleas, NY]

SKINNER, JOHNSTON, naturalised, court of Common Pleas, Philadelphia, 25 Apr.1809.

SLACK, MARY, wife of James Parlane from Bonhill, Dunbartonshire, died in Brooklyn on 7 July 1875. [EC#28333]

SLATER, JAMES, a carpenter in NY, son of John Slater in Paisley and his wife Ann Auld who died 13 Jan.1885. [NAS.SH.9.6.1885]

SLATER, THOMAS AULD, in Syracuse, NY, son of John Slater in Paisley and his wife Ann Auld who died 13 Jan.1885. [NAS.SH.9.6.1885]

SLIMMON, ROBERT, born in Sanquhar, Dumfries-shire, during 1819, settled inNY during 1840, a merchant who died on 8 Nov. 1870. [ANY#2.282]

SLOANE, DOUGLAS, second son of William Sloane of W. and J. Sloane, merchants, 655 Broadway, NY, died NY 2 Oct.1872. [S#9129]

SMALL, JAMES, married Margaret Pringle, Campknowe Cottage, Bowden, St Boswells, Roxburghshire, in Plainfield, NJ, 14 Oct.1872. [S#9147]

SMALL, MARGARET, born 1844, wife of William Keith a law accountant from Edinburgh, died in NY on 3 Nov. 1877. [S#10,717]

SMELLIE, THOMAS, born 1810, youngest son of Robert Smellie a grocer in Tobago St., Edinburgh, died in NY 28 December 1868. [S#7977]

SMITH, ALEXANDER, from Kintore, Aberdeenshire, died in NY, on19 Apr. 1852. [AJ:12.5.1852]

SMITH, ANDREW, son of Deacon Smith a tailor in Ayr, an agent in NY for McKnight and McIlwraith haberdashers in Ayr, in 1800. [NAS.CS29.178.42]

SMITH, ANN, wife of George Cleland an ironmonger in NY, 1812.[NAS.CS17.1.31/352]

SMITH, BERNARD, from Leith, then in NY, 1809. [NAS.CS17.1.29/218]

SMITH, CUNNINGHAM, born in 1813 second son of William Smith of Carbeth-Guthrie and Jane Cunningham, educated at Glasgow University 1827, merchant in Glasgow and later

in NY until 1850, died in Helensburgh 21 February 1890.
[ANY.2.172]

SMITH, ELIZABETH, born 1788, wife of William Smith, died at
259 William St., NY, on 23 June 1863. [S#2515]

SMITH, GEORGE, a sailor in NY, cnf 1857. [NAS.SC70.1.94]

SMITH, GEORGE B., in NY, 1870. [NAS.SC58.27.238]

SMITH, GEORGE, from Dumfries, a clerk on Coney Island, NY,
cnf 1888.[NAS.SC70.1.269]

SMITH, JAMES, born in Selkirk during 1797, a teacher,
naturalised NY,16 May 1825. [Court of Common Pleas, NY]

SMITH, JAMES, naturalised, Court of Quarter Sessions,
Philadelphia, 20 Oct.1825.

SMITH, JAMES, born on 24 Aug. 1816 son of Alexander Smith, a
shoemaker, and Isabella Main [1779-1827] in Old Machar,
Aberdeen, settled in Buffalo, NY, before 1827.[Banchory
Ternan g/s, Aberdeenshire]

SMITH, Reverend JAMES, late of the Secession Church,
Nicolson Place, Lauriston, Glasgow, and of Washington,
PA, died at 13 Surrey Street, Lauriston, Glasgow, on 12
Mar. 1845. [W#553]

SMITH, JOHN, late of HM Customshouse in Philadelphia, died in
Musselburgh on 24 Jan. 1789. [GM#XII.578/38]

SMITH, JOHN, naturalised, Court of Common Pleas,
Philadelphia, 1 Dec.1795.

SMITH, JOHN, born in Forres, Morayshire, a merchant in NY from
1791 to 1818, married Agnes Wetzell in 1793. [ANY#1.315]

SMITH, JOHN, a mariner then a merchant in NY, 1806.
[NAS.CS17.1.25/239]

SMITH, JOHN, son of Reverend Samuel Smith, [1757-1816] and
Janet Carruthers,[1758-1831], a merchant in NY. [Borgue
g/s, Kirkcudbrightshire]

SMITH, JOHN ELDER, son of John Smith and Ann Hutton Elder,
died in NY on 28 Apr. 1887. [St Monance, Fife, g/s]

SMITH, JOHN, 3rd Avenue, NY, cnf 1898. [NAS.SC70.1.368]

SMITH, Mrs MARGARET, in North Parma, NY, cnf 1876
Edinburgh. [NAS.SC70.1.181/449]

SMITH, PETER, born in 1792, a coppersmith from Aberdeen, died
in 16 Beaver Street, Albany, on 16 Feb. 1858.
[AJ:17.3.1858]

SMITH, THOMAS, born in 1746, son of James Smith a blacksmith
in Edingham, a minister of the Seceder Congregation in
Huntington, PA, died on 24 Aug. 1825. [Colvend g/s]

SMITH, THOMAS, born in Scotland during 1776, naturalised in NY city on 26 Dec. 1809. [Court of Common Pleas, NY]

SMITH, THOMAS, naturalised, US Circuit Court, Philadelphia, 29 Apr.1796.

SMITH WILLIAM, born in Aberdeen, educated at King's College, Aberdeen, from 1798 to 1802, a teacher in NY from 1806 to 1816, died in Port Jackson, Australia, during 1826. [ANY#2.41]

SMITH, ..., daughter of John Warrack Smith, was born in NY on 13 October 1867. [S#7566]

SMITH, ..., son of John Warrack Smith, was born in NY on 23 September 1869. [S#8173]

SMYLES, ELIZABETH, born 1809, widow of Alexander Kinleyside late parochial teacher in Coupar Angus, Perthshire, died in Rochester, NY, on 24 April 1875. [S#9924]

SNODGRASS, ANDREW, born in Scotland, settled in NY, later in Nova Scotia by 1792. [NAS.CS17.1.12/165]

SOMERVILLE, ALEXANDER, born in Roxburghshire during 1772 son of Dr Archibald Somerville, a bookseller in NY around 1798, died in New Orleans on 4 Sep. 1804. [ANY#2.342]

SOMMERVILLE, ARCHIBALD, naturalised, Court of Common Pleas, Philadelphia, 23 Sep.1826 and 25 Sep.1829.

SOMMERVILLE, GEORGE, merchant at Old Man's Creek, NJ, youngest son of James Sommerville of Kennox, Ayrshire, 1786. [GM#IX.431.112]

SOMMERVILLE, THOMAS, naturalised, Court of Common Pleas, Philadelphia, 13 Apr.1813.

SOMERVILLE, WILLIAM H., born in Glasgow during 1794, a butcher, to America via Liverpool, naturalised in NY on 30 Sep. 1819.[Court of Common Pleas Records]

SPENCE, ANDREW, died in St Andrew's, Philadelphia, during 1805. [AJ#3024]

SPENCE, ANDREW BISHOP, probably from Dunfermline, Fife, an accountant in Philadelphia by 1819. [NAS.RD5.175.635]

SPENCE, WALTER, a merchant in NY around 1789, son of David Spence a Writer to the Signet. [NAS.CS17.1.2/8/42]

SPIER, ALEXANDER, in Pishenlinn, Moon township, PA, 1816.[NAS.SC58.459.6.164]

SPROTT, MARGARET, in Hamfield, Westmoreland County, PA, [NAS.SC70.1.393]

STALKER, DUNCAN, born in 1782, son of Daniel Stalker a merchant in Comrie, Perthshire, educated at Glasgow University in 1799, a minister in Peebles from 1807 to 1830, to America, a minister in New Argyle, Washington County, NY, from 1831 to 1853, died on 5 Dec. 1853. [MAGU#189][IPC#1.572]

STAMPA, WALTER, second son of John Stampa in Edinburgh, died in NY on 20 Sept. 1873. [S#9424]

STARK, Reverend ANDREW, LL.D., of NY, died at Dennyloanhead Manse on 18 Sep. 1849. [SG#1858][AJ#5308]

STARK, JOHN C., born in 1812, died in Philadelphia on 29 Dec. 1838.[St Cuthbert's g/s, Edinburgh]

STEDMAN, HUNTER, born in Edinburgh on 20 Dec. 1812, to the West Indies in 1839, settled in Philadelphia as a wine merchant, returned to the West Indies in 1890, died in Rosseau, Dominica, on 2 Sep. 1900.[AP#333]

STEEL, JOHN, naturalised, Supreme Court of PA, 23 Jan.1823.

STEELE, WILLIAM, born in Dumfries during 1810, died in Shodack Landy, Renselaer County, NY, on 25 Aug. 1871. [AO]

STEEL, WILLIAM, a merchant in NY, 1850. [NAS.SC48.49.25.12/151]

STEEL, Miss ...., from Edinburgh, married M. Drury from Philadelphia, in NY on 14 May 1823. [EEC#17471]

STEEL, WILLIAM, a merchant in NY, 21 Feb. 1850. [NAS.SC371/59/12/151]

STEPHEN, PATRICK WILLIAM, in Philadelphia but from Aberdeen, married Jane Stewart Hay, third daughter of Peter Hay, farina manufacturer, Glen Eden House, Fife, in NY on 2 November 1876. [S#10,390]

STEPHENS, ..., son of David Stephens, a trunkmaker in Edinburgh, died in NY Sep. 1799. [NAS.CS233, Seqn.S1.19] [AJ#2718]

STEPHENSON, WILLIAM, born in Scotland during 1793, a carpenter, arrived in NY on the <u>Camillas</u> during 1821. [USNA.par]

STEVENS, WILLIAM, a lithographer from Edinburgh, married Emily, daughter of Joseph Le Jeune of Hoboken, NJ, in NY on25 November 1874. [S#9798]

STEVENSON, HAY, born in the Borders, later a merchant in NY from 1783, married Jessie Graham on 29 July 1790, father

of John Graham Stevenson, died on 24 Sep. 1799.
[ANY#2.189]

STEVENSON, JOHN, a tailor, with his wife Mary McNab, at
Champlain, Clinton Co., NY, 1830. [NAS.RS54.6300]

STEVENSON, WILLIAM, in NY, cnf 1889. [NAS.SC70.1.277]

STEWART, ADOLPHUS, a merchant in Brooklyn, NY, died in
1822, cnf 21 Apr. 1824. [NAS.CC8.8.150][NAS.SC70.1.27]

STEWART, ALEXANDER, a surgeon in Chambersburg, Franklin
County, PA, cnf 24 Jan. 1794. [NAS.CC8.8.129]

STEWART, CHARLES, in NY, 1798. [NAS.CS17.1.17/329]

STEWART, CHARLES, born in Airlie, Angus, on 3 Aug. 1783,
son of John Stewart and Isabel Ellis, married Isabella ....,
father of John (born 1810), a farmer who was naturalised in
NY on 2 Oct. 1819. [Court of Common Pleas NY]

STEWART, DAVID, naturalised, Court of Quarter Sessions,
Philadelphia, 24 july 1828, and Court of Common Pleas,
Philadelphia, 26 Sep.1832.

STEWART, DAVID, born in Auchterarder on 7 August 1810,
merchant and insurance company director in NY, died at
Hotel Champlain 17 July 1891. [ANY.2.164]

STEWART, ELIZABETH, dau. of James Stewart in Montrose,
married John Thompson, in Jersey City 8 Dec.1870.
[S#8556]

STEWART, ELIZABETH, in Philadelphia, cnf 1897.
[NAS.SC70.1.356]

STEWART, GEORGE, in NY 1806. [NAS.CS17.1.25/424]

STEWART, GEORGE, from South Uist, a book-keeper in NY, cnf
1892. [NAS.SC70.1.313]

STEWART, JAMES, naturalised, Supreme Court of PA, 13
Feb.1798

STEWART, JAMES, a partner in J. and J. Stewart merchants in
Paisley, by 1813 a merchant in NY. [NAS.CS230.S13.1]

STEWART, JANET, dau. of Jas. Stewart vintner in Glasgow,
married Thos. Walker, in Philadelphia on 24 May 1838.
[SG#675]

STEWART, JOANNA, born 1823, wife of William Kemp a
confectioner, died in Brooklyn, NY, on 11 July 1876.
[S#10,324]

STEWART, JOHN, eldest son of Alexander Stewart, tenant in
Foss, Perthshire, settled Albany, NY, by 1786.
[NAS.RD2.241/2.776]

STEWART, JOHN, born in 1798, a shipwright then a grocer, naturalised in NY on 8 Nov. 1826. [Marine Court Records]

STEWART, JOHN, died in Lucesco, PA, on 19 Dec. 1894. [Whithorn g/s, Wigtownshire]

STEWART, JOHN ANDREW, a master mariner in NJ, cnf 1896. [NAS.SC70.1.343]

STEWART, KINLOCH, a freeholder in Oneida County, NY, 1821. [NAS.RD5.218.326]

STEWART, MARGARET, in Brooklyn, cnf 1893. [NAS.SC70.1.16]

STEWART, PETER, in NY, 1798. [NAS.CS17.1.17/329]

STEWART, PETER, born 1787 in Perth, a mason, via Guernsey to US, nat. in NY on 25 Jan. 1827.[Court of Common Pleas]

STEWART, ROGER WYLLIE, from Paisley, died in NY on 24 Mar. 1877. [EC#28873]

STEWART, ROBERT, from Glasgow, died at 250 W, 49th Street, NY, on 19 Dec. 1883. [EC#30984]

STEWART, ROBERT DOUGLAS, naturalised, Court of Quarter Sessions, Philadelphia, 17 June 1819, Court of Common Pleas, Philadelphia, 10 May 1824.

STEWART, THOMAS, son of Robert Stewart of Yardhead of Barford, Lochwinnoch, now a baker in NY, 1820. [NAS.CS17.1.39/283]

STIRLING, JOHN, born on 20 Oct. 1786, son of Andrew Stirling of Drumpellier, educated at Glasgow University in 1799, married Elizabeth Willing in Philadelphia on 4 Feb. 1816. [MAGU#191][NAS.CS17.1.37/43]

STODART, ADAM, born in 1783, died in NY on 27 July 1872.[Covington g/s, Lanarkshire][S#9066]

STODART, JOHN, born in 1782, son of James Stodart [1757-1829] and Agnes Thomson [1757-1839], died in Uttica on 15 Dec. 1834. [Covington g/s, Lanarkshire]

STORRY, ALEXANDER, a merchant in NY, 1808. [NAS.CS17.1.28/86]

STORRY, ANDREW, a merchant in NY, 1808. [NAS.CS17.1.28/86]

STOTT, ..., daughter of William M. Stott from Edinburgh, was born at 3700 Irving Street, West, Philadelphia, on 18 September 1875. [S#10048]

STOTT, ..., son of W. M. Stott from Edinburgh, was born at 3700 Irving Street, West, Philadelphia, on 11 Apr. 1877. [EC#28889][S#10,540]

STRACHAN, Mrs HELEN, born in 1824, wife of James Strachan, from Fortree of Esslemont, Ellon, Aberdeenshire, died in Rochester, NY, on 8 Apr. 1874.[AJ:6.5.1874]

STRACHAN, JOHN, born during 1763, from Campfield, Kincardine O'Neil, Aberdeenshire, to America in 1819, died in Waterford, NY, 1850. [AJ#5340]

STRACHAN, SARA EMILY, youngest daughter of L. Strachan, Hilldsale, NY, married John Fraser Scott, second son of John Scott, Port Dover, Ontario, in Newark, NJ, 18 June 1879. [S#11,226]

STRAIN, JOHN, from Edinburgh, married Priscilla Robertson, from Edinburgh, at 410 West 55th Street, NY, on 11 May 1876. [EC#28600]

STRAIN, ..., son of John Strain, was born at 329 East 52nd St., NY, on 15 June 1879. [S#11,227]

STRANGEWAYS, CHRISTOPHER, from Leith, in Downingtown, PA, cnf 1899. [NAS.SC70.1.377]

STRATTON, EDWIN W., son in law of Dr W. A. Roberts, 30 Queen Street, Edinburgh, and eldest son of Isaac Stratton, West Swansey, New Hampshire, died in Titusville, PA, on 30 Nov. 1873. [EC#27832][S#9484]

STRATTON, ..., son of E. W. Stratton, was born in Titusville, PA, 22 June 1871. [S#8738]

STRONG, DUNCAN, born in Perthshire during 1776, a grocer who from Greenock to America, a baker on Front Street, NY, in 1812, naturalised in NY on 18 Apr. 1821.[1812][Court of Common Pleas Records]

STRYTHERS, ALEXANDER, naturalised, Court of Common Pleas, Philadelphia, 10 Jan.1824, and 24 Sep.1828.

STRUTHERS, JOHN, born in Irvine, Ayrshire, with his family to America in 1816, an architect in Philadelphia, died there in 1851. [AP#335]

STRUTHERS, WILLIAM, born in Irvine, Ayrshire, on 26 Jan. 1812 son of John Struthers, with his parents to America in 1816, a mason and builder inPhiladelphia, died there on 21 Nov. 1876. [AP#336]

STUART, ELISE THOMSON, second daughter of Robert Stuart in Glasgow, married F. B. Littlejohn from NY, in Glasgow on 19 Apr. 1876. [EC#28566]

STUART, WILLIAM, born in 1823, grandson of John Stuart a farmer in Old Castle of Balvenie, Mortlach, Aberdeenshire,

died in Belvidere, Warren County, NY, on 23 Feb. 1849.
[AJ:25.4.1849]

SUTHERLAND, ALEXANDER, formerly a druggist in Aberdeen,
then of Miller andCo., druggists in NY, died 12 July 1846.
[AJ#5143]

SUTHERLAND, Mrs ELIZA, daughter of William Robertson,
Cuttlebrae, Enzie, Banffshire, and daughter-in-law of William
Sutherland in Cullen, Banffshire, died in NY on 16 Jan.
1861. [AJ:13.2.1861]

SUTHERLAND, JOHN, born in 1818, a merchant, son of William
Sutherland late Fishery officer in Cullen, Banffshire, died in
NY on 25 July 1861.[AJ:14.8.1861]

SUTHERLAND, JOHN, from Falkirk, a boot and shoe maker in
NY, cnf 1888. [NAS.SC70.1.271]

SUTHERLAND, JOHN MACKAY, born in 1852, died in Ailsa,
Paterson, NJ, on 14 Nov. 1879. [St Cuthbert's g/s,
Edinburgh]

SUTHERLAND, MARY ANN, daughter of James Sutherland in
Aberdeen, married James, son of William Clark in Elgin,
Morayshire, in NY on 27 August 1875. [S#10018]

SUTHERLAND, WILLIAM, born in 1847, died in Ailsa, Paterson,
NJ, on 28 June 1895. [Edinburgh, St Cuthbert's g/s]

SUTHERLAND, Mrs, from Aberdeen, died on board the Isabella
on passage from Glasgow to NY on 1 Sep. 1852.
[AJ:13.10.1852]

SWAN, ANDREW, naturalised, Court of Common Pleas,
Philadelphia, 13 May 1822 and 2 Feb.1826.

SWAN, DAVID, naturalised, Court of Common Pleas,
Philadelphia, 13 May 1822 and 2 Feb.1826.

SWAN, JOHN, naturalised, Court of Common Pleas,
Philadelphia, 13 May 1822 and 2 Feb.1826.

SWAN, MARY ANN, born in Scotland during 1797, with children,
arrived in NY on the Camillas during 1821. [USNA.par]

SWAN, ROBERT, naturalised, Supreme Court of PA, 17 June
1799

SYME, ANDREW, born in Bo'ness, West Lothian, during 1788, a
merchant, via Liverpool to America to settle in New Orleans,
naturalised in NY,14 Oct.1817. [Court of Common Pleas
NY]

SYMINGTON, MARY, in Rocky Point, Suffolk County, NY,
cnf 1887.[NAS.SC70.1.259]

SYMON, ROBERT R., son of Adam Symon from Dundee, married Mattie A. Conover, daughter of Gustavus A. Conover in New York, there on 18 January 1871. [S#8594]

TAIT, DAVID, from Dumfries-shire, married Marie Alston Irving youngestdaughter of William G. Irving of Rosebank, Westchester, NY, there on 8 Nov. 1866. [AO]

TAIT, GEORGE, born in Leith, Midlothian, during 1815, a merchant in New York, died in NJ on 5 Aug. 1886. [ANY#2.241]

TAIT, ROBERT, late of Walls Corner, Geneva, NY, died in Geneva Cottage, Beechgrove, Moffat, Dumfries-shire, on 30 August 1863. [S#2566]

TAIT, WILLIAM, from Kilconquhar, Fife, died in Philadelphia on 18 February 1867. [S#7385]

TANNER, AUGUSTA GRAHAM, born at 14 President Street, Brooklyn, New York, on 12 Aug. 1859, daughter of James Tanner and his wife Margaret Barclay Allardyce. [GRH#159]

TARBAT, ALEXANDER, a plasterer from Forfar, Angus, then in NY, 1857. [NAS.RS.Forfar.18.206]

TARIES, JAMES, naturalised, Supreme Court of PA, 20 Feb. 1798.

TAYLOR, ALEXANDER, naturalised, Supreme Court of PA, 9 Oct.1802.

TAYLOR, COLIN FALCONER, born in Scotland during 1787, a teacher, a passenger on the <u>Sally</u> or on the <u>Isabella</u> from NY bound for Bermuda in Aug. 1812. [1812]

TAYLOR, ELLEN JEAN MORTON, daughter of William Taylor and Jean Armour, was born in NY 27 April 1830. [Paisley OPR]

TAYLOR, JAMES, naturalised, Court of Quarter Sessions, Philadelphia, 9 Oct.1802.

TAYLOR, JANETTE, born in Dumfries during 1776, a niece of John Paul Jones, to USA in 1828, died in NY on 5 Mar. 1844. [AJ#5021][EEC#20013]

TAYLOR, JOHN, a merchant in NY, died there on 1 Apr. 1840. [EEC#20052][S#24/2124]

TAYLOR, JOHN RAE, in 21 Vine Street, Brooklyn, NY, cnf 1885. [NAS.SC70.1.240]

TAYLOR, MICHAEL, from Perth, via Belfast to NY on the brig <u>Shannon</u> on 18 Nov. 1816, [PI]

TAYLOR, ROBERT EVELEIGH, naturalised, Court of Quarter Sessions, Philadelphia, 2 Nov.1819.

TAYLOR, WILLIAM, born 1790, son of William Taylor, a
merchant, to NY in 1803, died there on 23 Mar.1811.[Howff
g/s, Dundee]

TAYLOR, WILLIAM, son of John Taylor a farmer in Falkirk,
educated at Glasgow University in 1790, a minister in
Stonehouse, Lanarkshire, from 1798 to 1817, then miister of
Osnaburgh and Gwilliamsburgh in Upper Canada, later
minister of Madrid Church, NY, from 1823 to 1827, died in
1837. [MAGU#159][UPC#2.234]

TAYLOR, WILLIAM, and his wife Janet Armour, settled in NY,
parents of Ellen Jean Morton Taylor born there on 27 Apr.
1830. [Paisley Old Parish Register]

TEASDALE, JOHN, from Larkhall, Lanarkshire, settled in
Philadelphia by1848. [NAS.RH1.2.764]

TEDCASTLE, WILLIAM, second son of George Tedcastle in
Langholm, Dumfries-shire, died in Waverley, NY, on 18 Jan.
1866. [AO]

TENANT, Mrs MARY, wife of David Marshall, in NY 1809.
[NAS.CS17.1.28/556]

THOMS, ..., daughter of William Thoms from Edinburgh, was
born in Yorkville, NY, on 28 Feb. 1852. [FJ#1005]

THOMSON, ANDREW, of Kinloch, Writer to the Signet, died in
Easton, Saratoga, NY, on 19 Aug. 1831.
[AJ#4369][EEC#18705][GkAd#3688]

THOMSON, DAVID, eldest son of David Thomson a farmer in
Scotstoun, Forfar, Angus, and grandson of David Thomson
a merchant in Gallatown, Fife, settled in Oneida County, NY,
before 1821. [NAS.RD5.218.326]

THOMSON, DAVID, late of the Inverness Railway Parcel Office,
died in NY on 1 June 1876. [S#10,457]

THOMSON, ELIZABETH, third daughter of David Thomson a
farmer in Scotstoun, Forfar, Angus, and granddaughter of
David Thomson a merchant in Gallatown, Fife, also wife of
John Crichton a stonecutter, settled in Oneida County, NY,
before 1821. [NAS.RD5.218.326]

THOMSON, ELIZABETH, born 1869, eldest daughter of Arhur
Thomson a bricklayer, died in McKeesport, PA, 1 Oct.1872.
[S#9119]

THOMSON EUPHEMIA, in NY, 1821. [NAS.RD5.218.326]

THOMSON, HENRY LAWSON, in Brooklyn, NY, cnf
1880.[NAS.SC70.1.203]

THOMSON, JAMES, in NY, 1804. [NAS.CS17.1.23/90]

THOMPSON, JAMES MILLER, born 1861, son of William Thompson {1820-1892} and Roseanna McHarg {1824-1896}, died in Alleghany City, PA, 29 Dec. 1893. [Wigtown g/s]

THOMSON, JOHN, a joiner from Dalkeith, died in NY 19 Jan.1875. [S#10,152]

THOMSON, JOHN WALKER, born 1810, son of bDavid Jugurtha Thomson a leather factor, Niddry Street, Edinburgh, died in Clifton, PA, on 2 March 1878. [S#10,822]

THOMSON, Rev. JOHN, born St Andrews 7 Jan.1819, educated at St Andrews University, a minister in England, New Brunswick and in 1851 NY, to Scotland 1875, died 1 March 1893. [ANY.II.262]

THOMSON, Mrs MARIA ELIZABETH, wife of Alexander Thomson, Captain of the 46th Regiment, and granddaughter of Dr Samuel Guise, HEICS, from Montrose, Angus, died in NY 26 Aug. 1873. [S#9401]

THOMSON, PETER, born in 1770, son of Robert Thomson [1717-1783] and Agnes Lewers [1741-1811], died in Philadelphia on 16 July 1795.[Colvend g/s, Kirkcudbrightshire]

THOMSON, ROBERT, born in 1814, son of J. Thomson in Kilbank and Ann Scott [1783-1815], died in NY during 1840. [Lesmahagow g/s, Lanarkshire]

THOMSON, ROBERTSON, son of Robert Thomson a merchant of Brighton Street, Edinburgh, died in Meadville, PA, on 2 April 1870. [S#8345]

THOMSON, THOMAS ROSS, born 1848, second son of Rev. John Thomson in NY, died on passage to NY on the SS Scotia on 9 April 1868. [S#7726]

THOMSON, WILLIAM CONN, in Kingston, NY, cnf 1867. [NAS.SC70.1.136/542]

THOMSON, WILLIAM, third son of Peter Thomson a baker in Kirkcaldy, Fife, died in Poughkeepsie, NY, on 26 September 1874. [S#9744]

THOMSON, ..., daughter of Arthur Thomson a bricklayer, was born in McKeesport, PA, 23 Sept. 1872. [S#9115]

TOD, JOHN, naturalised, Supreme Court of PA, 20 Feb.1798.

TODD, JOHN, born 1807 in Anstruther, Fife, died in Brooklyn, NY, 1877. [S#10,506]

TODD, DAVID, naturalised, Supreme Court of PA, 17 Feb.1798.

TODD, JOSEPH, born in 1772, a merchant from North Berwick, East Lothian, to NY on the <u>George of New York</u> on 12 Aug. 1807. [PRO.PC1.3790]

TODD, ROBERT F., 31 York Place, Edinburgh, married Caroline B. Moxey Reeves, daughter of Joseph Reeves in Bridgeton, in Philadelphia on 11 Apr. 1874. [EC#27940][S#9588]

TORRANCE, JOHN, editor in NY, died on 2 June 1858, cnf 1860. [NAS.SC70.1.105]

TOWART, ROBERT, from Dundee, a hat manufacturer in NY, died in 1836, cnf 1839. [NAS.SC70.1.58]

TRAILL, ROBERT, born in Lady parish, Orkney Islands, on 29 Apr. 1744, son of Reverend Thomas Traill of Hobbister and Sibella Grant, settled in Philadelphia, died on 31 July 1816. [F#7.264]

TRUEFITT, HENRY PAUL, in Philadelphia, died on 12 May 1864, cnf 1865. [NAS.SC70.1.127]

TUDEHOPE, Rev. ARCHIBALD, born in Paisley on 19 Aug1801, graduated from the University of Glasgow in Apr. 1822, to NY in Apr. 1838, settled in Philadelphia in Sep. 1838, died on 6 Dec. 1861, buried at Mount Moriah, Philadelphia. [AP#340]

TULLIS, ROBERT WILSON, from Pittenweem, Fife, married Annie Thompson Greig, daughter of David Greig, grand-daughter of Alexander Reddie a merchant in Dunfermline, in NY 22 July 1871. [S#8751]

TULLIS, ..., daughter of Robert Wilson Tullis was born NY 18 Sept.1872. [S#9106]

TURNBULL, ADAM, born in Gladsmuir on 5 Apr. 1832 son of James Turnbull and Grace Patterson, to NY in 1852, a tea merchant, later in Philadelphia, died there on 14 Sep. 1861. [AP#341]

TURNBULL, ALEXANDER, naturalised, Supreme Court of PA, 20 Feb.1798.

TURNBULL, ANDREW, born in 1818, a printer from Edinburgh, died in NY on 15 May 1876. [EC#28605][S#10,256]

TURNBULL, ELIZA KINCAID MONTEITH, eldest daughter of Andrew Turnbull a bookseller, married William M. Connell at 879 Broadway, NY, on 23 Jan.1868. [S#7656]

TURNBULL, ISABELLA MCINTOSH, born in Scranton, PA, on 24 Jan. 1873, daughter of John Turnbull, a joiner, and his wife Elizabeth Stirling from Glasgow. [GRH#159]

TURNBULL, JOHN, in NY on 20 Dec. 1803.
[NAS.RGS.134.108.142]

TURNBULL, Dr LAURENCE, born on 10 Sep. 1821 in Shotts, Lanarkshire, to America in 1838, a pharmacist, died in Philadelphia on 24 Oct. 1900. [AP#346]

TURNBULL, ROBERT, naturalised, Supreme Court of PA, 20 Feb.1798.

TURNBULL, ROBERT, naturalised, Supreme Court of PA, 17 June 1799

TURNBULL, ROBERT WILSON, youngest son of James Walter Turnbull a draper of NY, in Jedburgh, Roxburghshire, died in NY, on 5 Jan. 1840. [EEC#20014]

TURNBULL, WILLIAM, second son of William P. Turnbull, died aged 18 months in Philadelphia on 23 Feb.1860. [S#1472]

TURNBULL, WILLIAM, born 1820, eldest son of John Turnbull a merchant in Galashiels, died in Amsterdam, NY, 5 Feb.1868. [S#7663]

TURNBULL, WILLIAM, of San Francisco, formerly a farmer in Lochend of Barra, Aberdeenshire, died in NY, on 18 Nov. 1869. [AJ:15.12.1869]

TURNBULL, WILLIAM P., born 1830, son of James Turnbull in Gladsmuir, East Lothian, died in Philadelphia 5 July 1871. [S#8735]

TURNER, ARCHIBALD, naturalised, Court of Quarter Sessions, Philadelphia, 21 Sep.1818.

TURNER, MARY, born at Lochaweside, Argyll, died at Port Jervis, NY, on 25 Jan. 1878. [EC#29135]

URQUHART, JOHN, son of Reverend John Urquhart, via Liverpool to NY on the William in 1815, a merchant in NY and by 1832 master of the Mobile packet ship Extio. [ANY#2.42]

URQUHART, MARY MINOT, born 1861, younger daughter of Robert Urquhart, died in NY on 16 October 1867. [S#7564]

URQUHART, WILLIAM D., MD, born in Aberdeen, a member of the medical staff at the Emigrants Hospital on Ward's Island, NY, died there on 28 Dec. 1849. [AJ#5325]

USHER, JAMES, a heraldic painter in NY, second son of James Usher a Solicitor to the Supreme Court in Edinburgh, and grandson of James Usher of Totfield, died in Union Hill, NJ, on 28 Feb. 1878. [EC#29164]

VANCE, WILLIAM, naturalised, Supreme Court of PA, 14 Feb.1798.

VEITCH, JAMES, born 1869, son of Thomas Veitch a mason from Edinburgh, died in Hermitage, PA, 6 November 1871. [S#8838]

VIVERS, ELIZABETH, daughter of John Vivers of Annan, Dumfries-shire, and wife of John Longston, died in Jersey City 1858. [AO]

VIVERS, RACHEL, from Annan, Dumfries-shire, died in Jersey City on 31 Aug.1866. [AO]

WALDIE, ADAM, naturalised, Court of Common Pleas, Philadelphia, 7 Sep.1820 and 13 Oct.1828.

WALDIE, ALEXANDER, from East Lothian, married Ann C. Mires, youngest daughter of Henry C. Mires in Leith, at the residence of the Hon. John Fisher in NY on 26 September 1867. [S#7555]

WALKER, AGNES, younger daughter of William Walker, Elderslie, Renfrewshire, married Robert Thomson, Braddocksfield, PA, in NY 25 Sept. 1873. [S#9433]

WALKER, CHRISTIAN, wife of Thomas Logan jr., died in Jersey City on 4 Aug. 1849.[SG#1850]

WALKER, DAVID, naturalised, Supreme Court of PA, 6 Jan.1795.

WALKER, DAVID, in Philadelphia 1812. [NAS.CS17.1.32/512]

WALKER, DAVID, a mason, married Helen Rait, fourth daughter of Robert Rait, St Andrew, Fife, at 19 Bethune St., NY, 12 June 1872. [S#9030]

WALKER, HENRY MELVILLE, fourth son of John McKenzie Walker, died NY 20 October 1877.[S#10,708]

WALKER, MARGARET, eldest daughter of John Walker a leather merchant in St Andrews, Fife, died in NY on 30 Aug. 1849.[SG#1857][St Andrews, Fife, g/s]

WALKER, MEGGIE E., fourth daughter of James Walker in Forderlye, Roxburghshire, married John Young, in Brooklyn on 28 April 1868. [S#7780]

WALKER, MARGARET, widow of John Walker, died in NY during Aug.1875. [St Andrews, Fife, g/s]

WALKER, PARTHINIA, widow of John Carmichael, died in NY during 1855. [St Andrews, Fife, g/s]

WALKER, ROBERT, born in Glasgow during 1795, a boot and shoe maker, his wife Christian born in Glasgow during 1795, and daughter Mary born in Glasgow in 1818, to America via Greenock, naturalised in NY on 19Mar. 1827. [Court of Common Pleas Records]

WALKER, WILLIAM, born in 1810, son of Andrew Walker and Isobel Landale, died in Williamburgh, NY, Sep. 1853. [Cupar, Fife, g/s]

WALKER, WILLIAM C., born in Dumfries during 1823, a merchant in NY by 1848, died in Hampstead, Long Island, on 3 Oct. 1873. [ANY#2.241]

WALLACE, DANIEL MCKIRDY, infant son of William Wallace from Leith, died in Pittston, PA, on 24 July 1876. [S#10,318]

WALLACE, DAVID, a corn merchant from Leith, then in Philadelphia 1800, son of John Wallace of Newton of Collessie.[NAS.CS17.1.19/125;CS26.909.9]

WALLACE, DAVID HUTCHESON, from , married Mrs Lizette Dupre from New Orleans, in NY on 7 June 1859. [NY Daily Times, 10.6.1859]

WALLACE, DAVID LAMONT, born on 25 July 1826 in Kirkpatrick-Durham, son of Reverend Robert Wallace and Elizabeth Smith, a merchant in NY who died in Louisville, Kentucky, on 2 Mar. 1895. [F#2.267]

WALLACE, JAMES, born in 1790, a laborer from Craigenfearn, Logerait, Perthshire, from Greenock on 4 Sep. 1817 bound for NY on the <u>William of New York</u>, arrived NY on 17 Oct. 1817. [NYMunicipal Archives][NY Commercial Advertiser, 18.10.1817]

WALTON, WILLIAM, in Bristol, PA, grandson of Michael Russell, writing master in Canongate, Edinburgh, 1787. [NAS.CS17.1.6]

WALLACE, WILFRED, born on 24 Nov. 1824 in Kirkpatrick-Durham, son of Reverend Robert Wallace and Elizabeth Smith, a merchant in NY who died on 12 Apr. 1893. [F#2.267]

WARDEN, JAMES, from Glasgow, died in Paterson, NJ, 1854 [S.29.1.1853]

WATERSTONE, JAMES R., in NY, cnf 1867 Edinburgh. [NAS.SC70.1.137/575]

WATSON, ALEXANDER, MA, late of White Plains, NY, died in NY on 17 December 1862. [S#2356]

WATSON, Dr GAVIN, born on 20 June 1796 son of John Watson and Janet McCrocket, in Pettinain, Lanarkshire, graduated from Glasgow University in 1817, to Philadelphia in 1823, died there on 28 Oct. 1858. [AP#352]

WATSON, GEORGE, born in 1791, son of Thomas Watson in Glasgow, educated at Glasgow University in 1807, a surgeon and lecturer in USA from 1818. [MAGU]

WATSON, HUGH, born in Mearns parish, , in 1778, a carpetweaver, his wife Elizabeth born in Kilwinning, Ayrshire, during 1785, their children all born in Paisley, , Robert born in 1805, Janet born in 1805, Matthew born in 1806, George born in 1809, and William born in 1811, Naturalised in NY on 18 Mar. 1822. [Court of Common Pleas Records]

WATSON, ISABELLA, wife of Peter Watson a flax dressr in Dundee, died in Philadelphia 4 Dec.1861. [S#2033]

WATSON, ISABELLA, in NY, cnf 1894. [NAS.SC70.1.329]

WATSON, JANET, in White Plains, NY, died on 12 Feb. 1859, cnf 1860. [NAS.SC70.1.103]

WATSON, PETER, born in Arbroath, Angus, on 30 Oct. 1816, educated at the University of Edinburgh, a linen manufacturer in Philadelphia, died there on 29 Jan. 1890. [AP#352]

WATSON, WILLIAM, naturalised, Supreme Court of PA, 16 Feb.1799.

WATSON, WILLIAM, naturalised, Supreme Court of PA, 22 May 1799.and Court of Common Pleas, Philadelphia, 26 June 1826.

WATSON, WILLIAM, son of Archibald Watson a cashier at Broadford Works, Aberdeen, of the Law Department, City of NY, died in Cooper Villa, Cranford, NJ, on 13 Oct. 1880. [AJ:3.11.1880]

WATSON, ..., daughter of Walter Watson a banker, was born on Staten Island, NY, on 30 November 1867. [S#7606]

WATT, EBENEZER, an ironfounder in NY, died in Jersey City, cnf 1881. [NAS.SC70.1.205]

WATT, GEORGE, born 1831, eldest son of George Watt, Broad Street, Fraserburgh, Aberdeenshire, died in Brooklyn 23 June 1868. [S#7788]

WATT, ROBERT LESLIE, born in 1789, a shoemaker from Aberdeen, died in Scranton, PA, on 9 Aug. 1859. [AJ:5.10.1859]

WATT, WILLIAM GEORGE, infant son of William Watt from Macduff,Banffshire, died in NY in 1857. [AJ:2.9.1857]

WEBB, AMELIA NORA, wife of Lt. George Webb 21st Royal Scots Fusiliers, died in Brooklyn 1853. [S.21.5.1853]

WEDDEL, JAMES, from Stockbridge, Edinburgh, died in NY on 1 April 1877, cnf 1877 Edinburgh. [NAS.SC70.1.185/404][S#10,530]

WEDDELL, MATTHEW, merchant in NY 1853. [ANY.II.263]

WEDDERSPOON, HERBERT, farmer in Otsego, NY, grand-nephew of Andrew Wedderspoon surgeon in Auchterarder, Perthshire, who died 1834; and grandson of James Wedderspoon a teacher in Blackford, Perthshire, who died 1831. [NAS.SH.18.4.1888; 29.6.1888]

WEDERSTONE, JAMES R., in NY, cnf 1867. [NAS.SC70.1.137]

WEILD, MARGARET, wife of Robert Clark from Windmill, Annan, Dumfries-shire, died Clark's Mills, Utica, NY, 11 Mar.1858. [AO]

WEILD, MARY, youngest daughter of James Weild, Carlyle's Place, Annan, Dumfries, married William Loudon, eldest son of William Loudon, 329 West 21st Street, NY, in NY on 15 Jan. 1872. [AO]

WEILD, ..., son of David Weild, was born at 307 Monroe Street, Brooklyn, on 9 Aug. 1874. [AO]

WEIR, ALICE, fourth daughter of Peter Weir, married P. C. Kracke from Bordeaux, in NY on 15 June 1875. [S#9975]

WEIR, ARCHIBALD, born in 1777, a farmer from Argyll, with his wife, arrived in America on 13 Sep. 1807, settled in Russia, Herkimer County, NY. [1812]

WEIR, JESSIE, daughter of James Weir a florist in King's County late of Hallyburton, Angus, married Otto Heinigke, at Bay Ridge, Long Island, NY, in October 1874. [S#9773]

WELLSTOOD, MARY, born 1818, eldest daughter of James Wellstood in Edinburgh, died in Vineland, NJ, on 30 November 1874. [S#9804]

WELSH, GEORGE, born during 1780, arrived in America on 30 Apr. 1811, a baker in Newark, NJ. [1812]

WELSH, ROBERT, from Peebles-shire, died in NY 10 November 1868. [S#7903]

WESTWOOD, J., a merchant from Torryburn, Fife, then in NY 1796.[NAS.CS17.1.15/403]

WESTWOOD, P., a merchant from Torryburn, Fife, then in NY 1796.[NAS.CS17.1.15/403]

WHITE, HENRY, naturalised, Court of Common Pleas, Philadelphia, 24 May 1810.

WHITE, JAMES FARQUHAR, born in Letham, Angus, during
1820, a merchant in NY before 1864, died in Balruddery,
near Dundee, on 5 Sep.1884. [ANY#2.200]

WHITE, JOHN W., born in Dunfermline, Fife, during 1820, a
merchant in Brooklyn, died in Plainfield, NJ, on 30 May
1890. [FFP]

WHITE, WILLIAM, naturalised, Court of Quarter Sesions,
Philadelphia, 21 Sep.1818.

WHITEHEAD, JOHN, naturalised, Supreme Court of PA, 20 Feb.
1796.

WHITEWRIGHT, WILLIAM, born in Balmaghie,
Kirkcudbrightshire, 8 July 1783, settled in NY by 1831, died
8 May 1874. [ANY#2.27]

WHITLIE, JOHN, born in 1800, son of James Whitlie, feur in
Ayton, [1766-1837] and Isobel Clark, died in South Trenton,
NJ, on 30 Apr. 1847.[Ayton g/s, Berwickshire]

WHYTE, CHARLES, naturalised, Court of Quarter Sessions,
Philadelphia, 15 Feb.1798.

WHYTE, HELEN, eldest daughter of Reverend James Whyte in
NY, died in Telford Street, Inverness, on 1 Jan. 1844.
[AJ#5019]

WHYTE, HELEN, born 1784, relict of John Scott who for 27 years
was head gardener to the Duke of Buccleuch at Bowhill,
died in Syosset, Long Island, NY, 10 August 1868. [S#7828]

WHYTE, JAMES, born in Kirkcaldy, Fife, during 1777, via
Liverpool to America to settle in Mississippi as a merchant,
naturalised in NY on 6 Jan. 1819.[Court of Common Pleas
Records] [NAS.CS17.1.25/45]

WHYTE, JAMES, born in 1795, son of Robert Whyte a farmer in
Muthill, Perthshire, educated at Glasgow University in 1810,
a minister in Salem, NY, from 1825 to 1827, died on 3
December 1827. [MAGU#250][UPC#663]

WILL, ROBERT, naturalised, Court of Quarter Sessions,
Philadelphia, 22 Mar.1820.

WILLCOX, EDWARD JOHN GRAY, infant son of William and
Jessie Willcox from Edinburgh, died in NY 18 April 1871.
[S#8664]

WILLIAMSON, CHARLES, born in Edinburgh, an officer in the
British Army, founded Bath, NY, in 1793, a militia officer and
public official, died during 1808.[SSA#38]

WILLIAMSON, DAVID, a nurseryman in NY, 1794.
[NAS.CS17.1.4,240]

WILLIAMSON, JAMES, born in Edinburgh on 13 Mar. 1810, a metal broker in Wall St., NY, 1837 to 1872, died at 23 Washington Place, NY on 23 Jan. 1872. [ANY#2.180][S#8904]

WILLIAMSON, JOHN, naturalised, Supreme Court of Pennsylvania, 17 Feb.1798, and Court of Common Pleas, Philadelphia 8 Oct.1808

WILSON, CHARLES, a distiller in Brooklyn, died 18 June 1858. [ANY.2.184]

WILSON, GEORGE, born in 1751, a farmer from Peebles, with his wife born in 1756, and daughter Mary born in 1781, to NY on the Draper of New York on 6 June 1801. [PRO.HO#102.18]

WILSON, GEORGE, naturalised, Supreme Court of Pennsylvania, 20 Feb.1798.

WILSON, GEORGE SIBBALD, born 1839, from Poughkeepsie, Adjutant of the NYS Volunteers, was wounded at the Battle of Fredericksburg and died in Washington on 7 February 1863. [S#2407]

WILSON, ISABELLA, wife of John Scott, sometime a builder in Golden Acre, Edinburgh, died in NY on 7 August 1875. [S#10012]

WILSON, JAMES, naturalised, Supreme Court of Pennsylvania, 16 Feb.1798

WILSON, JOHN, born in Leith during 1767, a cartman, via Portsmouth to America, naturalised in NY on 31 Mar. 1821. [Court of Common Pleas Records]

WILSON, JOHN BUCHANAN, born in 1790 son of Dr John Wilson, educated at Glasgow University 1805, to NY, a commission agent at 120 Water Street, NY, died on 30 May 1855, cnf 1855. [NAS.SC70.1.62][MAGU]

WILSON, JOHN, born 1820 son of Charles Wilson, a distiller in NY, died in Edinburgh 8 Juy 1867. [ANY.2.195]

WILSON, PETER, schoolmaster at Flat Bush village near NY, 1793.[NAS.GD170.1658]

WILSON, ROBERT, youngest son of Walter Wilson a draper in Jedburgh, Roxburghshire, died in NY on 5 January 1840. [S#24/2098]

WILSON, ROBERT, born in 1847, eldest son of John Wilson, 25 Napiershall Street, Glasgow, died in Philadelphia on 19 Jan. 1873. [EC#27568]; cnf 1873 Edinburgh. [NAS.SC70.1.162/419]

WILSON, ROBERT MOIR, born in 1861, second son of George Wilson from Glasgow, died in St Mark's Place, Bedford Avenue, Brooklyn, on 2 Sep. 1875. [EC#28384]

WILSON, THOMAS, born in Edinburgh around 1758, via Greenock to America, naturalised in NY on 16 Nov. 1818. [Court of Common Pleas Records]

WILSON, THOMAS, born in 1763, son of Robert Wilson [1737-1782] and Alison Darling, died Philadelphia 26 Jan.1830. [Preston g/s]

WILSON, THOMAS, born in Edinburgh during 1758, a gentleman, wife Matild, via Greenock to NY, naturalised there on 16 Nov. 1818.

WILSON, WILLIAM, born in 1755, son of Reverend Alexander Wilson, graduated MA from Glasgow University in 1775, a physician in Clermont, Columbia County, NY, in 1784, first Judge of Clermont County in 1804, died there in Dec. 1828. [MAGU#654]

WILSON, WILLIAM, a merchant in NY, 1806, husband of Agnes Ann Kerr, 1816.[NAS.RD5.85.713][GA.T-ARD#13/1]

WILSON, WILLIAM, in NY during 1820, [NAS.CS16.1.168/409]; on 18 Dec. 1829. [NAS.RD5.418.689]

WILSON, WILLIAM, a merchant who died in NY on 13 July 1844. [SG#1322]

WINNING, WILLIAM, born in Lanarkshire during 1790, a pocketbookmaker, to America via London, naturalised in NY on 29 May 1821.[Court of Common Pleas Records]

WITHERSPOON, THOMAS, a merchant in Philadelphia 1814. [NAS.CS17.134/450]

WOOD, GEORGE, born in Port Glasgow in 1794, a merchant who sailed to America via Greenock, nat. in NY on 3 May 1817. [Court of Common Pleas Records]

WOOD, GEORGE, eldest son of Lord Wood, married Emma Henry, eldest daughter of Bernard Henry in Philadelphia, there on 17 Apr.1845. [PC#1968] [EEC#21191][W#571]

WOOD, HENDRY, naturalised, Supreme Court of Pennsylvania, 16 Feb.1798

WOOD, JANET M., or Moxey, in Philadelphia on 6 May 1853. [NAS.RS.Edinburgh#64/4]

WOOD, MARY EMILY, born in 1847, daughter of George Wood, died in Philadelphia on 21 Jan. 1850. [W#1082]

WOODS, ELIZA G., youngest daughter of John Woods in Glasgow, married Alfred Pell, in NY on 17 Feb. 1848. [SG#1699]

WOOF, OLIVER, born in 1849, grandson of Mrs Oliver, Ednam Street, Annan, Dumfries-shire, died in Chester, Philadelphia, on 22 May 1876. [AO]

WOTHERSPOON, ELIZABETH, in NY, died on 17 Jan. 1853, cnf 1857. [NAS.SC70.1.94]

WOTHERSPOON, ROBERT, naturalised, Court of Quarter Sessions, Philadelphia, 23 March 1813.

WOTHERSPOON, THOMAS, a merchant in Philadelphia, 1811. [NAS.CS17.1.31/287]

WRIGHT, FRANCES, born in Dundee during 1785 daughter of James Wright a merchant, via Liverpool to America, naturalised in NY on 16 Nov. 1818, in NY in 1819. [NAS.RD5.228.341].

WRIGHT, JAMES, from Newton Stewart, Wigtownshire, via Sligo, Ireland, to NY on the Juno on 16 Aug. 1816. [NWI.2.368]

WRIGHT, MARY, born in 1787, married Francis Thompson a merchant, settled in NY by 1850, died on 31 May 1864. [Glasgow Necropolis g/s]

WYLD, JAMES, in NY, son of Robert S. Wyld, LL.D., Edinburgh, married Blandina Hasbrouck, youngest daughter of William C. Hasbrouck, Newburgh, NY, in Ellenville on 4 June 1878. [S#10,884]

YAIR, ARCHIBALD MCDOUGALL, born in Eckford, Roxburghshire, on 30 Dec. 1843, son of Reverend Joseph Yair and Helen McDougall, later a Customs House officer in NY, died on 6 July 1909. [F#2.111]

YOOL, WALTER, a merchant in NY, 1806. [NAS.CS17.1.25/136]

YOUNG, Reverend A. MCLAREN, from Southend, Campbeltown, Argyll, married Maggie Huntley Hartie lately a Presbyterian missionary in India, in Oakland, Pittsburgh, PA, 5 March 1877. [S#10,505]

YOUNG, ALEXANDER, born in 1785, a laborer from Methven, Perthshire, from Greenock to NY on the Pitt 14 Sep. 1803. [NLS~MS1053]

YOUNG, ALEXANDER, born in Perthshire 1783, a grocer in NY, died there on 15 Dec. 1826. [ANY]

YOUNG, ANNIE F., daughter of E. B. Young MD, married Edgar S. Hyatt, in New Brunswick, NJ, on 3 June 1874. [EC#28000][S#9652]

YOUNG, CHARLES, naturalised, Supreme Court of Pennsylvania, 16 Feb.1798.

YOUNG, ELIZABETH, in NY, died on 17 Jan. 1853, cnf 1857.[NAS.SC70.1.94]

YOUNG, GEORGE, born in Cortachy, Angus, during 1789, a merchant via London to America, settled in Alabama, naturalised in NY on 10 Nov. 1817. [Court of Common Pleas Records]

YOUNG, JAMES, naturalised, Supreme Court of Pennsylvania, 3 Feb.1798 and 19 Feb.1798, Court of Quarter Session, Philadelphia 23 Sep.1808.

YOUNG, JOHN, son of James Young in Beith, Ayrshire, educated at Glasgow University, to America in 1786, a minister in Schenectady and Currie Bush, NY, and in Canada, died in Truro, Nova Scotia, during 1825. [F

YOUNG, JOHN, of Culimore, Stirling, a Judge of the 10th Judicial District of PA, died in Greenburgh, PA, on 6 Oct. 1840.[FH#995][AJ#4865]

YOUNG, MARY, third daughter of Reverend Joseph Young in Haddington, East Lothian, married Rev. D. Duff of Brandt, Canada, in Haarlem USA, 15 October 1868. [S#7885]

YOUNG, THOMAS, son of Archibald Young a farmer in Ingliston, died in NY on 1 Sep. 1844. [EEC#210931]

YOUNG, WILLIAM, born on 27 June 1755 in Irvine, Ayrshire, son of John Young and Agnes Wallace, educated at Glasgow University, with his wife and child to America in 1784, a printer and publisher in Philadelphia, died there on 12 May 1829.[AP#372]

YOUNG, WILLIAM, naturalised, Supreme Court of Pennsylvania, 17 Feb.1798.

YOUNG, WILLIAM, born in Edinburgh, a British Army surgeon, married Elisabeth Clauson in Annapolis Royal, Nova Scotia, on 5 Jan. 1785, settled on Staten Island, NY, [ANY#2.43]

YOUNG, WILLIAM, born in 1783, a laborer from Methven, Perthshire, from Greenock to NY on the Pitt on 14 Sep. 1803. [NLS.MS#1053]

YOUNGER, JAMES, an engineer in Philadelphia, cnf 1895. [NAS.SC70.1.342]